CONFIGURING PSYCHOLOGY

Configuring Psychology offers a vibrant, multimodal sociological analysis of clinical psychology as a profession and practice in the United Kingdom. Starting from the widely accepted principle and goal of enhancing access to care, it examines how political, economic, legal, and social dynamics intertwine with clinical norms and expertise. These interactions configure broader healthcare contexts, defining not only entry into therapy but also exclusion from it.

Through close attention to policy developments, professional strategies, and psychologists' experiences, Martyn Pickersgill reveals how access reforms shape clinical knowledge, therapeutic practice, and understandings of psychology itself. He shows how expanding access has become both a moral imperative and a managerial project, with clinical psychologists balancing competing bureaucratic, ethical, and emotional demands in an increasingly strained National Health Service.

As such, *Configuring Psychology* provides essential insights for social scientists as well as clinicians and policymakers navigating reform.

This title is also available as open access on Cambridge Core.

MARTYN PICKERSGILL is Professor of the Sociology of Science and Medicine, University of Edinburgh. Known internationally for his scholarship on the sociology of psychology, psychiatry, and neuroscience, he is an elected Fellow of the UK Academy of Social Sciences and winner of the Royal Society of Edinburgh Henry Duncan Medal.

CONFIGURING PSYCHOLOGY

Access to Therapy and the Transformation of Psychological Care

MARTYN PICKERSGILL

The University of Edinburgh

CAMBRIDGE
UNIVERSITY PRESS

CAMBRIDGE UNIVERSITY PRESS

Shaftesbury Road, Cambridge CB2 8EA, United Kingdom

One Liberty Plaza, 20th Floor, New York, NY 10006, USA

477 Williamstown Road, Port Melbourne, VIC 3207, Australia

314–321, 3rd Floor, Plot 3, Splendor Forum, Jasola District Centre, New Delhi – 110025, India

103 Penang Road, #05-06/07, Visioncrest Commercial, Singapore 238467

Cambridge University Press is part of Cambridge University Press & Assessment, a department of the University of Cambridge.

We share the University's mission to contribute to society through the pursuit of education, learning and research at the highest international levels of excellence.
www.cambridge.org

Information on this title: www.cambridge.org/9781108494250
DOI: 10.1017/9781108664295

First published 2026

Cover image: shuoshu / DigitalVision Vectors / Getty Images

A catalogue record for this publication is available from the British Library

Library of Congress Cataloging-in-Publication Data
NAMES: Pickersgill, Martyn author
TITLE: Configuring psychology : access to therapy and the transformation of psychological care / Martyn Pickersgill, University of Edinburgh.
DESCRIPTION: Cambridge, United Kingdom ; New York, NY, USA : Cambridge University Press, 2026. | Includes bibliographical references and index.
IDENTIFIERS: LCCN 2025042862 (print) | LCCN 2025042863 (ebook) | ISBN 9781108494250 hardback | ISBN 9781108714228 paperback | ISBN 9781108664295 epub
SUBJECTS: LCSH: Mental health services–Great Britain
CLASSIFICATION: LCC RA790.7.G7 P53 2026 (print) | LCC RA790.7.G7 (ebook)
LC record available at https://lccn.loc.gov/2025042862
LC ebook record available at https://lccn.loc.gov/2025042863

ISBN 978-1-108-49425-0 Hardback
ISBN 978-1-108-71422-8 Paperback

Contents

Acknowledgements

I found these acknowledgements surprisingly stressful to write. I wrote and rewrote them, acutely aware of the plethora of people I wanted to thank – and the ensuing dangers of this section itself becoming a chapter of the book if I did. I was troubled by the question of how I could possibly acknowledge all who have spoken to me candidly about their personal experiences accessing or delivering therapy. These conversations with colleagues, friends, and strangers – at parties, during taxi rides, after seminars, and so on – have been deeply impactful and truly appreciated.

In the end, I found myself pressing the delete key on my initial efforts. Instead, I am electing to put forward a generalised Thank You. To the many clinicians who offered up spaces in packed schedules for interviews or more informal conversations about their work, and who spoke thoughtfully about the care they sought to provide and the constraints through which it is configured. To the patients, survivors, activists, advocates, and carers who have asked probing questions of my research – and of me, personally – and surfaced issues that contoured my approach to the sociology of psychological praxis. To the politicians, policymakers, and advisers who have given me much food for thought in relation to the realpolitik of national healthcare, in ways that have shaped and sometimes sharpened some of my critique. To the academics who offered insight on work-in-progress, including my manuscript reviewers for offering generous and valuable commentary on a prior iteration of this book, and of course the co-workers who have become mentors, supporters, and friends. To colleagues working in HR, finance, research governance, and grant administration within the University of Edinburgh, as well as the Wellcome Trust and the NHS, who collectively made this research possible. To everyone at Cambridge University Press for their faith in me and this book project, and the expertise they provided. And, most of all, to my family, to whom I owe everything. Thank you all so very, very much.

This book is based primarily on research undertaken through grants awarded by the Wellcome Trust (principally WT094205MA as well as WT106612MA; 209519/Z/17/Z; 209519/Z/17/A; 223615/Z/21/Z). It also draws on elements of the research and engagements I undertook through sponsorship by the British Academy (EN160164) and UKRI (AH/W011417/1ES/S013873/1; ES/G041415/1; MR/S035818/1; MC_PC_MR/R01910X/1). I am enormously appreciative of these funders for enabling my work.

Chapters 2, 3, and 4 were developed, respectively, from the following articles, revised and expanded for this book:

Pickersgill, M. (2019). Access, accountability, and the proliferation of psychological therapy: On the introduction of the IAPT initiative and the transformation of mental healthcare. *Social Studies of Science*, *49*(4), 627–650.

Pickersgill, M. (2013). How personality became treatable: The mutual constitution of clinical knowledge and mental health law. *Social Studies of Science*, *43*(1), 30–53.

Pickersgill, M. (2020). Uncertainty work as ontological negotiation: Adjudicating access to therapy in clinical psychology. *Sociology of Health & Illness*, *42*(S1), 84–98.

Acronyms

ACP-UK	Association of Clinical Psychologists UK
ACT	Acceptance and Commitment Therapy
ASPD	Antisocial Personality Disorder
BACP	British Association for Counselling and Psychotherapy
BPS	British Psychological Society
CAMHS	Child and Adolescent Mental Health Services
CAPA	Choice and Partnership Approach
CAT	Cognitive Analytic Therapy
CBT	Cognitive Behavioural Therapy
CMHT	Community Mental Health Team
CORE	Clinical Outcomes in Routine Evaluation
CQUIN	Commissioning for Quality and Innovation
DBT	Dialectical Behaviour Therapy
DClinPsy	Doctorate in Clinical Psychology
DCoP	Division of Counselling Psychology
DCP	Division of Clinical Psychology
DHP	Division of Health Psychology
DNA	Did Not Attend [a therapy appointment]
DSM	*Diagnostic and Statistical Manual for Mental Disorders*
DSPD	Dangerous and Severe Personality Disorder
EBM	Evidence-Based Medicine
GP	General [Medical] Practitioner
HCPC	Health and Care Professions Council
HEAT	Hospital Efficiency and Access Targets
IAPT	Improving Access to Psychological Therapies
ICD	*International Classification of Diseases*
LDP	Local Delivery Plan [Standards]
MHA	Mental Health Act [of England and Wales]
NHS	National Health Service
NICE	National Institute for Health and Care Excellence

NIMHE	National Institute for Mental Health in England
PHQ-9	Patient Health Questionnaire [nine-item version]
PTMF	*Power Threat Meaning Framework*
PWP	Psychological Wellbeing Practitioner
RCPsych	Royal College of Psychiatrists
RCT	Randomised Controlled Trial
SLA	Service Level Agreement
SSRI	Selective Serotonin Reuptake Inhibitor
TNA	Treatment Needs Assessment
UKCP	United Kingdom Council for Psychotherapy

Introduction
Psychology, Therapy, and Society

Much is said these days about the importance of mental health. It has risen as a policy priority internationally, reflected in and furthered by wider public and political interest across many countries. Associated epistemic and practical projects have likewise flourished, including the wide-ranging field of 'global mental health' (Ecks, 2016; Jain and Orr, 2016; Littoz-Monnet, 2022). This often takes as its focus a purported need to reduce the so-called treatment gap – the number of people deemed to require treatment minus the number in receipt of such – with this 'gap' playing a role in the consolidation of the field itself (Lovell et al., 2019; Mills, 2014; White et al., 2017). At the national level, policymakers, health professionals, and wider publics across much of the world are also staking clinical, moral, and economic claims to the need to enhance access to care for (some) people understood to be living with mental ill-health (Béhague and MacLeish, 2020; Crespo Suárez and Machin Suárez, 2021; Fassin, 2012).

This ethic of access in relation to mental healthcare is part of a broader set of activist, clinical, and political discussions about care and treatment more generally. Calls to improve access to therapies for different kinds of ill-health resound internationally, propelling changes to policies, practices, and people's lives. 'Therapy' is often taken to mean 'drug treatments', with campaigns and initiatives commonly associated with pharmaceuticals like antiretroviral therapies (ART) for HIV (Biehl, 2007; Cloatre, 2013; Greene, 2011). Often heated debates around the accessibility – or otherwise – of therapies are constitutive of the operations of global health and national healthcare. Concerns around access to mental healthcare, are not just about drugs, however; psychological modalities have attracted widespread interest and support, especially cognitive behavioural therapy (CBT).

Within the United Kingdom, psychological therapy came to particular attention over the past two decades or so, with political interest intensifying rather than reducing. First, it has been regarded by politicians and others as an important tool to address the 'societal burden' of mental ill-health. Second, it has been characterised as a major intervention to which patient access is deemed to require enhancement, with advocacy groups and clinicians making this point forcefully and repeatedly. Enhancing 'access' is generally rendered as developing additional mental health services, increasing the numbers of therapists available to provide care, offering a greater range of psychological therapies, and lowering waiting times for clinical assessment and treatment (with this latter point a matter of significant concern and activity) (Mental Health Foundation et al., 2006; Mind, 2024; Mind et al., 2013). There is also a growing emphasis on enhancing access in ways that address considerations of equity by explicitly focusing on the needs of a range of populations disadvantaged through structural prejudice and discrimination (Mad Youth Organise, 2025; Mind, 2024; Mind et al., 2013; National Collaborating Centre for Mental Health, 2023).

In this book, I examine how economic and social concerns, political and legal operations, and national and local policies interrelate with clinical knowledge, norms, and processes in relation to psychological therapy. I show how the interactions between these configure the broader contexts of healthcare, and the orientations and activities of those who deliver it. These configurations collectively shape the conditions of possibility for entry into – and exit from – therapy. Accordingly, I elucidate some of the wider effects of an ethic of access; in particular, I articulate the impacts on clinicians themselves. Finally, I reflect on what some of the implications of those could be for people seeking care.

Over the last two decades, the fields of the sociology of mental health, survivor research, and mad studies have grown significantly. Analysts within them have advanced important works focusing especially on lived experiences of distress – scholarship that holds both intellectual insight and normative force (Beresford, 2005; Beresford and Brosnan, 2021; Beresford and Russo, 2022; Broer and Chandler, 2020; Brossard and Chandler, 2022; Chandler, 2016; International Mad Studies Community, 2022; Lane, 2020; LeFrançois et al., 2013; McWade, 2020; Rogers and Pilgrim, 2021; Spandler, 2006; Staddon, 2013; Sweeney et al., 2009). I take a different path through the thicket of mental health and society here. I am principally interested in health professionals, and the profession of clinical psychology especially.

Clinical psychologists in the United Kingdom are doctorally trained psychological practitioners (generally holding a DClinPsy degree) specialising in the treatment of mental ill-health. They are often employed within the National Health Service (the NHS, which is devolved across England,

Northern Ireland, Scotland, and Wales), as well as in private practice. Yet, unlike their medical colleagues, psychiatrists, studies of the professional development and practical foci of clinical psychologists are rather rare (though see Pilgrim and Treacher, 1992). This is despite the fact that alongside psychiatry, clinical psychology holds considerable prestige within the landscape of mental healthcare. Entrance into the profession is extremely competitive, and by national standards clinical psychologists are well paid. They also often hold managerial roles within the NHS, such as leading services provided by other professions, including those associated with the prominent NHS Talking Therapies initiative (a significant endeavour to roll out psychological therapy at scale). Clinical psychologists contribute to shaping national and international debates about the meaning and practices of mental health and psychological therapy, and hence of wider understandings of the psychological. They surely merit our attention.

The Social Life of Psychology

The importance of clinical psychology is itself a function of the wider societal significance of psychology writ large. As a range of historians and social scientists have clearly demonstrated, psychological findings, ideas, and terminology flow through societies across the world (Brinkmann, 2008; De Swaan, 1990; De Vos, 2012; Duncan, 2018; Illouz, 2008; Jackson and Rees, 2007; Jimena Mantilla, 2023; Lemov, 2005; Madsen, 2018; Pfister and Schnog, 1997; Raikhel and Bemme, 2016; Rieff, 1966; Smith, 2013; Thomson, 2000, 2006). In so doing, they can help to animate or rework varied social, political, and therapeutic imaginaries (Armstrong, 1995; Pulido-Martinez, 2010; Grzanka and Mann, 2014; Herman, 1995; Hollin, 2014; McKay, 2016; Vaughan, 2016; Vorhölter, 2019; Whitehead et al., 2017; Younis and Jadhave, 2020). These can result in revised ways of understanding and managing subjects in the clinic, the classroom, the courts, and beyond (Barr-Haim, 2021; Erickson et al., 2013; Fassin and Rechtman, 2009; Jones et al., 2013; Ossa et al., 2021; Robcis, 2013; Weinstein, 2013; Yang, 2015; Zhang, 2020). Indeed, such arenas are important in their own right for generating psychological notions and knowledge that configure the subjects ensconced within them (Armstrong, 1983; Miller and Rose, 2008; Rose, 1996).

The configurations that might be implied by the advent and attempted instantiation of psychological knowledge are not, however, inevitable. Societal processes and concerns inform where and how psychological concepts and findings settle, if at all, within professional work, policy settings, popular media, and personal experience. Their reception depends on social circumstances and everyday epistemologies (Broer et al., 2020, 2022). Ideas about psychology configured through university research settings or inside the clinic cannot, then, be assumed to simply and straightforwardly diffuse into and instantiate within other discursive and practical sites (Capshew, 1999; Pettit and Young, 2017). In the case of specific therapies, as their use extends beyond national borders, their practices of deployment – and even the assumptions underpinning these – can shift and change (Amouroux et al., 2023; Wu and Wang, 2016). The arrival of behaviour therapy in France is one example (Amouroux, 2017; Amouroux et al., 2022). This 'American' therapy was hardly welcomed by French clinicians; however, over time, it imbricated with pre-existing imaginaries and practices, evolving in ways that saw some measure of acceptance. It is in part through ongoing transit, and via discursive roadblocks to this, that psychological concepts and practices morph, with the meanings ascribed to them rewritten in the process (Lloyd, 2006; Pettit, 2015; Turkle, 1978).

Different approaches to therapy, of the kinds practised by clinical psychologists and other psychological practitioners (like counsellors and some psychiatrists), also contain different models of the psychological. As these therapies and the ideas associated with them travel, they likewise entwine with other ideas about the self; for instance, those shaped through various biological idioms (Behrouzan, 2016; Ehrenberg, 2020; Loughran, 2016). For some therapists, this means that acting upon the psychological can be understood to take place through the brain, as well as vice versa: that stimulating the brain can sooth the soul (Brenninkmeijer, 2010; Moutaud, 2022; Rose, 2006; Vidal and Ortega, 2017). These reproachments between different ontologies and their enactments underscore the great extent to which different models of the psyche, and of being human more broadly, can sit together and articulate with one another in non-determinative ways (Craciun, 2018; Marks, 2017; Pickersgill, 2010; Pickersgill et al., 2011; Richert, 2019; Silverman, 2012; Shamdasani, 2017; Zhang, 2020).

The psychological knowledge that gives rise to and results from therapeutic intervention is also itself shaped through societal discourses and debates (Koczanowicz and Koczanowicz-Dehnel, 2021; Solovey, 2001). These impact what is researched, why, how, and by whom (Dehue, 1995; Kusch, 1999; Pandora, 1997). In turn, research contributes to configuring professional training in applied psychology, although the expertise of clinicians can by no means be reduced to knowledge trickled down from laboratories (Ashmore et al., 2005). Psychology, as Nikolas

Rose (1996) has put it, is very much a *social* science; equally, the social is undoubtedly a product of psychological praxis.

While psychology can be popularly celebrated for its contribution to care, it is also important to underscore that the sociality Rose points to can be regressive. Discriminatory societies and social institutions inflect the knowledge produced within them and the uses to which it is put (Asante and Vandi, 1981; Harding, 1986; Martin, 2022; Schiebinger, 1993). Psychology, then, has not merely been impacted by discrimination and oppression: it has been constituted through these processes (Caplan, 1993; Guthrie, 1976; Howitt and Owusu-Bempah, 1994; Morawski, 1994; Richards, 1997). As a range of academics and activists have pointed out, including many psychologists themselves, psychology both inscribes and contributes to social ills and structural violence (Capella Palacios and Jadhav, 2020; Fine, 1985; Henriques et al., 1984; Morawski, 1997a; Parker, 2015; Rutherford, 2018; Spandler and Carr, 2020; Tyson et al., 2011) such as homophobia, transphobia, racism, and sexism (Chaparro and Prado, 2022; Cokley and Garba, 2018; Hegarty, 2018; Hird, 2003; Hubbard, 2017; Hubbard and Griffiths, 2019; Kitzinger, 1987; Parlee, 1979; Pyne, 2020; Spandler and Carr, 2022; Valasek, 2022; Waidzunas, 2015; Young and Hegarty, 2019). Psychological knowledge has also long been instantiated within, and generated through, practices of colonialism, war, and torture (Balfe, 2016; Capshew, 1999; Linstrum, 2016; Oakes, 1994; Orr, 2006; Reyes, 2008; Rohde, 2022; Samelson, 1977; Soldz, 2011). Clearly, psychology cannot be neatly separated from the social and normative practices through which it is configured.

As historians like Danziger (1997, 1990), Morawski (1997a), Richards (1996), and Smith (1997, 2013) have discussed, the traffic between psychology and wider society puts psychologists in a particularly tricky position in relation to their role as authoritative crafters of knowledge about, and technicians of, the self. If psychological knowledge is constituted through social and interpersonal processes, and if the outputs of psychological research impact societies, subjectivities, and how we come to know them, then the self-making potential of psychology as a science and practice is dizzying. Likewise, the associated responsibility and reflexivity required from practitioners is considerable, not least given the issues outlined earlier (Brinkmann, 2005; Hearnshaw, 1987; Morawksi, 1997b; Richard, 1996). Many psychologists take seriously both the power of their discipline and the need to wield it thoughtfully. Nevertheless, there can be gaps between laudable therapeutic goals, for example, and the lived realities of those who encounter psychological knowledge and expertise.

Today, discriminatory logics continue to be discernible within psychological research and practice (Adams et al., 2018; APA, 2021; Riggs et al., 2019). They have ramifications for how therapeutic practitioners come to understand and relate to those with whom they work (Carr, 2010; Charura and Lago, 2021; Constantine, 2007; Hodges and McManus, 2006; Pilgrim and Patel, 2015). With regards to access to psychological therapy, for instance, it would be unwise to assume that assessments of whether someone is 'ready' for therapy, as various clinical psychologists put it, are somehow free from raced, gendered, and classed assumptions that might pave the way to access to care and treatment for some and not others. Better understandings of both how psychologists enact clinical decision-making and the wider context in which therapy is delivered can provide evidence and insight for activists and campaigners lobbying for more equitable access to care.

Introducing Clinical Psychology

What today is referred to in the United Kingdom as clinical psychology has its origins in a range of traditions, not least educational and industrial psychology (Stewart, 2015). Over its existence, the profession has been configured through – and helped to configure – wider initiatives in the NHS, health policy, and academia. Early training programmes included initiatives at the Maudsley Hospital and the Tavistock Clinic (both in London, England) alongside the Crichton Royal (Dumfries, Scotland), the scope and intent of which were shaped by the inauguration of the NHS in 1948 (Stewart, 2015). The Maudsley programme has long attracted particular attention, not least because of the significance of its founder to the history of psychology: prominent and controversial psychologist Hans Eysenck. Established in 1947 at the behest of psychiatrist Aubrey Lewis (Buchanan, 2010; Derksen, 2001; Yule, 2015), the programme developed in the context of a wider professional buoyancy for psychiatry and psychology following the Second World War (Jones, 2004; Loughran, 2016; Thomson, 2000). Psychological medicine, often practised by physicians, had for some time been institutionalised within the United Kingdom (Crichton-Browne, 1861; Jones, 2010). However, Eysenck's programme was a significant moment in the consolidation of clinical psychology as a distinct discipline that long exerted influence on the nascent profession (Derksen, 2000).

The style of clinical psychology fostered by Eysenck drew from the influential field of educational psychology (Rose, 1985). It underscored the import of psychological testing, the cultural traction of which had been a key mechanism for the professionalisation and expansion of psychology (Thomson, 2000). This focus on testing purposely framed out therapy (Buchanan, 2010; Derksen, 2000); Eysenck (1949, 1953, 1959) was especially critical of the kind of therapy expounded by Freud and psychoanalysts, noting often and at length its limits as a scientific practice. This was in contrast to some of the early members of the British Psychological Society (BPS), founded at University College London on 24 October 1901 as the then and still principal professional society for UK-based psychologists (Hearnshaw, 1964). Many BPS members were physicians orientated to psychological treatment, including psychoanalysis (Pilgrim and Parry, 2015). Consequently, the establishment and rollout of the Maudsley programme over its early years entailed a slightly rocky relationship with the BPS (Yule, 2015), before the highly influential Eysenck gained traction there too (Buchanan, 2010).

The focus of psychological testing via psychometrics, rather than therapy, had professional as well as epistemic advantages. Serving as a form of practical boundary work (Gieryn, 1983) between the disciplines, it ensured that psychology avoided a direct contest with physicians (Pilgrim, 2010) while also contributing to the reification of psychological science (Stewart, 2015). By framing their identifies around testing, psychologists could demarcate an increasingly autonomous space for themselves in ways that highlighted their unique skills and utility. Since this zone of praxis did not overtly threaten the far more powerful profession of medicine, there was plenty of scope for it to further expand.

Still, professional context changes over time, in a dynamic interrelationship with the epistemic content that fills it. Eventually, Maudsley psychologists came to engage in therapeutic practices as well. This was, in part, through the rising influence of Eysenck's colleague Monte Shapiro in the early 1950s, with whom he had a somewhat challenging relationship at times (Buchanan, 2010). Shapiro had a rather different approach to psychology than Eysenck (Derksen, 2001) and helped to initiate psychological treatment within the Maudsley (Yule, 2015). As the years went by, the import of a more overtly therapeutic emphasis for psychology was increasingly asserted across the profession. Eysenck himself ended up becoming a vocal supporter of empirically orientated behaviour therapy (Eysenck, 1959; Yule, 2015), following long-standing interests in behavioural conditioning, and in 1965 he co-authored the first major textbook in this area with Stanley Rachman (Marks, 2012).

At the same time, the BPS more generally was embroiled in what historian Roderick Buchanan has called 'the somewhat tortuous process of professionalization' (Buchanan, 2010, p. 220). To this end, it engaged extensively with the government and with the evolving NHS. In 1965, a Royal Charter was granted to the Society, and then, in 1966, the BPS Division of Clinical Psychology (DCP) was founded (Hall and Wang, 2015). That year saw membership of the Division stand at only 163, while the BPS as a whole had 3,300 members (Hall et al., 2015). As the 1960s progressed, psychologists working clinically only numbered in their hundreds (Buchanan, 2010). Nevertheless, alongside the establishment of the DCP, the 1960s saw a range of other clinical psychology programmes develop within the United Kingdom, and the demands for psychologists within the NHS grew (Hall et al., 2015). In the 1950s, aside from the London Institute of Psychiatry, the Tavistock Clinic and the Crichton Royal were the only 'approved' training courses for clinical psychologists seeking work within the NHS (Hall et al., 2015). By the end of the 1960s, however, the BPS had formalised a Diploma in Clinical Psychology, and 'in-service' NHS training programmes were also operating (Lavender and Turpin, 2015).

The lot of clinical psychologists improved further in the 1970s and, to an extent, into the 1980s. The call for clinical psychologists, and psychological practitioners more generally, continued, including within both primary care and outpatient settings (Burns and Hall, 2021). Clinical psychology separated further from psychiatry, heartened in this respect by a significant 1977 Department of Health document, the Trethowan Report (DHSS, 1977). Led by William Trethowan, a psychiatrist at the University of Birmingham, this entailed a significant review of clinical psychology services. Clinical psychologists were, for instance, regarded as fully competent to accept referrals from general medical practitioners (GPs; what some countries refer to as family doctors/physicians), with recommendations made to expand service provision (Hall and Wag, 2015). By the end of the decade, clinical psychology training was provided through either two-year Masters programmes, or the aforementioned in-service diploma route (Lavender and Turpin, 2015). At the same time, psychologists also themselves became involved in the training of physicians and psychiatrists via the establishment of posts within medical schools (Hall, 2015). Through this, psychological knowledge became increasingly interpolated within medical curricula. The therapies these emboldened psychologists were delivering, and the theoretical debates to which they contributed, also became increasingly heterogeneous (Parry, 2015; Pilgrim and Patel, 2015). This heterogeneity tended not to result in particularly seismic professional ructions, although the applications of behavioural techniques in relation to the ethically troubling aversion therapy became increasingly contested (Carr and Spandler, 2019; Marks, 2015).

During the 1980s, clinical psychologists continued to enjoy a significant degree of professional autonomy in the NHS (Hall et al., 2015), despite the challenges of NHS reforms and budgetary issues under a Conservative government. So-called deinstitutionalisation through the closures of 'mental hospitals' (Scull, 2021) meant that, in theory, clinical psychologists were better integrated into the wider NHS workforce. With the rising influence of managerialism in the NHS, they also came to occupy sometimes powerful positions leading large, multidisciplinary teams (Pilgrim and Patel, 2015). The BPS supported this through DCP management training (Hall and Wang, 2015). Professional debate and knowledge production were also furthered via periodicals such as the *British Journal of Clinical Psychology* (first issue 1981), which evolved from the long-standing *British Journal of Social and Clinical Psychology*; *Clinical Psychology Forum* (first issue 1986), developed from its forerunner, the *DCP Newsletter*; and, *The Psychologist* (first issue 1988), a rebranding of the *Quarterly Bulletin of the British Psychological Society* (established in 1948) (Hall and Wang, 2015). The reconfiguration of these texts reflected an increasingly ambitious profession of psychology in general and of clinical psychology especially. The ambitions of the latter were also furthered through the Manpower Planning Advisory Group of the Department of Health (Richardson, 2015). Under the leadership of psychologist Derek Mowbray, this produced a key report foregrounding the importance and expertise of clinical psychology for the NHS (Management Advisory Service, 1989), galvanising many hopes and expectations about the future (Pilgrim and Treacher, 1992).

The authority and autonomy of clinical psychology were further consolidated in the 1990s through the reconfiguration of core training from a two-year Masters qualification to a three-year doctorate (although not without considerable debate; Lavender and Turpin, 2015). In a medically dominated NHS, much benefit was seen to be afforded through the title of 'Dr' in relation to prestige and professional recognition (Cheshire and Pilgrim, 2004). Following the 1997 general election and the coming to power of a Labour government, investment in mental health services also improved and the numbers of clinical psychologists employed within the NHS grew (Richardson, 2015). During this decade, it also became clear that some clinical psychologists were beginning to engage in more dialogic ways with people to whom their therapeutic expertise had been applied (Foster, 2015). This move was powered by an increasingly organised and influential advocacy sector and service-user movement (Beresford and

Brosnan, 2021; Campbell, 2005; O'Donnell and MacLean, 2019; MacLean, 2021; Rogers and Pilgrim, 1991), even if this itself faced a range of obstructions and practices of relegation (Carr, 2007; Lambert and Carr, 2018; Lewis, 2009, 2014; Sweeney, 2016). While engagement with people who use psychology services was not a significant feature of clinical psychology in the 1990s, subsequently there has been a gradual shift in this respect (Foster, 2015; Soffe et al., 2004). That said, organisations and individuals involved in mental health advocacy and the user and survivor movements continue to demonstrate that too many of their critiques of existing services and concrete suggestions for reform go unheeded (Farmer and Blackshaw, 2021; Russo and Sweeney, 2016; Sapouna et al., 2019).

Other challenging matters around which the profession is increasingly concerned are the stigma and marginalisation of a range of groups within and by clinical psychology, including in relation to race and ethnicity as well as gender and sexuality. Since the 1990s there has been an intensification of attention within psychology to the forms of prejudice that can exist in the profession (Adetimole et al., 2005; Hodges and McManus, 2006; Wood and Patel, 2017). Some progress has been made to address this: for instance, the much campaigned-for Lesbian and Gay Section of the BPS was finally established in 1998 (Kitzinger et al., 1998), which became the Psychology of Sexualities Section in 2009 (Hubbard and Griffiths, 2019). In the face of ongoing structural, institutional, and interpersonal forms of racism that impact access to mental healthcare (Bowl, 2007; Burr, 2002; Haarmans et al., 2022; Halvorstud et al., 2018; Nazroo et al., 2020), there is also increasing problematisation of the fact that clinical psychologists are overwhelmingly a white, middle-class (Palmer et al., 2021) workforce (Odusanya et al., 2018). With this, there has been some recognition too of how a lack of demographic diversity within clinical psychology configures the logics of healthcare delivery and the subjects of therapy (Wood and Patel, 2017). However, discourse in relation to the whiteness of psychology has often been articulated through the idiom of diversification rather than the more direct register of discrimination or racism (Pilgrim and Patel, 2015; Wood and Patel, 2017). While the volume of calls to address power and privilege within clinical psychology is increasing, much work remains to be done (Cohen-Tovée, 2020; Fernando, 2017; Wood and Patel, 2019).

Professional competition and relationships with other disciplines also continues to be a challenge for clinical psychology. Besides psychiatrists, clinical psychologists have long worked with other health professionals, not least of which are other kinds of psychological practitioners, such as counselling psychologists. Maintaining good relations while securing professional autonomy and advancement can involve some delicate organisational and personal manoeuvring. This relationship work became more pressing as policy in the late 20th century (notably the Department of Health's (2007) 'New Ways of Working' agenda) came to emphasise the important place of clinical psychologists within multidisciplinary teams, as well as supervisors of other kinds of therapists, for example people with a diploma in CBT who were specifically hired to deliver that particular therapy (Cheshire and Pilgrim, 2004). Clinical psychology also found itself in a slightly tricky position with the formation of the Health Professions Council (now the Health and Care Professions Council (HCPC)) in 2003 as a legal regulator of professional practice. While the formal regulation of psychology was in many respects welcome – and legal restrictions on who could use the 'protected title' of clinical psychology particularly so – worries circulated, and still do, that more bespoke regulation for psychologists remained lacking.

Today, clinical psychology is firmly established as a therapeutic profession – one necessarily engaged, to varying degrees, with policymakers, academia, other mental health professions, and advocacy groups. Clinical psychologist David Harper (2010, p. 13) reads the shift away from testing to therapy as 'a bid for autonomy from psychiatry'. In this respect, clinical psychology has had clear success. With a distinct doctoral training route which can result in a well-renumerated, relatively autonomous, and commonly secure job in or beyond the NHS, clinical psychology will look to many like a profession that has done well for itself. No longer simply an adjunct to psychiatry, through contributing to healthcare policymaking and clinical guideline development, clinical psychologists now shape the work of psychiatrists themselves (Parry, 2015). Still, the originating purpose of the Maudsley programme is not without contemporary impact. Furthermore, for all its evident import, and to the understandable chagrin of some practitioners, the social and economic standing of clinical psychology is not parous with psychiatry. These issues appear to reverberate in some of the discord that can at times remain discernible between the professions, and which contributes to the professional politics – and thus instantiation within healthcare services – of the psychological disciplines.

Introducing (Cognitive Behavioural) Therapy

If clinical psychology is a therapeutic profession, what therapies are practised, where, and with what foci? As noted, many clinical psychologists work in the NHS, where they draw on a range of therapies to address a variety of forms of disease and subjective distress: addiction, eating disorders, low mood, psychosis, and more. Different therapeutic approaches can be used alongside each other, and the assumptions underpinning these are wide-ranging. Take, for example, cognitive-analytic therapy: this draws on elements of psychoanalysis and cognitive psychology in ways that might be anathema to some specialists in either tradition.

The ontological variety and complexity between and within therapies generally does not, however, get in the way of actual therapeutic work. Rather, clinical psychologists take what they need, interweave what they regard as helpful, and leave the rest behind (cf. Luhrmann, 2000). As such, practitioners of clinical psychology commonly describe their therapeutic style as 'integrationist'. Implicit to this characterisation of professional practice is an epistemic claim to know about a range of techniques, and to know (best) how to braid and deploy them in different ways for particular patients. This claim itself helps to support the position of clinical psychologists within the wider NHS ecosystem, within which there exists a great many other providers of psychological therapy.

At the same time, many clinical psychologists also draw significantly on the widely regarded, if also sometimes hotly contested, technique of CBT. This is one of the most popular psychological treatments in the world, used in diverse ways in a range of contexts (Marks, 2015). A preference towards CBT is marked out from training onwards, if not before – for instance, during pre-doctoral work within psychological services. While students on clinical psychology doctorates must acquire competencies in two therapeutic modalities, one of these has to be CBT (BPS, 2019). Consequently, although CBT is by no means a therapy clinical psychologists can uniquely claim as their own, it is nevertheless central to their work – with that centrality enjoined by the BPS itself.

CBT entails psychological and behavioural strategies aimed at lessening the subjective impact of what are considered 'maladaptive' patterns of thinking about and relating to the self and the world. It has developed over successive 'waves' and builds on various pre-existing therapeutic approaches, including rational therapy (Craciun, 2018; Pilgrim, 2011; Stark, 2017). As its name indicates, it has origins in both behaviourist and cognitivist traditions of psychology (and psychiatry). CBT consequently represents an amalgam of approaches that draw from figures such as Hans Eysenck, psychologist Albert Ellis, and psychiatrist Aaron Beck (both trained in the Eastern United States) (Marks, 2012; Pilgrim, 2009). The conjoining, and even blurring together, of the 'C' and the 'B' of CBT became essentially taken granted in the United Kingdom by the early 1990s, and the influence of the therapy grew and grew (Marks, 2012).

Professionals who centre CBT within their practice commonly locate as their primary concern 'patient's thoughts and actions' rather than placing emotions as salient (Craciun, 2018, p. 985). Relatedly, CBT tends to have a relatively immediate temporal focus as compared to a deep dive into distant personal histories that characterises many other therapies (although childhood experiences, for instance, are not necessarily disregarded) (Craciun, 2017). It is generally a more targeted and shorter-term modality than techniques such as psychodynamic psychotherapy or psychoanalysis. Within the United Kingdom, this temporal structure has contributed to the consolidation of CBT within an overstretched NHS (as well as in public and private healthcare elsewhere; Lakoff, 2005; Scott, 2006; Zhang, 2020), where psychologists and other practitioners are often asked to undertake their work within fewer therapy 'sessions'.

Many professionals regard this situation as undesirable – as do numerous people who are asked to engage in such 'brief interventions' as the sum total of their psychological care (Greener and Moth, 2022; Moth et al., 2015). Likewise of concern has been the alignment of the temporalities of CBT with managerialist approaches to organising services. For instance, when a certain number of sessions are commonly anticipated by NHS managers as being appropriate for a particular presenting issue – for example, anxiety or low mood – targets can be set for professionals in relation to how many sessions of CBT should take place. Consequently, CBT is also easily aligned with the kind of audit culture (Power, 1999) that anthropologist Paul Brodwin (2013) has characterised within US community mental health, and which many clinical psychologists and other therapeutic professionals in the United Kingdom frequently lament. This is not least because extended modes of audit and accountability contribute to the reconfiguration of that which is to be audited (Miller and Rose, 2008), ostensibly impacting the autonomy of practitioners and underscoring in turn how this is itself always shaped through relations of power (Dingwall, 2016).

As a highly standardisable intervention, CBT has been particularly valued within the international move towards 'evidence-based medicine' from the late 20th century onwards (Craciun, 2018; Pickersgill, 2019a). At the same time, CBT is flexible enough to be worked up as a specific treatment for particular kinds of formally recognised psychiatric disorders. This has meant that clinical trials could be conducted on its efficacy in ways that rendered it comparable with pharmaceutical interventions (Harper and Townsend, 2021; Sadowsky, 2021), in turn helping to ensure its wider acceptability in the NHS and in privatised healthcare systems beyond the United Kingdom (Craciun, 2018; Lester, 2019; Zhang, 2020). This ambiguous existence as standardised yet flexible means that it is well suited for use by practitioners with a range of trainings and ontological commitments. While some regard CBT as a fruitful treatment for psychiatric disorders, many in clinical psychology are wary of, and sometimes antagonistic towards, what they see as a medical model of ill-health. These practitioners would be disinclined to position CBT as a specific, tailored treatment for a discrete, defined disorder, even as they might make use of the therapy for their own ends.

With its focus on recasting rather than deciphering patterns of thought, it has been feasible to constitute CBT as suitable for practitioners to use via the telephone, as well as through online modalities. It is in this computerised form that the therapy is sometimes recommended as a first step to people seeking psychological care through the NHS (Pickersgill, 2019b) – as well as to divert people away from stretched face-to-face services (Lane, 2020). Apps for managing experiences of anxiety and depression can also make use of CBT, and are used in a context where some people are electing or being encouraged not to seek access to NHS services due to concerns about long waiting lists for therapy (Crosby and Bonnington, 2020). Self-directed delivery both online and through handbooks is also common (Zeavin, 2021), and 'CBT-like' conversations with generative artificial intelligence such as ChatGPT are now feasible (Ellis and Tucker, 2021). CBT has escaped the confines of the clinic in other ways as well, and in a range of countries: for instance, it is deployed as an ostensibly humanitarian intervention within resource-restricted settings internationally; is a feature of the criminal justice system; is situated within or accessed through employment centres; and is inscribed within popular self-help texts (Armstrong, 2002; Brownlie, 2004; Frayne, 2019; Friedli and Stearn, 2015; Madsen, 2018; Torre, 2021). All these settings and uses have elicited a range of concerns from within and beyond the psychological professions, not least clinical psychology.

Initiatives to enhance access to psychological care often emphasise the provision of CBT. But this does not always sit well with clinical psychologists, nor with some other professionals. Concerns circulate widely that CBT is sometimes used as a quick and, in the eyes of some, even simplistic approach to therapy orientated primarily towards the rapid movement of people into and then out of services, rather than at substantively addressing their individual needs. Prominent arguments around its economic effectiveness as a treatment modality (Layard et al., 2007) have raised alarm bells for many; as senior clinical psychologists John Marzillier and John Hall

(2009, p. 399) put it in BPS periodical *The Psychologist*, 'Psychological therapy should be not be travestied as routine application of particular methods or techniques that can somehow deliver happy, adjusted people at low cost' (see also Binnie, 2015; Dalal, 2019; Mollon, 2009; Moloney, 2013; Ratnayake, 2022, among a range of other critiques from within and beyond psychology). Clearly, while some practitioners, such as the highly influential clinical psychologist David Clark (Clark, 2018; Layard and Clark, 2014), speak often of the benefits of mass CBT, not everyone agrees.

Descriptive and normative statements can easily blur together within the professions (Dingwall, 1977). As such, criticisms from clinical psychologists especially cannot be neatly separated from wider disciplinary politics (Cheshire and Pilgrim, 2004). Claims made about the limits of CBT often implicitly and sometimes explicitly underscore the importance of other varieties of therapy (and therapists), and the need to go 'beyond' CBT, especially in cases deemed to be particularly 'complex'. Consequently, they lend important support to clinical psychologists as well as counsellors and other practitioners who generally prioritise a longer-term therapeutic relationship than an exclusively and narrowly CBT approach is usually supposed to enjoin. This relates back to my earlier point about the epistemic claim of clinical psychology to be expert not only in CBT but also in knowing how and why to go beyond it and entwine other therapeutic approaches – to be 'integrationist'. None of this is to say that clinical psychologists' concerns reduce simply and straightforwardly to professional self-interest. Rather, these overlapping forms of claims-making illuminate how ideas about who should receive therapy, what kind of therapy should be administered, what services are for, who should deliver psychological care, and what makes a good therapist are synthesised together and reciprocally configured.

Taking a Step Back

I have used the word 'configure' and its derivatives several times now – including, of course, in the title of this book itself. Some readers will have spotted that I employ it in a similar way to how humanities and social science scholars tend to use the word 'construct'. Historian of psychology Kurt Danziger (1990) provides a key example of this in his pathbreaking book, *Constructing the Subject*. Why, then, use 'configure' at all? For one, I appreciate its connotations of ordering or rearrangement so as to get something to work. This aligns with how I think about clinical psychology. I understand this field to operate through an assemblage of material and semiotic entities and devices – policies, guidelines, waiting lists, and so on. Changes to them reorder or rearrange the nature of professional work, how it is delivered, and thus what psychology is (cf. Woolgar and Neyland, 2013). My view of therapy is that it is a form of praxis largely geared towards (re)configuring the psychological in ways that aim to ease distress – and, in so doing, (re)frames and (re)configures subjectivities (rather than building these up from scratch). In effect, and in line with the writers I drew upon earlier, I see psychological power as transformative but not unlimited, nor completely determinative.

I am also drawn to the word 'configure' because of its association with technologies (alongside its use within the sociology of technology). Consumers and/or users configure technologies, and professionals also configure the infrastructures within which these are employed – and are themselves also configured in the process. Think of the configuring of a computer, for instance, and the circuits and networks that enable its operations for purposes of work, leisure, or both. Most users do not build or construct these from scratch; rather, they configure what already exists for their own ends, and there are material and practical limits to what these might be. These artefacts likewise contour how users themselves operate and relate to technologies (Woolgar, 1990). Further, configuration does not necessarily have a clear endpoint: software is updated, and computer usage changes over time, resulting in an interplay between use, user, object, and the contexts within which all of these are situated. Processes of configuration are consequently non-linear and potentially multidirectional, since they always happen within social and economic milieu which shape what is imaginable and actionable (Mackay et al., 2000; Oudshoorn and Pinch, 2003; Oudshoorn et al., 2004; Suchman, 2012). Similarly, psychological praxis is configured and made manifest through particular organisational and epistemic environs, while at the same time psychologists can contribute to shaping the semiotic and even material settings within which configuration occurs.

Resonant metaphors have long existed within critical work on the history and philosophy of psychology (Derksen et al., 2018). This is exemplified by Michel Foucault's (1988) phrase 'technology of the self': as in, an operation or set of operations that people engage in alone or with others as an exercise in constituting selfhood (Esteban-Guitart, 2014). Like Craciun (2018), Pilgrim (1997), Rose (1992), and many others, I consider psychological therapy to be such a technology. As with other forms of technology, it is configured through use and configures both its principal users and the institutions wherein that use plays out.

The arrival of Foucault into the text seems like a good point to be even more explicit about some of the concepts and debates through which this book has itself been configured. Foucault (1988, 1989) certainly influenced my work, although I owe more immediate intellectual debts to those who have experimented with and expanded his ideas, especially Nikolas Rose (1985, 1989, 1996) as well as Ian Hacking (1995, 2002). I am, however, mindful of the concerns of feminist psychologists and others that structural power relations are occluded within some writings by analysts inspired by Foucault (Busfield, 1991; Kitzinger, 1991; Morawski, 2015). Further, I am more reluctant than some post-Foucauldian scholars to characterise processes and techniques as intrinsically new or novel (given that such characterisation is itself a sociological process; Pickersgill, 2021). While not completely opposed to this, I remain wary of over-reliance on attributions of fundamental novelty as an analytic pivot. Instead, I am more interested in the social work entailed in, for instance, how, in what sense, and with what effects a given object, practice, or institution comes to be feted as novel (a disposition which perhaps also takes some inspiration from Foucault). More generally, I find myself in alignment with historians of psychology (e.g. Smith, 1988; Thomson, 2006) who have implicitly or explicitly cautioned against embracing too tightly or interpreting too literally theorists like Foucault. Such practices can constrain analyses and reproduce their own form of scholarly conservatism.

The arguments set out in these pages, then, are informed by a range of histories and sociologies of psychology specifically, and – as will become evident over the chapters that follow – of clinical knowledge and healthcare practice more generally (most notably from traditions like the sociology of the professions and the sociology of science). Such scholarship collectively demonstrates the significance of psychology to societies while also showing that the psychological does not pre-exist the social in straightforward ways. Rather, what we take to be the psyche, and what counts as expert knowledge about it, is accomplished via a range of social and technical operations (Byford, 2016; Hayward, 2014; Miller and Rose, 1988; Young, 1995). These can be regarded as forming what Rose (1985, p. 9) terms the 'psychological complex': an intersecting matrix of 'discourses, practices, agents and techniques' through which the psychological is known and understood to be. Clinical psychology and the provision of psychological therapy more broadly are vital to understand, then, not only because they are key yet often understudied elements of healthcare. They also require our attention because they have ramifications in turn for how the subjects of therapy – which, partly because of an ethic of access, are very many of us – might be configured.

What Lies Ahead

This book draws on a range of texts and interviews (predominantly with clinical psychologists) to examine the dynamic relationships between policy and law, norms and categorisation, and knowledge and expertise within psychology vis-à-vis the enhancement of access to therapy. I show how health research, professional politics, governmental pressures, and everyday exigencies reciprocally configure the contexts of psychological care and the experiences of healthcare workers. In doing so, I also demonstrate the troubling ambivalence of an ethic of access. First, this entails a reconfiguration of praxis in ways that create professional and affective challenges even as policy to enhance the accessibility of therapy is deemed broadly desirable. Second, it creates the conditions of possibility for an increase in care for some while curtailing it for others, in part through giving clinical psychologists both more and less power.

Clinical psychologists often play senior roles in mental health services, managing different kinds of staff. This includes within NHS Talking Therapies services, formerly the Improving Access to Psychology Therapy (IAPT) initiative, one of the key programmes to expand the numbers of people receiving therapy in England. Within these and other services based in primary care settings across the United Kingdom (i.e. places generally serving as the 'first port of call' for accessing healthcare, such as a local general medical practice), therapy is very often delivered by other, less well-paid professionals. This is part of the broader logic of cost effectiveness that configured the initial instantiation of IAPT. However, clinical psychologists also contribute significant amounts of therapy, especially within secondary care (i.e. more specialist services which generally require a referral and are commonly located in hospitals). Given the prestige the profession has worked so hard to attain, clinical psychology also shapes the psychological complex more widely through its epistemic practices, ontological assertions, and strategic activities. As such, the narrative of the book moves, in the earlier chapters, from an exploration of clinical psychology as a profession to a broader consideration of psychological therapy, before refocusing later on the experiences and accounts of clinical psychologists specifically.

Accordingly, this book is divided into two parts. Part I focuses on national shifts and debates. It is grounded primarily in textual sources:

scientific articles, policy documents, and charity campaigns materials as well as blogs, newsletters, and other, more informal media. The analysis is also undergirded by a small number of interviews (conducted over 2012–2014) and informal conversation with various policy actors including civil servants, policy advisors, and charity leads. It is additionally informed by scores of encounters with different kinds of mental health professionals and discussions with a range of people who have lived experience of mental ill-health. I have been engaged to varying degrees for around 20 years now with different constituents of the psychological complex – including people receiving or/and contesting healthcare, as well as advocacy and campaign groups – through formal research interviews and focus groups as well as more everyday and personal interactions. Some of the people closest to me also work within the NHS delivering therapy, including as clinical and health psychologists. Further, alongside undertaking the sociology *of* the psychological complex I am also increasingly an actor *within* it through active research collaborations with psy-practitioners. The arguments made in this book are deeply impacted by all those engagements.

In Chapter 1, I elaborate further on the introductions to clinical psychology I made earlier in this Introduction. I demonstrate how professional claims-making operates as a form of boundary work that both configures and is configured by the evolving identity of clinical psychology. The keenness of many in the field to position it as different from psychiatry is illuminated, with the 'diagnostic' approach deemed particularly problematic by a variety of leading clinical psychologists. Likewise, I spotlight how some in clinical psychology also labour to differentiate it from other psychological traditions (like counselling psychology and health psychology), including through the development of a professional body solely for clinical psychologists: the UK Association of Clinical Psychologists (ACP-UK). Ultimately, these forms of boundary work help to configure the nature and practices of clinical psychology. Accordingly, they also have implications for the values and perspectives of individual therapists and the kinds of care people are (or are not) able to access.

Chapter 2 explores the rise of the English IAPT programme. This flagship initiative aimed at enhancing access to psychological therapy has drawn international acclaim – alongside critique and concern. In attending to its underpinnings, I highlight the managerial and clinical trends IAPT drew from and extended to proliferate therapy at scale. I examine how features of IAPT understood to be novel came to be regarded as vital forms of infrastructure around which other psychological services should be built.

I also illustrate how the economic logics that underpinned IAPT initially resulted in particular kinds of therapy being rolled out for certain types of conditions experienced by specific groups, most notably CBT for anxiety and depression diagnosed in working-age adults. The chapter reflects on the ramifications of IAPT, including in relation to the understandings of the nature of ill-health that result from it.

The narrative then turns to explore and historicise attempts to review the 1983 Mental Health Act of England and Wales. In Chapter 3, I focus on the traffic between clinical affirmations about the need to enhance access to treatment – increasingly understood to be psychological therapy – for people diagnosed with a personality disorder and political aims to detain criminal offenders living under this diagnosis for longer periods. The rewriting of the Act and the significance of personality disorder among these represent a key yet underacknowledged moment in the unfolding story of access to psychological care, while also demonstrating how improved access is not necessarily an unproblematic social good. The chapter demonstrates how legal and professional discourses contoured each other such that an understanding of personality disorder as treatable through psychological intervention was produced. Doing so improved the accessibility of therapy for some people; however, this was often as a consequence of their involuntary confinement.

Part II of this book returns to focus specifically on clinical psychology and how the activities of its practitioners have been configured though an ethic of access. It attends to clinical psychologists' negotiations of patient access to their care, including via the management of waiting lists and the rejection of referrals. I draw primarily on 40 interviews conducted over 2013–2015 with clinical psychologists who worked across a range of services in both rural and urban localities in both England and Scotland. These are interpreted against a backdrop of an assortment of conferences and professional events held by or convened for mental health professionals in general or clinical psychologists in particular. I took part in these on and off for more than a decade (with some respite during and following the COVID-19 pandemic). Some I arranged myself, with the explicit aims of bringing activists, clinicians, patients, and policymakers into conversation. The interview data are further contextualised by the materials and data that informed Part I. Again, the arguments advanced are additionally shaped by my ongoing research into, and increasing participation within, the psychological complex. Unfortunately, these continuing engagements confirm that many of the concerns discussed in Part II – such as long waiting lists and associated challenges – have only worsened since the interviews were conducted.

Chapter 4 analyses how clinical psychologists preface (potential) care through negotiations of referrals and acts of assessment prior to any kind of therapy. I regard these as key 'uncertainty moments', in which practitioners must decide whether to see a someone for therapy. This decision-making process depends on far more than an 'objective' evaluation of the person in front of them. Resolution of uncertainty entails the reciprocal configuration of at least three kinds of ontologies: the ontology of a potential patient; the ontology of the service in which they work; and the ontology of their profession. These are not necessarily stable; rather, they can be remade over time and in relation to particular service users (demonstrating how visions and adjudications of therapeutic need are highly contextualised). Such 'prefacing practices' contribute to the denial of access for some people, although even exclusions might themselves sometimes be accounted for by professionals as a form of care.

In Chapter 5 I move to consider some of the challenges of waiting lists and associated targets that configure clinical psychology. Taking the position that targets operate as a technology of government (Rose, 1996), the chapter indicates some of the affective and material consequences of their instantiation. In particular, I show how clinical psychologists rework processes of entry into therapy, and the aims and character of care, to meet – and sometimes accommodate – targets. While professional autonomy is often regarded as being constrained through these technologies of government, practitioners nevertheless find ways of performing autonomous action in a manner that can advantage some patients over others. I illuminate how shifts in psychological care in response to targets might recast clinical psychologists' relationships with their work and with people seeking therapy. In so doing, implications arise for the subjectivities that are (not) assembled through therapy.

Chapter 6 centres clinical psychologists' perspectives on and responses to 'did not attend' (DNA) policies. Patient non-attendance at clinical appointments has long been regarded as troubling within healthcare, particularly so in light of pressures and targets to see more people for therapy and more quickly. DNA policies are also an object of often latent concern by professionals and patients in relation to how they ostensibly improve access for some people through the potentially strategic exclusion of others. I analyse how clinical psychologists account for and navigate such policies, exploring how (in)formal rules around attendance can prompt the involuntary discharge of patients. DNA policies often provide space for clinical discretion and are even sometimes elided by practitioners. Their negotiations can involve highly moralised configurations of both patient and professional subjectivities. These contribute to legitimising exclusion from services, as well as the expertise leveraged to do so.

Finally, I conclude with a short coda. In it, I describe some of the ambivalences that come with an ethic of access. I reflect on the procedural and ethical challenges that can be propelled by ostensibly progressive healthcare initiatives, and consider what could perhaps be done about these. In light of the arguments made throughout the preceding chapters, I decline to advance discrete recommendations in what is already a crowded policy space. Rather, I urge an ethos of reconfiguration within mental healthcare that fosters variability and mutability in services through direct and ongoing engagement with communities. In so doing, psychological practitioners might be enabled to better comprehend, articulate, and serve the needs of those with whom they undertake therapeutic work.

PART I

Configuring Contexts

CHAPTER 1

Positioning Psychology

Configuring Professional Boundaries and Identities

A whole range of ideas, practices, and institutions intersect and reciprocally shape one another to give life to the psychological. The overarching discipline of psychology itself, with all its constituent traditions (including clinical psychology), is of course key among these. Significant too, though, are fields such as psychiatry, counselling, social work, and education. These and much more – everyday notions, actions, and relations – form what Nikolas Rose (1985) has called the psychological complex. Attending to how clinical psychology is configured with respect to its close neighbours within this multifaceted and dynamic matrix offers insight into how its practitioners conceive of themselves. This production of professional identities, in turn, has ramifications for the people with whom psychologists work. Disciplinary claims making and straightforward politicking contour the psychological complex, informing the kinds of knowledge and expertise through which subjects are known about, acted upon, and configured through.

As we saw in the Introduction, the role of the clinical psychologist in the United Kingdom over the last 70 years or so has shifted from that of a psychometrician embedded in psychiatric contexts to being an autonomous therapeutic practitioner and authoritative figure within the mental health ecosystem. In considering this change, it is important to underscore that – as practitioners themselves have argued – clinical psychology 'cannot be understood in isolation' (Cheshire and Pilgrim, 2004, p. 5). Accordingly, this chapter explores how the profession engages in what sociologists term 'boundary work' (Gieryn, 1983) in relation to other psychological specialisms and psy-professions. How, for example, are boundaries drawn between the nature, remit, and function of clinical psychologists vis-à-vis these other experts (Goldie, 1977; cf. Buchanan, 2003; Schlett, 2022; Scull, 2015)? Assuming this boundary drawing can be read as a form of 'occupational identity work' (Allen, 2000, p. 345; Snow and Anderson, 1987), what kinds of claims about and understandings of clinical psychology emerge in the process?

Boundary work is a strategy for generating and controlling status and resource (Lamont and Molnár, 2002), including through the modulation of relative prestige inside a broader professional milieu where this has economic connotations (Burri, 2008; Comeau-Vallée and Langley, 2020). Within healthcare, both inter- and intra-professional boundaries serve important roles in the configuration of specialities and practices (Goodwin et al., 2005; Jenkins, 2020; Lindberg et al., 2017; Martin et al., 2009; Nancarrow and Borthwick, 2005). In what follows, my focus is, primarily, on the relationship between clinical psychology and psychiatry – one that was vital to the consolidation of clinical psychology and which remains significant (Derksen, 2000; Hall, 2015). I attend especially to the discursive configuring of psychiatry by clinical psychology, and how this acts to demarcate the disciplines and to underscore the singularity of the latter. Towards the end of the chapter, I then move to reflect on how clinical psychology navigates boundaries between, and asserts its distinctiveness and autonomy in relation to, other psychological professions in the NHS – focusing on health, as well as counselling, psychology. This is in light of both long-standing and recent 'jurisdictional disputes' (Abbott, 1988, p. 74) between these psychological professions and clinical psychology, and various attempts to manage these by the British Psychological Society (BPS). By examining how clinical psychology positions itself in relation to other disciplines, a brighter light can be cast on how professional identities, discourses, and practices are reciprocally configured.

Clinical Psychology and Psychiatry

> That a strong, respected and highly competent profession of psychiatry is essential to the growth and flourishing of clinical psychology appears obvious; it is perhaps no less true to say that the existence of a large group of well-trained, competent, and friendly clinical psychologists can be of the utmost value to psychiatry.
>
> (Eysenck, 1950, p. 714)

These comments were made by the influential psychologist Hans Eysenck in an article outlining 'The Function and Training of the Clinical Psychologist'. Eysenck (1950) asserted that the Maudsley clinical psychology training course (discussed in the Introduction) sought 'to facilitate such a rapprochement' (p. 714) between clinical psychology and psychiatry. More than 70 years later, the kind of mutually beneficial relationship between disciplines outlined in the section-opening quote seems, more or less, to have developed. The professions work closely together within mental health services, as well as often within universities. However, there have been many bumps along the way as clinical psychology and psychiatry have sometimes moved apart yet remained connected (Burns and Hall, 2021; Cheshire and Pilgrim, 2004; Samson, 1995). Today, flare-ups between them remain not altogether uncommon, and within the literature and especially on social media those sometimes burn brightly.

Before examining some of those tensions, I want to step back for a moment to consider some of the salient (dis)similarities between clinical psychology and psychiatry. Within popular culture, distinctions between these professions can often be elided: the terms 'psychological' and 'psychiatrist' – not to mention 'therapist' and even 'shrink' – are sometimes used synonymously. Boundaries can inadvertently be further blurred by practitioners themselves: some psychiatrists are consultants in medical psychotherapy, for which they have received advanced training in psychological treatments (Royal College of Psychiatrists, 2019). Certainly, both professions are orientated towards intervening in psychological distress. The stated and enacted differences between them are important, however (Abbott, 1988).

In the United Kingdom, prospective clinical psychologists must study for a Doctorate in Clinical Psychology (DClinPsy). This is achieved through a combination of teaching, research, and therapeutic provision. Applicants for doctorate programmes are commonly only successful after some years working as an assistant psychologist or in a similar role, usually within the NHS (following undergraduate training in psychology and often an MSc degree as well). For their part, psychiatrists are, by definition, medically qualified. After a degree in medicine, further training is then undertaken in psychiatry. Following examination, this eventually leads to membership and then later perhaps fellowship of the Royal College of Psychiatrists. As medical practitioners, psychiatrists can legally prescribe pharmaceuticals; clinical psychologists cannot. They also tend to be more diagnostically orientated than clinical psychologists. Nevertheless, the differences between professions with respect to diagnosis can sometimes be overstated, and – as we will see – also deployed to underscore the distinctiveness of clinical psychology.

Prescribing is a useful starting point to think about the discursive boundary work that helps to configure clinical psychology. Perhaps unsurprisingly, debates about whether psychologists should have some kind of prescribing rights occasionally foment. The legal authority to prescribe would bring clinical psychology in line with other key health professions, such as nursing. However, opinion on this matter varies greatly (BPS,

2020; Cohen-Tovée, 2020). Rebecca Courtney-Walker, Chair of a BPS Group charged with considering this issue, reflected during her work that the question of prescribing rights for psychologists has long 'been a controversial topic with strong views on both sides of the debate' (Courtney-Walker, 2019, p. 2). Responses to a 2019 consultation with psychologists about prescribing 'showed', in her view, 'considerable passion' (Courtney-Walker, 2020, p. 3). Some judged prescribing rights as representing an opportunity for 'evolution' – 'especially as other professions have evolved and now routinely practice as psychological therapists, which was previously one of our unique selling points' (Courtney-Walker, 2020, p. 3). Concerns were raised by other respondents, though, 'that prescribing rights would mean psychologists may become more medicalised, posing a potential threat to their identity and practice as a profession' (Courtney-Walker, 2020, p. 2).

Alison Clarke, then Chair of BPS Practice Board, noted in 2020 that the diverging views about prescribing rights suggest 'the need for a wider debate about the future shape of our profession and what our trajectory towards that future may look like' (Clarke, 2020, p. 4). As Courtney-Walker's summary of consultation responses indicated, this is because negotiating a consensus on prescribing rights also involves negotiating what psychology is and what it should be doing. Discussions around pharmaceuticals are particularly volatile in this respect, since debates about their potential or proper roles within clinical psychology invite – and for some, even many, demand – deep reflection on what their use implies for how the profession conceptualises the ontology of psychological distress. If clinical psychologists are to prescribe the same drugs as psychiatrists, for example, does it mean that they must regard the targets of that intervention in the same way? Should clinical psychologists be urged to think more like psychiatrists?

This question speaks to a bigger concern within clinical psychology about what many practitioners see as the quintessentially biomedical epistemology shaping psychiatric thought and treatment. Unease about, critique of, and explicit opposition to this has been increasingly evident within a range of reports and commentaries over the past decade or so. This includes a high-profile BPS report produced by the Division of Clinical Psychology (DCP) and led by Anne Cook, titled *Understanding Psychosis and Schizophrenia*. In it the authors write that there is a 'need to shift from seeing ourselves as treating disease to seeing ourselves as providing skilled help and support to people who are experiencing understandable distress' (BPS DCP, 2017, p. 102). Accordingly, clinicians 'need to move beyond the "medical model"' (BPS DCP, 2017, p. 103). It seems likely that for the authors of this report, the answer to the question 'Should clinical psychologists be urged to think more like psychiatrists?' is a 'no' – as it is for a significant number of others as well.

We can see, then, that while clinical psychology and psychiatry can have broadly similar professional foci, the former can express considerable unease about mimesis with the latter. This is both despite and because of what Eysenck (1950, p. 714) referred to as the 'inseparable destinies' of these professions: what happens to one has implications for the other. Professional tensions between psychiatry and clinical psychology can at times be deeply felt. These can reflect much deeper ontological and epistemological disjunctures that through their proclamation and rehearsal come to be further enacted and more deeply entrenched.

Diagnosis and the 'Medical Model'

Clinical psychologists critical of medical approaches to mental healthcare sometimes posit that their profession works with a fundamentally different ontology of distress compared with ostensibly diagnostically orientated psychiatry. For these psychologists – and, it should be noted, quite a few psychiatrists – the complexities of subjective experience escape straightforward categorisation through diagnostic terms such as *bipolar disorder* or *schizophrenia*. Indeed, two of the authors of the aforementioned *Understanding Psychosis and Schizophrenia* report have argued that 'psychiatric diagnosis has the potential to be particularly damaging' when deployed in relation to experiences associated with psychosis (Cooke and Kinderman, 2018, p. 47). Such comments articulate with other statements around diagnosis in outputs from the BPS, and especially the DCP, in recent years. These assertions have occasionally been to the chagrin of some clinical psychologists who judge them to be made as part of intellectual debates and professional turf wars in which they profess varying degrees of disinterest.

Clinical psychologists who position themselves against biomedical – or, more specifically, diagnostic or pharmaceutical – approaches to mental health have held powerful roles within the BPS. Although many BPS documents suggest that psychologists should not be "anti" diagnosis in any straightforward way, these figures have helped to inflect wider debate within the Society and the profession. Peter Kinderman, for instance, is a professor at the University of Liverpool who has held a range of BPS leadership roles, not least BPS President (2016–2017) and, for two terms,

DCP Chair (2004–2005 and 2010–2011). He is also the author of a range of texts critical, to varying degrees, of biomedical approaches to mental health, including the books *A Prescription for Psychiatry* (2014) and *A Manifesto for Mental Health* (2019). For Kinderman, 'diagnoses are often unreliable, invalid and separate inappropriately the person from their experiences' (Kinderman, 2015, p. 156).

Other high-profile clinical psychologists, such as Richard Bentall (2009) and Mary Boyle (1997), have also written critically, and sometimes for a wide audience, about psychiatry, psychiatric diagnosis, and pharmaceuticals. Probably one of the best-known critics in clinical psychology of psychiatric diagnosis is Lucy Johnstone, a senior practitioner in Bristol. She is a key contributor to, and occasionally an architect of, a variety of highly visible BPS policy statements and guidance (including some described later here). In a range of writings, such as her monograph, *Users and Abusers of Psychiatry* (Johnstone, 2021), she has set out clearly and powerfully the harms that can result in the adoption of a disease-focussed conception of subjective distress. Johnstone has sought to actively further the separation of clinical psychology from diagnostically orientated approaches to mental health. In her view, 'We are close to recognising the traditional psychiatric model of "mental illness" for the failed paradigm that it is' (Johnstone, 2016, p. 732).

Beyond Diagnosis

A particular focus of psychological critique has been the American Psychiatric Association's *Diagnostic and Statistical Manual for Mental Disorders* (the DSM). This is widely judged to be emblematic of a diagnostic approach to psychiatry with which many in clinical psychology take issue. The fifth edition of the DSM, the *DSM-5*, was released in 2013. Over the course of its writing, and immediately following its release, there was a proliferation of critical discourse centred upon this text (Kinderman et al., 2017). As we will see, this critique was a key feature of the boundary work that informed the positioning of clinical psychological within the psychological complex.

Prior to its release in 2013, the BPS, among others (Kamens et al., 2017), wrote to the American Psychiatric Association to express concern that by classifying 'problems as 'illnesses'', the *DSM-5* 'misses the relational context of problems and the undeniable social causation of many such problems' (BPS, 2011). Subsequently, and a matter of days before the manual was released, the DCP released a Position Statement titled

'Classification of Behaviour and Experience in Relation to Functional Psychiatric Diagnoses: Time for a Paradigm Shift' (BPS DCP, 2013). If the title of this document left some room for interpretation, the opening sentences made its point crystal clear:

> The DCP is of the view that it is timely and appropriate to affirm publicly that the current classification system as outlined in DSM and ICD [the World Health Organization's International Classification of Diseases], in respect of the functional psychiatric diagnoses, has significant conceptual and empirical limitations. Consequently, there is a need for a paradigm shift in relation to the experiences that these diagnoses refer to, towards a conceptual system which is no longer based on a 'disease' model. (BPS DCP, 2013, p. 1)

The Position Statement garnered considerable attention – including, and in advance of its release, from the left-leaning broadsheet, *The Observer*. An article therein framed the BPS document as an 'attack' on a 'rival profession', noting that it 'effectively casts doubt on psychiatry's predominantly biomedical model of mental distress – the idea that people are suffering from illnesses that are treatable by doctors using drugs' (Doward, 2013).

Unsurprisingly, this coverage and framing were not well received by many in psychiatry, but also generated concern, frustration, and even anger from some BPS members. Prominent academic psychologists Essi Viding and Uta Frith, for example, rebuked the authors of the DCP Policy Statement for 'attacking the *DSM-5*' and biomedical approaches. They wrote in a letter to *The Psychologist*,

> The DCP representatives in the media appear to predicate their argument on a false dichotomy between genes and environment, which seems to presume that search for genetic risk factors equals drive for medication and that demonstration of environmental risk calls for psychological therapy. We do not know of any informed researchers who would make a simplistic proposal like this. (Viding and Frith, 2013, p. 382)

Viding and Frith went on to outline links between genetics, psychology, and environment – conclusions about which, apparently, 'anyone who has done their homework in keeping up with the research in the past 20 years should be able to draw'. As far as they were concerned, 'representatives of the DCP should know better' (Viding and Frith, 2013, p. 382).

Viding and Frith's letter stimulated, in turn, its own spirited responses. Refuting claims made within Viding and Frith's contribution, Mary Boyle, for one, found it 'surprising' that they 'should use the words "attacking the DSM"', given 'the importance they attach to evidence' (Boyle, 2013, p. 466). Other psychologists also defended the Policy Statement, including a letter by Mel Wiseman and 209 other signatories which stated their clear 'support [for] the DCP's call for a paradigm shift in how we think about mental distress and the need to move away from psychiatric diagnosis' (Wiseman, 2013, p. 469). As far as Wiseman and colleagues were concerned, 'We need to step out from the shadow of biological reductionism' (Wiseman, 2013, p. 469). Richard Pemberton, Chair of the DCP, also contributed to the debate. He noted that the Statement was not seen by the DCP 'as an "attack" but as a thoughtful critique based on a two-year process of reviewing the evidence and consulting within all the DCP Faculties, where it has widespread support' (Pemberton, 2013, p. 467). He did, however, 'regret that some of the reporting has badged this as a psychiatry versus psychology battle'.

Pemberton's comments reflect a wider rhetorical position in some of the critique of biomedical approaches to psychiatry emerging from the BPS and, especially, the DCP; specifically, that it is not psychiatry per se that is being criticised, but rather a particular approach within that profession. However, some psychiatrists (and clinical psychologists) see diagnosis as so quintessential to psychiatry that flare-ups can and do happen, contributing to the demarcation of boundaries between these professions.

Since 2018, a focal point of frictions has been the *Power Threat Meaning Framework* (hereafter *PTMF*), which itself embeds and extends critical discourse around the DSM. Led by Lucy Johnstone and Mary Boyle, the *PTMF*, as it is commonly known, drew from and developed a range of long-standing activities and agenda-setting texts produced by the principal and contributing authors (including Peter Kinderman). Rather than serving as another kind of handbook for clinical practice, it sought to provide 'an over-arching structure for identifying patterns in emotional distress, unusual experiences and troubling behaviour, as an alternative to psychiatric diagnosis and classification' (Johnstone and Boyle, 2018, p. 5; see also Boyle and Johnstone, 2020; Harper and Cromby, 2022). Concerned with distress in its social and political contexts as well as individually experienced, and as the outcome of interactional 'relational, social, cultural and material factors' (Johnstone and Boyle, 2018, p. 8), the authors cast the *PTMF* as distinct from a more DSM-orientated approach. Johnstone, Boyle, and colleagues noted, for example, that the Framework 'allows provisional identification of general patterns and regularities in the expression and experience of distress and troubled or troubling behaviour, as opposed to specific biological or psychological causal mechanisms linked to discrete disorder categories' (Johnstone and Boyle, 2018, p. 8).

The *PTMF* has attracted considerable praise alongside a great deal of critique, much of which has played out across social media. The authors have reflected on concerns raised around their text (Johnstone et al., 2019), for instance in relation to how, and the extent to which, it focuses on trauma. Some criticism has also related to an assumed orientation of the *PTMF* towards 'anti-psychiatry' – although its authors appear keen to eschew accusations that the document is part of a strategy for asserting professional dominance (Johnstone et al., 2019). Indeed, psychology itself is taken to task by the authors, along with psychiatry, including for its 'reluctance to acknowledge positivism as a philosophy rather than a set of self-evident rules for discovering facts about the world' (Johnstone et al., 2019, p. 49). Still, it is hard not to read the *PTMF* as a kind of strategic resource for enacting boundaries between clinical psychology and psychiatry, given the latter is so often understood to have diagnosis at its heart.

Formulating Clinical Psychology

A primary concern for many psychological critics of psychiatric diagnosis – and, it should again be noted, for some psychiatrists (Pickersgill, 2024) – is that it represents a 'loss of meaning' (Johnstone, 2017, p. 31). As Johnstone summarises,

> By divesting people's experiences of their personal, social, and cultural significance, diagnosis turns 'people with problems' into 'patients with illnesses.' Stories of trauma, abuse, discrimination, and deprivation are sealed off behind a label as the individual is launched on what is often a lifelong journey of disability, exclusion, and despair . (Johnstone, 2017, p. 31)

As a counterpoint to this, the BPS supports the practice of psychological formulation. This is a skill in which the regulatory body, the Health and Care Professions Council (HCPC), requires all varieties of practitioner psychologists to be proficient (HCPC, 2023). 'Formulation' has increased in prominence over the last two decades; however, it has a much longer history – as the DCP themselves point out (BPS DCP, 2011). Indeed, this history is itself deployed by proponents to emphasise its importance (Johnstone and Dallos, 2014).

The central role of formulation in clinical psychology was underscored through the 2011 DCP *Good Practice Guidelines on the Uses of Psychological Formulation*. The development and writing of the Guidelines were led by Johnstone herself, and they attracted considerable attention and celebration. According to Johnstone, formulation 'is considered to be the core skill of the profession of clinical psychology' (Johnstone, 2018, p. 31). Through such statements, formulation can be leveraged as an important means of bounding and defining the profession.

What, though, is formulation? Like many questions within psychology, the answer depends in part on who one is asking, why, and in what contexts. Further, as Johnstone, writing with Rudi Dallos, has described, there are also a multitude of ways through which psychologists can produce formulations (Johnstone and Dallos, 2014). In the aforementioned DCP Guidelines, formulation was defined as 'a hypothesis about a person's difficulties, which links theory with practice and guides the intervention' (BPS DCP, 2011, p. 2). In a 2019 leaflet aimed at people undergoing psychological therapy, the DCP described it as 'a joint effort between you and the psychologist to summarise your difficulties, to explain why they may be happening and to make sense of them'. A metaphor of a jigsaw was used to further articulate this process:

> Working on a formulation is like two people putting together a jigsaw. The pieces of the 'jigsaw' are pieces of information such as:
>
> - How you feel at the moment;
> - What's going on in your life now;
> - When the difficulties or distress started;
> - Key experiences and relationships in your life;
> - What these experiences and relationships mean to you.

Formulation was presented as providing 'a starting point' for psychological therapy, which 'can be updated to respond to new information or changing circumstances'. Accordingly, 'a formulation is never static – it will keep evolving throughout your work with a psychologist as you find out more about yourself'.

Depending on how and why it is used, the practice of formulation may or may not align with diagnostic approaches to mental health. It does, however, have a particular resonance for clinical psychologists who seek to move away from the use of diagnostic categories, and is increasingly recommended in place of diagnosis (Bowden et al., 2020). Lucy Johnstone, for instance, has argued that formulation is a 'credible alternative' (Johnstone, 2018, p. 30) to diagnosis; indeed, best-practice formulation is deemed to be 'based on fundamentally different principles from psychiatric diagnosis' (Johnstone, 2018, p. 39). Peter Kinderman, too, has urged the use of a formulation-based approach rather than diagnosis (e.g. Kinderman, 2015; Kinderman et al, 2013). In his words,

> [W]e must move away from the 'disease-model', which assumes that emotional distress is merely symptomatic of biological illness, and instead embrace a model of mental health and well-being that recognises our essential and shared humanity. (Kinderman, 2015, p. 160)

Since, for Kinderman (and others), 'diagnostic entities lack validity, it is much easier and more appropriate to develop formulations' (Kinderman, 2015, p. 157).

An enhanced focus on formulation also aligns with wider moves on the part of some psychologists over the last decade or so – including Johnstone, Kinderman, and more activist groups like Psychologists Against Austerity – to revitalise a focus on social and economic inequality as part of psychological work (indeed, the BPS Annual Conference 2019 was specifically themed around 'The Psychological Impact of Inequality'). McClelland (2013, p. 121), for instance, argued that attention to inequalities within the process of formulation 'goes beyond the traditional boundaries of psychology in emphasising the role of social and cultural contexts in shaping problems'. This focus on inequality itself speaks to concerns within clinical psychology that mental health practice can individualise patient distress – with psychiatric diagnosis commonly seen as a key mechanism of reifying such individualisation.

Despite its historical and more recently underscored role in clinical psychology, formulation has not necessarily been a consistently significant strand of psychological discourse. As Harper and Moss reflected at the turn of the century, while 'formulation is now considered central to the professional practice of clinical psychology' neither recalled 'it being mentioned in any detail during our training as clinical psychologists in the late 1980s and early 1990s' (Harper and Moss, 2003, p. 6). Drawing on Crellin (1998), they likewise noted that formulation had been presented as rather distinct to clinical psychology and 'this, no doubt, serves a function of promoting clinical psychology as a unique discipline' (Harper and Moss, 2003, p. 6). To rewrite their proposition through a more explicitly sociological idiom: presenting formulation as both central and (reasonably) distinct to clinical psychology is a form of boundary work. In particular, it acts to distinguish the profession from other forms of psychological expertise within an economically challenging context (i.e. the NHS) which drives different therapeutic practitioners to compete for status and resource.

Yet, although clinical psychology dominates much discourse in mental health in relation to formulation, many psychiatrists – as well as other mental health professions – also engage in formulation (Pickersgill, 2024). A senior psychiatrist once described to me his surprise at what he saw as some clinical psychologists presenting formulation as a radical break from diagnosis. This particular interlocutor, a clinical academic specialising in biological research, noted that he had been formulating for decades and that it had been central to his training (see also Armstrong, 1980). Other psychiatrists I have spoken with have likewise invoked this term and its importance to their clinical practice, and the potential to engage in formulation alongside diagnosis (Baird et al., 2017; Owen, 2023). Indeed, there are those who regard claims-making about formulation as sometimes comprising a rather unhelpful form of assault on psychiatry (Mohtasshemi et al., 2016). These contemplations and assertions are also a kind of boundary work, however. Specifically, they act to buttress against, and to an extent dismantle, claims of clinical psychological exceptionalism, and so serve their own professional ends as well.

Clinical Psychology and Other Psychologies of the Clinic

While clinical psychology is a significant focus of the work of the BPS, the membership of the society goes far beyond this profession. Currently, the BPS recognises several branches of psychology, and the Society is structured along 11 divisions that reflect these. Alongside the Division of Clinical Psychology, which as we have seen is very active in terms of producing policy statements and practice guidelines, there are also the Divisions of Academics, Researchers and Teachers in Psychology; Coaching Psychology; Counselling Psychology; Educational and Child Psychology; Forensic Psychology; Health Psychology; Neuropsychology; Occupational Psychology; Sport and Exercise Psychology; and the Scottish Division of Educational Psychology.

The DCP is the largest of the BPS divisions. Its members include clinical psychologists both in the NHS and in private practice, alongside some whose role is primarily research. The DCP is currently subdivided into 13 'Faculties', which are largely orientated to foci of particular clinical concern and expertise, such as Addictions, Eating Disorders, and Psychosis and Complex Mental Health (an outlier is the DCP Faculty of Leadership and Management). Notably, some of the Faculties overlap with the interests of other BPS Divisions: the DCP Faculty of Clinical Health Psychology and the Division of Health Psychology, for instance. Indeed, there can be some overlapping orientations at the divisional level itself, most notably between the DCP and the Division of Counselling Psychology (DCoP). These intersections can be key sites of boundary work among professional psychologists, and are a further means through which clinical psychology configures itself.

The challenge of demarcation between clinical and counselling psychology has been an issue at times for both professions. The latter has long roots in counselling in the United States and the United Kingdom;

however, the BPS only approved a Division of Counselling Psychology in 1994 (Strawbridge and Woolfe, 2003). Even then, 'fierce resistance', as clinical psychologist Glenys Parry (2015, p. 190) put it, had to be overcome for this to happen. While technically a much younger profession than clinical psychology, counselling psychology nevertheless had considerable and long-standing evidence, concepts, and embodied experience from which to draw. Further, unlike clinical psychology, counselling psychology had always been configured around the therapeutic.

What is the difference between counselling and clinical psychology? As the authors of the introductory chapter of one handbook for the former remarked back in 2003, this question 'is not easy to answer' (Strawbridge and Woolfe, 2003, p. 4). More than a decade later, counselling psychologists Jessica Jones Nielson and Helen Nicholas argued that 'it is becoming more difficult to differentiate counselling psychologists from clinical psychologists' (Neilson and Nicholas, 2016, p. 211). Today, both groups deliver some kind of psychological intervention to a range of populations. Both, too, will be expected to have a (critical) understanding of psychiatric diagnosis, risk assessment, therapeutic relationship, and a range of other similarities.

Like clinical psychology (Cheshire and Pilgrim, 2004), counselling psychology has come to engage with a 'scientist-practitioner' model of practice (Corrie and Callahan, 2000). This is a popular phrase, if sometimes a little ambiguous. Holding it close, though, enables fully qualified psychologists across BPS Faculties to assert a keenly honed and sophisticated ability to engage closely with – and produce – research evidence about therapeutic mechanisms and efficacy. Part of this sophistication is knowing when to creatively interpret, move beyond, or elide 'the evidence' when doing so is deemed to be implied by the calculus of clinical judgement. The term also helps to draw boundaries between, for instance, both clinical and counselling psychologists and other providers of psychological care, implicitly elevating their status through the cultural, professional, and epistemic legitimacy that the term 'scientist' bestows.

Of course, despite all this there are also a range of differences between clinical and counselling psychology. Not least of these is the requirement for trainees of the latter profession to undertake personal therapy. Despite the assertions and recommendations of key figures in the DCP, there are also some in counselling psychology who feel that clinical psychologists espouse a more 'biomedical model' (Neilson and Nicholas, 2016, p. 211) through their work. The articulation of this position can be regarded as, in part, a strategy for differentiating the disciplines in ways that are advantageous to counselling psychologists. Since this group 'often compete[s] for similar jobs in the NHS' (Neilson and Nicholas, 2016, p. 211) as clinical psychologists, it makes good sense to present counselling psychologists as already practising in the ways DCP leaders are encouraging their own members to embrace.

The phrase 'reflective practitioner' has also been framed as perhaps especially important within counselling psychology. For Ray Woolfe (2012, p. 72), author or editor of several textbooks in this field, the notion of the reflective practitioner has 'offered a distinctive identity which articulated the special quality of counselling psychology'. It is one that is concerned with the thoughtful and critical analysis of clinical activities, with a view to ensuring that deep and open-minded reflection contributes to enhancing therapeutic and other kinds of practice (Carmichael et al., 2020). It is also a professional identity that is explicitly inculcated as part of training. For instance, the BPS *Handbook for Candidates* (BPS, 2022), for people seeking qualification in counselling psychology, describes how by the end of the qualification candidates are expected to 'embody the identity of the Reflective Practitioner' (BPS, 2022, p. 34). In contrast, while candidates are expected to be familiar with the scientist-practitioner role, no such embodiment is required. The aforementioned therapy that trainee counselling psychologists undergo is commonly framed as a key mechanism to develop and configure an identity as a reflective practitioner (Hanley and Amos, 2017).

Such an identity is not, though, one which clinical psychologists are willing to leave solely for counselling psychology. A range of writings on, training in, and encouragements towards reflective practice exist in the former field, commonly with a view that this should be imbricated with a scientist-practitioner approach (Carmicheal et al., 2020). Clinical psychologists have come to assert the values of reflection increasingly and publicly (Wigg, 2009), such as in the DCP guidelines on formulation (BPS DCP, 2011). As we can see, then, there are elements of a reciprocally iterative mimesis between clinical and counselling psychologies. This process can be regarded as powered, to a degree, by economic aims to secure posts for their members in an expanding but by no means limitless mental health workforce.

The Growth of Health Psychology

Just as the Divisions of Clinical and Counselling Psychology have their overlaps and potential for frictions, so too do the Divisions of Clinical and Health Psychology. The latter group are principally orientated to the study and mitigation of psychological issues associated with physical ill-health. Like counselling psychologists, health psychologists become chartered psychologists through a training route distinct to clinical psychology (BPS, 2021). The instantiation of health psychology within the BPS was first via the establishment of a Section in 1986, which became a Special Group in 1993, and then, ultimately, a Division in 1997- many members of which were initially trained as clinical psychologists (Bennett, 2015; Quinn et al., 2020). This gradual formalisation and growth followed interest by a small number of UK psychologists in the 1970s in the establishment of the American Psychological Association Health Psychology Division in 1978 (Wallston, 1997). Thereafter, a growing research and evidence base developed within universities and, more slowly, the NHS in the 1980s and beyond (Quinn et al., 2020).

While health psychology was professionalising in the 1990s, many clinical psychologists continued to consider physical health part of their territory. Some characterise themselves as 'clinical health psychologists' and work in services relating to, for instance, oncology, physical trauma, and pain management. The DCP supports a Faculty of Clinical Health Psychology for such practitioners, best regarded as 'a special interest group for all clinical psychologists practising in physical health settings' (Bennett, 2015, p. 304). This focus has obvious resonances with the activities of the BPS Division of Health Psychology (DHP), given its purposes to support and develop the discipline of health psychology and individual health psychologists – some of whom are indeed 'psychologists practising in physical health settings' (Bennett, 2015, p. 304), although many work in academia or public health. Given that the Faculty of Clinical Health Psychology was established in 1998 – a year after the formalisation of the DHP – it is hard not to regard its inauguration as, at least in part, a form of professional boundary work by the DCP.

When speaking informally to DHP members, I have sometimes encountered frustration about the position the larger and more established professional group of clinical psychology has held within what increasing numbers of health psychologists see today as their purview. This can centre on, for instance, the use by some DCP members of the aforementioned moniker, 'clinical health psychologist'. Notably, this is not a 'protected title' – that is, one of the professional titles legally protected by the HCPC in its role as the professional regulatory body for psychology in the United Kingdom (whereas 'clinical psychologist' and 'health psychologist' are). Some health psychologists feel that they are being implicitly, and on occasion explicitly, excluded from NHS jobs that advertise health-related posts through the terms 'clinical psychologist' or, more rarely, 'clinical health psychologist' (Bull et al., 2020) (despite BPS guidance about the use of inclusive job titles; Dooley and Farndon, 2021). Such advertisements can be explained, in part, by service leads who might be clinical psychologists that are perhaps unaware of the therapeutic expertise professed by some more recently trained health psychologists, or who are sceptical about the nature, extent, or potential applications of health psychology training. Regardless, health psychologists can at time feel discounted or marginalised within NHS settings where clinical psychology continues to hold considerable power and influence as compared to other psychologies (Asimakopoulou, 2022; Bull et al., 2020).

At the same time, some clinical psychologists can be disquieted by the increasing move of DHP members into what they have long seen as their domain, rather than that of health psychology: the provision of psychological therapy itself. For many years, health psychology was orientated far more towards academia than the NHS (Quinn et al., 2020). The non-therapeutic emphasis of health psychology was in fact part of the repertoire of persuasion and compromise that ensured support for the establishment of the DHP in the face of DCP members uncomfortable with the notion that health psychologists might deliver therapy (Bennett, 2015; Quinn et al., 2020). In recent years, however, ever more inroads are being made by health psychologists into the NHS and the delivery of psychological interventions (Forshaw, 2022; O'Carroll, 2014; Quinn et al., 2020).

Within BPS documents, the work of health psychologists is commonly carefully framed in terms of 'behaviour change interventions' or 'therapeutic intervention techniques' (e.g. BPS, 2021, pp. 5, 30), rather than more directly as 'psychological therapy' per se. Nevertheless, health psychologists can now be found in services orientated to, for instance, pain management and addiction, and employing psychological technologies like acceptance and commitment therapy (ACT) and CBT. Accordingly, characterising the interventions of health psychologists as lying outside of the realm of the therapeutic requires a particular framing of therapy that seems challenging to sustain. Unsurprisingly, this configuration of health psychology as a practitioner discipline can create friction with clinical psychologists.

The overlaps and tensions between clinical and health psychology, as with clinical and counselling psychology, underscore how, while psychological disciplines configure themselves through their professional self-image and foci, others in turn come to draw on similar language or practices to morph their own ontologies. A form of ratcheting is one result of this, with declarations of expertise and authority in a given field resulting in similar assertions from another, only to be met with fresh claims-making. Boundaries between psychologies are thus constantly being worked up through intra-professional praxis: they are built, partially dissolved, and redrawn. Importantly, this occurs within a notoriously competitive professional field, underscoring the need for psychologists within and beyond clinical psychology to stake claims to distinctiveness and significance.

Clinical Competition

Competition in clinical psychology starts early: training programmes are highly oversubscribed, and have been for a long time (Cheshire and Pilgrim, 2004). Application success rates are low, and those candidates who are not rejected are predominantly white and middle class (Palmer et al., 2021). Thereafter, career progression can also be challenging, although notably easier for white men, despite their proportionally far smaller numbers within the clinical psychology workforce (Palmer et al., 2021). Yet, despite many people seeking training in clinical psychology, NHS services can still sometimes struggle to recruit for a post (e.g. due to where a service is based geographically or institutionally). When this happens, these roles can be downgraded, or in some circumstances the funding for the job can be relocated or withdrawn (Dooley and Farndon, 2021).

Different employment pressures thus articulate and encourage what some critics of clinical psychology see as a shielding of that profession's interests by its more senior members, who can hold powerful roles within academia and the NHS. Some other kinds of psychologists consider that a corollary of this is the disadvantaging of their own specialisms (and perhaps, as a consequence, patients as well). Clinical psychologists are not necessarily unaware of the conversations that can circulate about them in this regard. As one noted in their reflections on working for 25 years in the NHS, clinical psychologists 'can be perceived as being precious or protectionist' (Fleming, 2012, p. 185) in relation to how they conduct their therapeutic work. This characterisation certainly aligns with some of the comments and assertions I have heard or seen made by other psychological practitioners, and even a few clinical psychologists themselves.

Over the past few years, issues around NHS employment for psychologists have come to be a focus of activity both for the BPS as a whole and for its individual members. Clinical psychologists have sometimes lamented the aforementioned downgrading of clinical psychology posts; at the same time, some other psychological practitioners have questioned why some jobs are earmarked for clinical psychologists in the first place (BPS Practice Board, 2019). The BPS Workforce Planning Advisory Standing Committee has been exploring these and related issues, which have also entered into discussions at the BPS Practice Board (one of the five activity-orientated boards of the BPS, reporting to the overarching Board of Trustees). In particular, there has been a desire expressed by some psychologists to move away from using protected titles (and unprotected titles, like clinical health psychologist) in job adverts and towards 'more inclusive' titles such as applied and practitioner psychologist (BPS Practice Board, 2020). This would enable a wider range of psychologists to apply for certain posts if they could evidence relevant expertise that might not be encapsulated by their route of chartership alone.

This move to 'recruitment by competence', as it is framed by the BPS, has generated various tensions since at least 2017 when moves began to be made towards refreshed recruitment guidance. According to some of my interlocutors, the shift has had support from some prominent members of the BPS over the years. However, while jobs advertised for 'applied psychologist' or 'practitioner psychologist' are more common, not everyone supports this move – and change has been slow. Job adverts are still not always framed inclusively, and the BPS Practice Board (2022) continue to consider how movement on this front might be encouraged. At the same time, various clinical psychologists have expressed concern about guidance around competency-based advertising which they read as potentially damaging to practitioners in their field (Kat and Yang, 2021). Concerns are on occasion also articulated, often less publicly, that people seeking therapy might not encounter psychologists with the necessary range of expertise. As we might expect, this charge can be hotly contested by BPS members beyond the DCP.

Tensions around changing recruitment guidance relate, in part, to the place that clinical psychologists have within the mental health workforce. For many years now they have been the dominant branch of applied psychology within the NHS, and a greater proportion are employed at senior levels that other kinds of psychological practitioner (Palmer et al., 2021). In Scotland, for instance, about 60% of the psychological workforce are clinical psychologists (NHS Education for Scotland, 2022). Across the United Kingdom, they also represent over half of the psychologists registered with the HCPC, whereas health psychology, for instance, comprises only around 2% (Palmer et al., 2021). Still, despite this dominance, these percentages indicate that there must be plenty of other professionals competing with clinical psychologists for jobs, influence, and prestige. We can see why clinical psychologists might want to defend their position within the NHS, despite widespread respect and regard for the knowledge and skills of – and a frequent management role in relation to – other psychological practitioners.

Therapeutic techniques common to clinical psychologists, particularly CBT, are also increasingly practised by other professions, including counsellors and psychotherapists (Parry, 2015). These groups are not necessarily BPS- and HCPC-recognised counselling psychologists, but instead tend to be members of the British Association for Counselling and Psychotherapy (BACP, founded in 1977 as the British Association for Counselling) and/or the UK Council for Psychotherapy (UKCP, founded in 1993). The additional boundary work between clinical psychologists, counselling psychologists, and counsellors (and, indeed, between the BACP and UKCP, and between both and the BPS) represents another means through which the psychological complex is further torqued (see, e.g. Hall, 2015; Parry, 2015).

However, the ramifications for clinical psychology of the place and role of counselling and psychotherapy within the NHS (and private sector) seem generally not to be felt so acutely as those associated with psychiatry and other BPS divisions. One possible reason for this is that clinical psychologists are often paid more than other providers of psychological therapy; for instance, within the NHS Talking Therapies initiative (although, as we will see in Chapter 3, this also has corollaries for clinical psychology). Still, the provision of CBT by people who are not clinical psychologists has occasionally raised concerns.

These tensions have collectively contributed to the launch of a professional society specifically for clinical psychologists: the Association of Clinical Psychologists UK (ACP-UK). Incorporated as a Community Interest Company in 2018 following an initial launch in the summer of 2017, in some ways the ACP-UK was a long time coming. Since at least the 1980s, some DCP members were dissatisfied with their relationships with the wider BPS, with various plans bubbling at different points to develop a professional society dedicated to the needs of clinical psychologists (Hall and Wang, 2015). The ACP-UK has expanded rapidly in size and has various member networks within it to support practitioners. Some of these have resonances with the DCP Faculties, such as the Clinical Health and Neuropsychology Psychology Network. It has also swiftly grown in influence, undertaking meetings with stakeholder organisations like the HCPC and the Royal College of Psychiatrists and putting out joint statements with other professional societies – including the BPS.

Nonetheless, the relationship between the ACP-UK and BPS is not always easy. Peter Kinderman (2017), for instance, felt that he had to resign as a Trustee of the BPS given his support of the ACP-UK and what he described as a contrasting view on the part of other Trustees that the BPS 'needed to press forwards with one message; that the Society (and only the Society) was the natural home for psychology and psychologists'. Later, in 2020, the BPS Practice Board declined to approve a Memorandum of Understanding to shape collaborative working between the DCP and the ACP-UK, noting among other factors in the decision that the latter was 'a competitor organisation' (BPS Practice Board, 2020, p. 9). Relations seem to have improved, with the websites of both organisations proudly displaying news items relating to co-working on different campaigns. However, the very existence of the ACP-UK as is a reminder that the psychological complex is a matrix of many shifting facets, and that the actions of clinical psychologists themselves are key to many of those shifts.

Persistence through Reconfiguration

As sociologist Andrew Abbott (1995, p. 876) has noted, 'no social entity ever takes shape in a vacuum'. The social entity that is clinical psychology operates within a wider complex of psy disciplines, discourses, and practices (Rose, 1985) which inform what it has been and what it could become. In this chapter, I have reflected on how recent and ongoing shifts in clinical psychology are both powered through and have impacted claims-making and boundary work in relation to other professions, configuring the discipline in particular ways. Boundaries shift both iteratively and dynamically in response to changing contexts and professional evolution (Lindberg et al., 2017) while also helping to maintain a professional whole (Abbott, 1995). Practitioners labour to sketch out or even remake modalities of distinction within clinical psychology, such that the whole might retain its uniqueness and so help it to endure. Boundary work ensures that clinical psychology persists, rather than fracturing into further emergent professional realms or collapsing completely into the domain of applied psychology. At the same time, the reification of certain visions of clinical psychology provides a fleetingly stable referent in relation to which other fields might configure themselves.

Debates, discussions, and proclamations about diagnosis and the 'medical model' comprise one form of boundary work in which clinical psychology is presented as being distinct in orientation and approach to (a certain style of) psychiatry. This particular working of boundaries is significant by virtue of the prominence and influence of many claims-makers. When senior figures within the BPS advance assertions about what clinical psychology is like and what it *should* be more (or less) like, these do not float unacknowledged into the ether. While the transport of these proclamations through the circuits of discourse constituting the profession cannot necessarily be taken for granted, my encounters with clinical psychologists (and psychiatrists) working at the coalface of practice nevertheless indicate their traction. Not everyone agrees with every statement made by the DCP or senior clinical psychologists in relation to diagnosis, yet their quantity and prominence are often noted by Division members. Demarcations from psychiatry help to refine how the praxis of clinical psychology can be recognised as distinct, and so contribute to shaping practitioners' understandings of themselves and others (Hacking, 1995, 2002).

Clinical psychology is not, however, configured solely through professional, epistemic, and ontological politics with an 'external' competitor for resource and prestige. It is also shaped through more 'internal' negotiations with other kinds of explicitly psychological practitioners. As professions like health psychology place increasing emphasis on their skills as therapists, and as lower-paid professionals such as nurses with CBT training become ever more visible within the NHS, the need for clinical psychology to assert its novelty and significance increases. Clinical psychologists are well paid compared to the average UK wage and often to others who deliver psychological care, are highly qualified by anyone's standards, and enjoy associated social prestige. However, changes to the overall landscape of healthcare have left some within clinical psychology concerned that the value of their expertise is being diminished and the uniqueness of their training and skill-set downplayed. Organisations like the ACP-UK consequently today represent a compelling alternative to the BPS, which also continues to support professionals like counselling psychologists who can be direct competitors to clinical psychologists (e.g. for NHS jobs).

Clinical psychology, then, is at once a prestigious and influential profession while also being increasingly called upon to justify itself within a healthcare system ever more subject to an economic calculus of value. In these circumstances, the unique skillset of clinical psychologists vis-à-vis other therapeutic practitioners is not always apparent to healthcare commissioners and policymakers. This striving for singularity, and the role of boundary work within that, has a long history; as Derksen (2000) has argued, the boundaries between clinical psychology and psychiatry in the 1940s and 1950s were productive for the former profession in terms of helping to configure what exactly it offered in relation to its competitor/

patron – stimulating innovation as a result. We can see similar dynamics operating over the 21st century, as discursive and institutional manoeuvring help to configure clinical psychology not only with respect to psychiatry but also in relation to other psychological specialities. The tensions that result are themselves propellants for sociotechnical reconfiguration within the profession.

Given what we know about the interpellations between psychology, society, and the self, we can reasonably assume that the ontological and epistemic machinations of clinical psychology have material and subjective effects. The ways in which this field seeks to (re)position itself and is positioned by – and positions – other fields have professional and economic ramifications in terms of what clinical psychologists are enjoined or permitted to do within the NHS, and (relatedly) how many are employed. These outcomes in turn affect investments in staffing and the nature of job roles for other experts in the psychological. Ultimately, the "success" (or lack thereof) of clinical psychology undergirds what kinds of professionals and forms of care people seeking support are able to access, and how they are configured through these (e.g. truncated forms of CBT as opposed to longer-term integrative therapies, or diagnostic versus formulation-based ontologies of distress). As wide-ranging psychological expertise continues to flourish and proliferate, the meaning and nature of therapy – and its subjects – likewise continue to change.

CHAPTER 2

Proliferating Therapy

The Rise of the Improving Access to Psychological Therapy (IAPT) Initiative

At the turn of the century, an adult in England who felt very down, lacking in hope, and unable to enjoy everyday pleasures, might have made an appointment with their primary care General (Medical) Practitioner (GP). The GP would then, perhaps, have concluded that their patient should receive a diagnosis of depression, with that in turn resulting in a prescription for a pharmaceutical such as a selective serotonin reuptake inhibitor (SSRI). Today, there is a good chance that some kind of psychological therapy would be recommended. In fact, a GP appointment is not always necessary at all: often people can call a local NHS therapy service and refer themselves directly. Such services are likely to have developed from something called the Improving Access to Psychological Therapies (IAPT) initiative – rebadged in 2023 as NHS Talking Therapies (Clark and Whittington, 2023). This much-lauded public health programme has had many millions of pounds invested in it, with the objective of making treatment for mental ill-health more accessible (Department of Health, 2012).

The advent of IAPT is largely associated with the campaigning of (among others) London-based academic and clinical psychologist David Clark alongside health economist and member of the House of Lords, Richard Layard. Through the English IAPT initiative, the number of clinicians delivering therapy has proliferated, and ideas about the salience of the psychological within the NHS across the United Kingdom have been reshaped. During the early days of IAPT, its therapists targeted men and women of working age and focused on depression and anxiety, employing psychological interventions to treat those conditions. IAPT later began to include older adults (Ghosh, 2009), and since 2011 children and adolescents have been the focus of a linked initiative (Fonagy and Clark, 2015). Some services further extended into the terrain of 'severe and enduring mental illness' (Jolley et al., 2015) – although IAPT, and now NHS Talking Therapies, continued to emphasise depression and anxiety. IAPT gained substantial media coverage in the United Kingdom and subsequently abroad, with one *New York Times* article describing it as 'the world's most ambitious effort to treat depression, anxiety and other common mental illnesses' (Carey, 2017). An editorial in the journal *Nature* (2012, p. 473) asserted that IAPT 'represents a world-beating standard thanks to the scale of its implementation and the validation of its treatments'. Such comments have acted to stimulate, and have been stimulated by, significant international clinical and policy attention to and mimesis of the initiative.

In this chapter, I examine the instantiation, operations, and ramifications of IAPT – perhaps the most striking and significant materialisation of an ethic of access in the United Kingdom, and a singular example internationally. I draw on interviews with professional and policy actors working in organisations that shape the wider field of psychological care, alongside interviews and conversations with dozens of NHS practitioners (especially clinical psychologists, from whom we will hear much more in the second part of this book). My sources also include an array of English, UK, and international policy papers, journal articles, clinical guidelines, and charity campaign materials (from 2005 onwards). Through these I sought to better understand the development and reception of IAPT, and the repertories of accountability through which it has been both celebrated and critiqued.

I focus on some of the movements in healthcare the IAPT initiative reflected, helped to stabilise, and further propelled. IAPT was a specifically English initiative, given the devolution of healthcare provision to the constituent nations constituting the United Kingdom of Great Britain and Northern Ireland. Yet, its logics and effects are readily apparent beyond England, with IAPT contributing to revivifying psychological framings of pathology and therapy across the United Kingdom. However, it has achieved this in ways that are more familiar within biomedical contexts, for example through recourse to randomised controlled trials (RCTs) studies (cf. Healy, 2004; Horwitz and Wakefield, 2007; Kitanaka, 2012; Lee, 1999; Luhrmann, 2000; Rose, 2007; Rosenberg, 2006).

Following its success, IAPT was held up as a model for other psychological services and augmented the legitimacy of public bodies that have the capacity to shape healthcare (most notably the National Institute for Health and Care Excellence (NICE)). Lessons from it have been widely deemed valuable to learn, and clinical psychologists sometimes speak – often critically – of the influence of IAPT on their profession and the services they provide (e.g. its focus on patient throughput). Consequently, IAPT has enjoined wider shifts in the landscape of UK – and international – mental healthcare. I suggest that IAPT morphed from being one ostensibly novel component of this terrain into an element around which other services are constituted (cf. MacKenzie and Pardo-Guerra, 2014). In effect, it has moved from being content to context (MacKenzie, 2015), with its renaming as NHS Talking Therapies signalling its expansive remit and effects. IAPT has played a significant role within mental healthcare, producing standards against which other ventures have been held to account.

Problematising Access

As noted earlier, IAPT per se can be largely – though clearly not wholly – traced to the actions of two key individuals: David Clark and Richard Layard. Currently a professor at the University of Oxford (previously King's College, London), Clark is also National Clinical and Informatics Advisor for NHS Talking Therapies. He is prominent for his research around anxiety disorders and as a major innovator of CBT. Layard is an emeritus professor at the London School of Economics and Political Science (LSE) and a very influential economist. He has played a number of major policy roles relating to mental health and well-being. In 2000, Layard was made a life peer by Prime Minister Tony Blair and remains a member of the Labour Party in the elite UK House of Lords. Both Clark and Layard were elected Fellows of the British Academy in 2003, and it was at the Academy that they first met (Evans, 2013a, 2013b; Layard and Clark, 2014). Subsequently, they came to work together closely to try and move access to therapy further up the policy agenda. To do so, they actively sought to expand their own influence regarding how issues of access and therapy should be understood and addressed. Their research and campaigning found favour within the Department of Health and at Downing Street, helping to impel reconfigurations of the matrix of clinicians, services, guidelines, treatment sites, and more that comprise mental healthcare. Ultimately, they played vital roles in orchestrating the development and rollout of IAPT.

However, the campaigning of Layard and Clark did not emerge de novo. In the 1990s and during the early 2000s, many patients and clinicians were troubled by ever more testimonies that people experiencing mental ill-health were not receiving the care they needed, including because of shockingly long waiting times. As a result of considerable charitable and clinical advocacy work, policymakers became more sensitised to these issues, with admission to services noted in (for instance) the major NHS policy document, *A National Service Framework for Mental*

Health (Department of Health, 1999a). This Framework also stated a requirement to expand the numbers of professionals deemed competent to deliver mental health interventions. Wider concerns were furthermore emerging about the economic 'costs of mental illness' (Sainsbury Centre for Mental Health, 2003, p. 1), which likewise attracted attention.

Layard proved adept at steadily entwining these discourses of access and economy, focusing on depression specifically, and ultimately delimiting a straightforward framing of the (economic) problem(s) of access. In the early 2000s, he was an active publisher across a range of discursive spheres, and his widely reviewed trade book, *Happiness: Lessons from a New Science* (Layard, 2005b), argued that depression was a social problem that could be addressed through psychological therapy at scale. Following the publication of *Happiness*, Layard also authored various clinically oriented writings (e.g. Layard, 2006a) and was a regular discussant on related issues with journalists and policymakers. Through such activities, he worked to at once characterise the nature of the problem of access and to articulate its solution (cf. Callon, 1986).

Layard's messaging generated policy traction. For example, in January 2005, he was invited to present a report to the Prime Minister's Strategy Unit, in a seminar at which Clark was also present (Evans, 2013b). Titled 'Mental Health: Britain's Biggest Social Problem?' (Layard, 2005a), this document claimed that mental illness 'imposes heavy costs on the economy'. It asserted – in bold typeface: 'There are now more mentally ill people drawing incapacity benefits than there are unemployed people on Jobseeker's Allowance' (Layard, 2005a, p. 1). An apt response, Layard argued (like the Department of Health before him), was a massive expansion of the mental health workforce.

Senior Labour figures seemed to have been receptive to Layard's arguments: following his presentation, *The 2005 Labour Party Manifesto* committed to improving mental health through 'behavioural as well as drug therapies' (p. 65). The phrasing of the manifesto promise presented psychological services as a kind of addition to the (pharmaco)therapeutic status quo. It thus underscored neurobiology as a key aspect of the UK mental health landscape (see Pilgrim and Rogers, 2005; Rose, 2007). Yet, the commitment also reflected increasingly outspoken voices (such as Layard's) in support of proliferating specifically psychological therapy. As we will see, the Labour Party pledge ultimately materialised as the IAPT initiative.

Layard's 2005 paper was subsequently expanded into *The Depression Report* (Centre for Economic Performance, 2006). Released on 19 June 2006, this was also widely termed the 'Layard Report', indicating the importance ascribed to Layard in developing IAPT. Though principally associated with him, the report advertised its authority through a list of impressive signatories from mental health research and practice, including David Clark. It further demonstrated epistemic accountability through its digestible number of endnotes linking the claims it made to relevant academic literature. Immediately prior to publication, Layard promoted *The Depression Report* in the UK left-leaning broadsheet *The Guardian* (Layard, 2006b), with the online edition linking to the LSE website where the report could be downloaded. It was also heralded on its release date in *The Observer* (the Sunday counterpart of *The Guardian*), which later, in September 2006, circulated a hardcopy (with support to do so from the mental health charity, the Charlie Waller Memorial Trust). Such widespread dissemination enabled *The Depression Report* to act as a rhetorical and collectivising device for articulating a particular problematisation of access to therapy, and expanding discussion on depression more generally (cf. Callon, 1986).

The overall message of *The Depression Report* was straightforward: depression negatively impacts the economy, it should be treated, and treatment was affordable. Economics was a key apparatus through which the normative and clinical claims contained with the Report were assembled. Readers were, for instance, told that 'the total loss of output due to depression and chronic anxiety is some £12 billion a year – one per cent of our total national income' (Centre for Economic Performance, 2006, p. 5; in bold type for emphasis in the original). The word 'cost' appeared 24 times in the main text of the 14-page report, including in a section subtitle that added the prefix 'cost-effective' to the word 'therapies'. Pound signs were scattered throughout, and – like in Layard's 2005 paper – the number of people diagnosed with mental illness receiving state benefits appeared on the first page. Even the subtitle of the report – 'A New Deal for Depression and Anxiety Disorders' – gestured towards the economy, reminding some readers of the culturally resonant 1930s US New Deal economic development programme. Altogether, it constructed a vision of a society full of despondent individuals whose despair impacted not only themselves but also (the wallets of) the wider citizenry.

More than any other text of the time, *The Depression Report* braided mental health and the economy within public discourse, relating expertise associated with the latter as an essential feature of (evaluating) attempts to understand and manage the former. Such an economistic framing attracted criticism from many mental health professionals, not least clinical psychologists (articulated across a wide range of blogs, newsletters, and journals).

Nevertheless, it also garnered support for the therapeutic options it outlined, specifically psychological therapy. As noted, drug treatments for and a neurobiological understanding of depression were prominent within broader popular discourse at the time (Rose, 2007), even if these were never hegemonic (Pickersgill, 2014). *The Depression Report* instead urged the NHS to adopt psychological therapies for redressing the economic, social, and personal costs of depression. It stated that 'hundreds of clinical trials' had helped to show that 'therapy is as effective as drugs in the short-run', and that psychological treatment 'has more long-lasting effects than drugs' (Centre for Economic Performance, 2006, p. 6). This promotion was seemingly a consequence of economic calculation rather than overt ontological partisanship over what depression 'really' was and hence how it should be treated. Overall, psychological therapy was presented as the most (cost-)effective solution to a pressing social problem.

Clinical psychologists and other health professionals I have spoken with often mention Layard as significant in helping to shift the mental healthcare landscape, with IAPT itself referred to as, for instance, the 'Layard initiative'. Nevertheless, important as he was, Layard by no means acted alone. As illustrated earlier, his arguments took considerable cues from policy reports and charitable briefings. Aside from David Clark, Layard also worked with colleagues at the LSE (e.g. Layard et al., 2007), and the underscoring of psychological therapy within his campaign put him in dialogue with wider advocacy that operated to direct change in policy.

In this regard, a range of largely London-based actors and networks were producing documents and statements about access to psychological therapies. For instance, one third-sector report, *We Need to Talk* (Mental Health Foundation et al., 2006), was published one month after *The Depression Report* and served as a de facto companion text to it. Commissioned by five major mental health charities (The Mental Health Foundation, Mind, Rethink, The Sainsbury Centre for Mental Health, and Young Minds), the report emphasised the effectiveness of psychological treatment, the long waiting times for accessing it, and the economic costs of lost work (for coverage, see Frauenfelder, 2006). A loose association of major figures in UK mental health research, policy, and practice also formed under the banner of the 'New Savoy Partnership'. This included social psychologist Pam Maras (then President of the British Psychological Society), clinical psychologist Peter Fonagy (Chief Executive of the prestigious Anna Freud Centre), and campaigner Paul Farmer (Chief Executive of the leading mental health charity Mind). In 2007, they released the 'New Savoy Declaration'; this called 'on the NHS to offer appropriate psychological therapies free at the point of delivery to all people who need them' (New Savoy Partnership, 2007). Hence, the widely circulated *Depression Report* served to publicise the goals and further the momentum of a diffuse and diverse undertaking that was already beginning to gain interest and investment within Westminster.

In sum, from 2003 to 2006, an intense campaign from elite metropolitan academics and clinicians and well-known organisations and charities sought to move mental health higher up the policy agenda. This also related to, and was reciprocally informed by, wider governmental strategy and commitments to work and (psychological) well-being (Edwards and Imrie, 2008; HM Government, 2005; Rick et al., 2010). These stakeholders – among whom Layard and Clark were significant – helped to set and propel a programme for expanding access to psychological care. In doing so, they contributed, via a particularly economic problematisation, to the reconfiguration of the mental health landscape from which IAPT emerged. At an early point in the campaigning, this landscape – configured through extant policy and clinical praxis – was one within which a thing called 'depression' could be straightforwardly delineated and operated upon by certain techniques, with those suffering from it understood to be disadvantaged by public health infrastructures that limited access to care. The activities of Layard and others helped to reshape it such that both economic and psychological rationalities became vital features. Depression itself was configured as something that should be treated primarily through psychological therapy, and which could be accounted for in terms of its economic costs (with calculations of cost also justifying psychological rather than pharmaceutical interventions). Accordingly, depression came to be increasingly understood as an object of concern not only to individuals categorised as living with the disorder but also to the State and the body politic more broadly.

Remaking Infrastructures and Expertise

Following their commitment to improve mental health services (The Labour Party, 2005), in 2006 the re-elected Labour government granted over £2 million for trialling a programme for enhancing access to therapy within primary care: IAPT (Department of Health, 2012). A few weeks prior to the dissemination of *The Depression Report* through *The Observer*, two IAPT pilots were launched, in the city of Doncaster and in Newham, East London. The Doncaster site focused on depression, with Newham dealing with depression and anxiety disorders. Newham was part of the geographic area covered by the East London and City Mental Health Trust, chaired by Baroness Molly Meacher, Layard's wife and a co-signatory of *The Depression Report*. The IAPT pilots were rapidly subject to various kinds of elaboration and attention, and in November 2006 a business case was advanced to expand IAPT nationally (Rick et al., 2010). Funding was then confirmed in 2007. By 2008, the vision of enhancing access to therapy outlined in *The Depression Report* (and elsewhere) was made manifest.

Though ostensibly a bounded initiative dedicated to improving primary mental health care in England, IAPT became, in the words of one Scottish mental health policy actor I spoke with, a '*hugely* influential' programme. This has been partly in light of what they termed the 'fundamental economic argument' that 'Richard Layard and Dave Clark put forward', and 'the way it's [IAPT] been done'. In this section and the next, I will sketch out the contours of IAPT and examine how its novelty and legitimacy were configured and accounted for to maximise the material and symbolic investment that generated such influence. In setting out 'the way it's been done', I demonstrate how the 'economic argument' justifying the initiative became tightly imbricated with the practices of care and accountability performed through the programme.

In my interviews, informal conversations, and documents I inspected, five key features of IAPT were regularly foregrounded: the introduction of 'self-referral', the multiplication of therapists, the development of 'stepped care', a focus on evidence-based therapies, and the measurement of outcomes. To begin with, I attend to the first three of these significant characteristics of IAPT; these comprise the infrastructural innovations of the initiative most directly geared towards its stated aims of making psychological therapy 'accessible'. After that, the chapter turns to the design and nature of the therapeutic provision of IAPT, and how this was rendered (ac)countable. The use of evidence-based therapies and outcome measures were central to the construction, management, and maintenance of (what has been often regarded as) the success of IAPT. Hence, these features played a somewhat different, though seemingly vital, role in configuring and proliferating psychological care. As we will see, they also responded to – and had ramifications for – the broader psychological complex (Rose, 1985) within which it was situated.

In IAPT, and now NHS Talking Therapies, people can generally contact services directly to request an appointment. This process of 'self-referral' was regarded as significant by many of the policy and clinical actors I spoke with. Deemed to avoid the 'barriers' to accessing therapy that GPs were often (and still sometimes are) seen to impose, self-referral was widely perceived as a 'radical shift' (Brown et al., 2010, p. 365). The hope was that it would help many more individuals who understood themselves to be depressed and in need of treatment. So important was self-referral to the leaders of IAPT that the number of people self-referring served as a key performance indicator for services within the initiative (Department of Health, 2011). Hence, self-referral represented a means by which IAPT could simultaneously contribute to addressing its core problematic (i.e. enhancing access) and account for the extent to which this was achieved. In problematising referral and offering a targeted solution, the architects of IAPT were further able to present their initiative to policy and clinical communities as a logical, rational endeavour with respect to the managerial and therapeutic mores of UK healthcare. Subsequently, the apparent success of the self-referral processes of IAPT was argued to support the need for this mechanism in other UK mental health services (e.g. Brown et al., 2010). This is despite some evidence suggesting that self-referral can itself act as a barrier for potential service users (Thomas et al., 2019).

Alongside such efforts to make care more directly accessible, the IAPT initiative greatly increased the number of health professionals able to deliver treatment by positioning large numbers of clinicians within specially commissioned services. A considerable proportion of the IAPT investment was spent on training several thousand cognitive behaviour therapists and new 'psychological wellbeing practitioners' (PWPs) (Clark, 2011, p. 318). Today, they work across more than 100 NHS Talking Therapies services. As part of the increasingly complicated interplay between the public and private sectors within England, these are provided by a range of charitable and private healthcare organisations (including Mind) partnering with the NHS. Practitioners commonly deliver highly prescriptive forms of CBT, which can sometimes be referred to as 'manualised' therapy. Clinicians were initially tasked with treating individuals diagnosed with 'mild to moderate' anxiety and/or depression for a discrete (6–10) number of therapeutic encounters. Therapy was not regarded as requiring the expertise of doctorate-holding clinical psychologists, who were also more highly paid and demanded more autonomy. Hence, the training and employment of less expensive cognitive behaviour therapists and PWPs, who worked within closely defined clinical parameters, further optimised IAPTs economic outcomes.

The clinical foci and professional makeup of the IAPT/NHS Talking Therapies workforce are indicative of how the economic rationalities inherent in the conception of the initiative continued to be emphasised within programme delivery. IAPT – along with other NHS policy that enjoined so-called New Ways of Working (e.g. CSIP/NIMHE, 2007) – also affected how therapeutic expertise and therapy configured more widely. In IAPT and elsewhere, psychologists came to be decreasingly viewed as the primary professionals who should deliver psychological therapy. Rather, other psychologically trained clinicians were able to claim sufficient expertise, assuming therapeutic protocols were closely followed. This shift helped to shape the meanings of therapy beyond that delivered through IAPT per se. Gradually, therapy has become progressively characterised in a range of settings as a kind of pre-packaged tool that professionals, sometimes with relatively limited credentialed psychological expertise, can be trained to use in specific, predetermined ways.

Unsurprisingly, many working in clinical psychology have lamented this widespread recasting of expertise and therapy, resulting in various performances of professional boundary work. One senior psychologist told me how IAPT had 'caused a lot of disquiet' – something evident during my conversations with various mental health professionals – with, for instance, the 'deskilling' (in the words of another) of psychological services registering as a concern. In terms of the therapeutic orientation of IAPT, a policy advisor to the initiative described how he had been 'besieged' by criticisms about its focus on CBT. With the rising prominence of IAPT and restrictions in wider healthcare funding, clinical psychologists increasingly displayed their clinical and economic worth (as compared to PWPs, for example) by underscoring their skill in disassembling manualised therapies and recombining them on a patient-by-patient basis. This is in relation to a specific clinical formulation of a presenting problem and the psychosocial milieu inhabited by the person seeking therapy. Such reconfigurations of psychological knowledge and action are not reducible to IAPT; nevertheless, they have been propelled and authorised through the initiative, given its scale and the attention its architects have attracted and demanded.

Connected to shifts in therapists and therapy were reconfigured institutional logics regarding the subjectification (Rose, 1996) of populations suitable for therapy. Since the inception of IAPT, the care apportioned through its services has been undertaken in a self-consciously ration(alis)ed fashion that is ubiquitously described as 'stepped'. For example, a 'low-intensity' CBT intervention (such as guided self-help, including computerised CBT) can be initially provided to patients, who might then be 'stepped up' to a more 'high intensity' treatment in the absence of recovery. Levels of care relate to different kinds of intervention administered by professionals with differing (kinds and degrees of) expertise. Seen as sitting 'at the heart of the IAPT clinical model' (Gyani et al., 2013, p. 605), stepped care was constituted through a conception of what we might term therapeutic wastage. It is deployed to prevent the loss of expertise, time, and, consequently, money to the treatment of mild depression, when these could be more swiftly applied and purportedly better spent (and accounted for) to and on other individuals understood to be experiencing more severe forms of distress.

IAPT did not, in fact, introduce the notion of stepped-care (e.g. Bower and Gilbody, 2005). However, its use was significantly extended through the salience of this model in what has been a very well-resourced and highly promoted programme. Many of my interlocutors were employed by psychological services structured through a kind of stepped-care approach, with implications for managing waiting lists. This form of care generally relates closely to values of cost effectiveness. While these have long been part of British clinical life (e.g. Department of Health, 1999a), their presence has been particularly apparent since the austerity policies enacted by the Conservative Government in the wake of the 2008 financial crisis, and almost every psychologist with whom I spoke expressed anxiety regarding service capacity vis-à-vis post-2008 budget restrictions. It was around this time that the infrastructures of IAPT were being touted as therapeutically and economically effective by key clinical proponents, such as Clark (e.g. Clark et al., 2009).

Stepped care, then, represented an answer to more than one problem. Through it, economic practices of accounting and clinical practices of accountability could entwine to synthesise the same ends: in principle, more people could be seen for therapy at ostensibly lower costs. Stepped-care systems also resonate with a certain notion of mental ill-health, one in which severity is not an abstract dimension of distress but is quantifiable through diagnostic language (e.g. 'mild to moderate' and 'severe and enduring' depression). Hence, stepped care represents a further example of how, through IAPT, economic understandings of care provision became increasingly enmeshed within clinical considerations.

Knowing What Works

In my interviews and conversations with policy actors, IAPT was commonly presented as a rational approach for intervening in a concrete economic, social, and clinical problem. Increasing access to psychological therapies was 'the sensible thing to do', as one policy advisor put it, not least because it would generate 'a cross-ministry saving'. Relating to such economic rationalism, the stated goal of IAPT was 'to greatly increase the availability of *NICE recommended* psychological treatment' (Clark, 2011, p. 318; emphasis added) – not therapy in general. A public body, NICE was originally the National Institute for Clinical Excellence before becoming the National Institute for Health and Clinical Excellence and, from 2013, the National Institute for Health and Care Excellence. It has a significant role within England (with implications for the wider United Kingdom) as a producer of NHS clinical guidelines. These are authored by expert Guideline Development Groups, and within them RCT evidence and assessments of cost effectiveness are salient (Moreira, 2011). Key to how the organisation presents and performs accountable action are the visibility of its processes of knowledge production and the managerial and clinical applicability, scientific veracity, and public and political palatability of its recommendations.

By framing the operations of IAPT as mandated by NICE, its advocates were enabled and emboldened to make claims about the clinical and epistemic legitimacy of the initiative. In doing so, the programme could be constructed as economically and politically durable. As the policy adviser above put it, NICE had 'an authority that goes beyond the authority of any particular professional group'. Another interviewee described how, by following NICE, IAPT could deliver 'treatments that we *know work*'. A further senior policy actor told me that although 'not everyone welcomes or *accepts*' NICE, it 'is the only show in town, at least at this stage, to keep the investment flowing'. Indeed, Layard and Clark (2014, p. 206) have asserted that 'the expansion of psychological therapy would never have happened at all without NICE'. CBT was prominent within the 2004 NICE guidelines for depression (and the subsequent 2009 and 2022 guidelines), and the architects of IAPT elected to emphasise this modality in their initiative. By ascribing dominance and import to NICE, this decision-making can be reframed as no choice at all: as the previously quoted interviewee asserted, 'in terms of a largescale programme we are almost *obliged* to go from where the evidence sits'.

Nevertheless, NICE is not an uncontested organisation. Over the last decade or so I have encountered wide-ranging dissatisfaction about it from clinical psychologists and others working in mental health. One senior figure associated with NICE noted, for instance, that 'a number of people' have regarded it as being 'too focused on CBT, to the exclusion of other psychological therapies'. Concerns have been, and continue to be, advanced within peer-reviewed and more informal literatures, with frustration about the calculative style of NICE commonly articulated. One critical journal article nicely summarises some of the concerns in its title: 'The NICE guidelines are misleading, unscientific, and potentially impede good psychological care and help' (Mollon, 2009). Part of a wider critique of NICE (Moreira, 2011; Syrett, 2003), these debates have developed a certain character through their refraction across the mental health professions. This relates especially to the occlusion of non-RCT treatment studies by the Guideline Development Groups, long-standing debates about the role diagnostic constructs (e.g. 'major depression') should play within clinical psychology, and the related use of manualised therapeutic approaches to CBT targeting categorical pathologies (Pilgrim, 2011). Despite these critiques, logics of quantification of the kind NICE is underpinned by and contributes to reifying are increasingly configuring UK psychological and wider mental health praxis.

The framework of evidence-based medicine (EBM) has long had traction within the United Kingdom (Armstrong, 2007); likewise, health economics has shaped healthcare delivery for many years (Mulkay et al., 1987). Still, these trends towards EBM and the deployment of economic expertise have intensified. Early in the 21st century, NICE – then a young organisation – operated at some distance from the everyday concerns of clinicians at the coalface of practice (cf. Hedgecoe, 2004). The first depression guidelines were only produced in 2004; prior to this, just three guidelines in mental health were available: on schizophrenia, eating disorders, and self-harm. In 2004, key players within NICE felt the need to write an article for the Royal College of Psychiatrist's *Psychiatric Bulletin* introducing their organisation and its activities (Kendall et al., 2004). Suffice it to say, these days NICE requires no introduction to UK-based clinicians whose practice is marked deeply by its recommendations.

The import of NICE in mental health has thus grown alongside the expansion of IAPT itself, with both increasingly interacting with one another. For example, Clark chaired the Guideline Development Group for the 2013 NICE social anxiety disorder guidance, which also emphasised the cognitive model of this construct (and subsequent treatment regimens) that Clark developed with Adrien Wells (Clark and Wells, 1995; NICE, 2013). Further, the perceived successes and practices of IAPT informed the evidence examined and generated by subsequent NICE Guideline Development Groups (e.g. BPS/RCPsych, 2011; NICE, 2011). More than two decades since Kendall and colleagues sought to raise awareness of NICE, its dominance can still inspire voluble criticism. Through this, health professionals reassert their authority to define subjective distress and therapeutic expertise in the face of the organisation doing so on their behalf, and following the expansion IAPT and the trumpeting of the styles of practice associated with it.

With the endorsement and encouragement of NICE, CBT has come to be widely promoted and operationalised within clinical psychology and mental health services across the United Kingdom. Over the years I have asked dozens of clinical psychologists about their therapeutic practice; they almost always reply that, at minimum, they draw on CBT, even as they generally integrate these with other approaches. IAPT itself has regularly been taken to task for its perceived (over-)reliance on this modality. One frequent criticism I encountered related to the notion that CBT has a good evidence base (which was seen to explain its promotion through NICE guidelines). Critics argue that trials for therapies that already indicate effectiveness in some populations are more likely to be sponsored for further research than untested modalities are. Accordingly, further evidence is generated, with which NICE's Guideline Development Groups might engage. In effect, knowledge about the effectiveness of CBT is presented as partly an artefact of a positive feedback loop. This is further accelerated by the readiness to which manualised forms of CBT could be subjected to evaluation through RCTs. Again, such critiques illustrate a shifting landscape in which 'evidence' (of a particular sort) has come to be central to the configuration of practice; hence, the nature of that evidence is reflexively subject to uncertainty and debate.

In interviews with policymakers, policy advisers, and key clinicians, I sometimes invited reflections on the criticisms that IAPT, CBT, and NICE had attracted. These interlocutors largely responded by presenting the widespread instantiation of CBT, the import of NICE, and the necessity of IAPT operationalising NICE guidelines as rational and reasoned. One asserted: 'if you think you should be trying to invest in evidence-based things then you need to be pushing the things that have evidence'. A senior member of the British Psychological Society asked, rhetorically: 'If one draws on the evidence base . . . what else could you do?' Concerns about CBT were sometimes reframed as an indication that those working in other therapeutic traditions needed to generate evidence for their preferred interventions in ways that NICE would recognise as legitimate. A more diverse array of therapies might then be included in future recommendations, and thus within IAPT. One interviewee argued that this perspective was 'not *unreasonable*, particularly in these straitened circumstances'. Even as evidence around CBT is decoupled from the social, technical, and economic contexts of its generation to justify its deployment, the reality that evidence must be actively made is therefore used as a means to critique the critics. This kind of shifting register was, I found, common in defences of IAPT: criticised on epistemic, economic, or humanitarian grounds, responses could readily be assembled from one of the other dimensions of the programme that reconstructed challenges as unreasonable or ill-informed.

Quantifying Success

Clark and Layard, as well as other IAPT leaders, have articulated the import and originality of their initiative through health economic forecasts, the synthesis of clinical guidelines, invocations of human need, and evaluation via the monitoring of clinical and socio-economic outcomes. Healthcare evaluation represents a key means of establishing intervention efficacy and demonstrating political and economic accountability (Broer et al., 2017), and was leveraged extensively within IAPT. During the programme rollout, for instance, various projects were developed to adjudicate its success, including an evaluation led by Clark et al. (2008) (see also Clark et al., 2009). Information collection was codified within the IAPT Data Standard (i.e. the list of data each IAPT service must collect), and voluminous monthly data collection continues to enable the comparison and evaluation of individual NHS Talking Therapy services. This has long been publicly available, and currently so through the NHS Digital webpages (NHS Digital, 2024). Data include referral dates for calculating waiting times, the number of referrals who have completed a course of treatment, and the average number of treatment sessions (Clark et al., 2009; Department of Health, 2011). Submitting data is itself a complicated process which involves considerable work in terms of the collection, anonymisation, and authorisation of the data and decision-making with regards to who monitors and controls this. Though this mass collection of data, the effectiveness of IAPT was made quantifiable.

Quantification can represent a solution to enduring issues of legitimacy and accountability in healthcare (Hogle, 2019) and beyond (Porter, 1995), and patients within mental health settings have long been subject to diverse forms of calculation (Grob, 2009; Hirshbein, 2009). Within IAPT, though, the variety and consistency of data collected on the characteristics of individuals engaged in therapy and their 'outcomes' from this was commonly argued to be unprecedented. Initially communicated to practitioners through the *IAPT Data Handbook*, the rationales for data collection indicated the range of intertwining clinical, economic, and political uses to which metrics are put (Department of Health, 2011, p. 10):

1. Ensure equitable use of IAPT . . . by people experiencing depression and anxiety disorders from all communities within the local population, actively advancing equality [. . .]
2. Actively use data collection as part of the clinical process . . . to enhance patients' and IAPT workers' engagement in collaborative decision making and treatment plan reviews [. . .]
3. Provide objective case-load and outcomes data for supervisors to enable them to review the clinical work of IAPT workers [. . .]
4. Provide IAPT workers with information that will help identify appropriate targets for intervention in the next therapy session [. . .]
5. Monitor the extent to which IAPT workers and services are providing evidence-based treatments which are consistently applied in the manner recommended by NICE
6. Measure people's experience and benefits from IAPT services
7. Assist commissioners and service providers in monitoring and improving the quality and cost effectiveness of their services for all communities
8. Build a robust data archive to inform evolving service improvement strategies [. . .]

The production and harnessing of data for different but connected ends also served to represent IAPT as a departure from more traditional means of undertaking and evaluating psychological therapy. One senior psychologist involved in the programme, for instance, told me how therapy delivered outside of IAPT could be 'very ineffective and very poorly monitored'. He claimed that this 'shouldn't really be allowed to carry on', given the risk of 'adverse effects' from poor practice. Such morally laden talk about the potential negative effects of therapy – and hence the need to scrutinise the expertise and performance of professionals – was also articulated in formal IAPT policy (e.g. Department of Health, 2011). Indeed, the very fact that measures were taken at all, notwithstanding the nature of the data itself or the uses to which it is put, helped to perform the novelty and legitimacy of IAPT.

One means through which different forms of accountability came to be enmeshed in IAPT was through the ongoing employment of a tool called the Patient Health Questionnaire (PHQ-9). Designed in the United States in the late 1990s to screen for and assess depression (Kroenke et al., 2001), it asks a series of questions about aspects and occurrences of depressed mood. Possible responses are 'not at all', 'several days', 'more than half the days', and 'nearly every day'. These correspond to a number, with responses summed to produce an overall severity score: 0–5 is taken to indicate mild depression, 6–10 is moderate, 11–15 is moderately severe, and 16–20 is severe. Following their (self-)referral to IAPT/NHS Talking Therapies, an individual hoping to access therapy will often be sent the PHQ-9 to complete. The score produced confirms suitability for the service, provides the therapist a starting point for the first appointment, and acts as a benchmark for therapeutic progress. By rendering depression quantifiable, the PHQ-9 enables judgements of severity to be deemed reasonable and therapeutic gains to be recordable, rendering clinical action accountable (to patients and service leads). Accordingly, the PHQ-9 acts as a significant apparatus for consolidating understandings of 'depression' as a bounded and discrete disorder, and hence has subjectivising effects on individuals completing it (Hacking, 1995, 2002). It aligns well with CBT, which as Stark (2017, p. 70) has observed, itself intertwines 'an emphasis on numerical quantification with an ordinal schema of rationality, clarity and self-fashioning'. By configuring patent subjectivities as calculable and surveillable, the PHQ-9 also enabled the evaluation of the therapist, the service, and ultimately IAPT (and now NHS Talking Therapies) itself.

Layard and Clark (2014, p. 205) stated that 'outcome measurement is probably the most important single feature of IAPT', arguing that it 'is really the only ultimate guarantee of quality'. Presented as descriptive statements, such comments are normative proclamations. An interviewee closely involved with the initiative told me that one reason why IAPT was 'successful' was 'because from the start' it was decided 'you have to actually demonstrate that what you do is worthwhile'. This meant 'that we just *had* to be able to have outcome data on more or less everyone who was treated'. Outcomes measures continue to be framed as providing epistemic and procedural credibility, which translates into political legitimacy. Without them, I was told, 'I don't think [IAPT] would have continued political support'. Despite clinical and normative claims about the import of outcome measures in IAPT, it is the economic and (consequently) political accountabilities relating to these that leaders of the initiative have often portrayed as particularly significant.

Given the salience of outcomes monitoring to IAPT – and their subsequent promotion by initiative leaders and other key healthcare figures and institutions – it is worth noting that this practice was not introduced by the programme. Rather, monitoring and evaluation have been advocated since at least the 1990s (e.g. Department of Health, 1999a; see also Roth and Fonagy, 1996). This has often been on the grounds of (political pushes towards) clinical accountability (e.g. Margison et al., 2000; NIMHE,

2008), generating tension and conflict within therapy communities (Power, 1999). IAPT was thus constituted within a landscape where measurement was already encouraged.

The calculation of outcomes has come to be even more forcefully mandated by policymakers, including as a key element to service commissioning and provider reimbursement (so-called payment by results) in an increasingly privatised English NHS (Department of Health, 2013). My interviews and conversation with clinical psychologists outside of IAPT/NHS Talking Therapies indicated that routine, systematic, and standardised outcomes measurements have become common following the advent of the initiative (such as the Clinical Outcomes in Routine Evaluation (CORE) framework; Evans et al,, 2000, 2002). I was even sometimes told (e.g. by one key civil servant associated with IAPT, as well as by various clinicians) that people engaged in psychological therapy 'like' outcome measures. Hence, outcome measures do not just ensure that the direction of accountability travels "up" to service and initiative leaders, and ultimately policymakers and politicians, but also "down" to patients themselves. Given policy emphases on patient choice (Greener, 2009), augmenting accountability to service users also enhances its political legitimacy.

The implications of IAPT for mental healthcare do not, then, lie in the introduction of outcomes monitoring per se. Rather, the ramifications of the English IAPT initiative can be seen in how it has contributed to establishing data collection in a range of mental health services across the United Kingdom as a necessary and ever more routine practical task for psychological practitioners and services to build and demonstrate clinical and economic legitimacy. Consequently, though generally presented by IAPT leaders as appropriately responsive to the demands of technocratic governance (Porter, 1995), claims about the collection and evaluation of therapeutic outcomes have also contributed to the consolidation of this authority.

Contextification

Almost two decades after its emergence, the reach of IAPT continues to be extensive, not least through its 2023 renaming as NHS Taking Therapies and subsequent promises of further expansion (HM Treasury, 2023). Its operations have been held up as examples from which other psychological services might learn, and policymakers and clinicians beyond the United Kingdom have expressed considerable interest in embedding similar models within their own health systems (not least Australia and Norway; Cromarty et al., 2016; Knapstad et al., 2018). In England and the wider

United Kingdom, many researchers, clinicians, and patients have praised IAPT for attending to both scientific evidence and human need. Layard and Clark (2014) followed up the 2006 *Depression Report* with a book for a general readership, *Thrive*, in which IAPT was presented as a 'great humanitarian project' (p. 207) and 'has shown that it is possible in a short time to make big improvements in the lives of hundreds of thousands of people' (p. 201). Perhaps unsurprisingly given their earlier messaging, Layard and Clark described prompt access to therapy as simultaneously 'morally right' and 'vital for our economy' (p. ix).

Nevertheless, criticisms of IAPT have been plentiful. Many clinical psychologists and other mental health professionals – including IAPT therapists and managers – have expressed concerns about the programme: to me directly in interviews and casual conversations, and across the academic and professional literature, blogs, and social media (see also Bruun, 2023; Marks, 2012). Their disquiet relates to the widespread use of CBT (and sometimes to its elite advocates), challenges to therapeutic quality that might result from prioritising particular kinds of outcomes measures, and how economic rationales impinge upon – and reconfigure – clinical care. Even some of the key health economic claims made about psychological therapy have been contested (McCrone, 2013), and antidepressant prescriptions continue to rise (Health and Social Care Information Centre, 2016; NHS Business Services Authority, 2022).

When IAPT was criticised, its advocates framed the various choices made during the development of the initiative as almost inevitable. Justifications related to the accountabilities that Clark, Layard, and colleagues emphasised through the initiative, and the measures and means chosen to demonstrate them. The accountabilities constitutive of IAPT were, chiefly, economic, epistemic, and clinical. They were built into the operations of the programme in ways that enabled its advocates to present it as reasonable and rational, and hence any naysayers as uninformed, misguided, or even self-interested (e.g. Fonagy and Clark, 2015). Their integration with the programme has served as a robust shield with which to deflect critique.

The decisions made by IAPT leaders when responding to the broader healthcare landscape during the development phase of the initiative have come, to a significant extent, to be reified as not merely *a* way of developing public mental health, but as *the* way to proliferate therapy. Elegantly advanced justifications for and defences of IAPT align closely and resonate with a seemingly ever more economistic framing of the public good by successive UK governments, further closing down spaces within which the problematisations that might propel alternative therapeutic futures can be developed. This discourse of inevitability (Leonardi, 2008; Pickersgill, 2024) has helped to authorise and legitimate the decisions of the early IAPT proponents and leaders, and consequently the situation of the initiative has itself morphed. From being but one feature of a wider public health ecosystem with roots in some existing practices, IAPT reshaped its environment and emerged as a principal entity to which other services must respond. It is in this sense that the imitative moved from 'content to context' (MacKenzie, 2015; MacKenzie and Pardo-Guerra, 2014).

Such "contextification" has been highly reliant on an economic problematisation of ill-health. This underscores: (1) a certain kind of psychological ontology for subjective distress, (2) the operationalising of this in categorical terms (e.g. depression, anxiety) that are off-putting to traditions like clinical psychology, (3) the possibility of swiftly quantifying such constructs in terms of severity, (4) the necessity of standardised and readily applicable forms of therapy, and (5) the significance of therapists of varying kinds with assorted psychological credentials. This economic problematisation also foregrounds the vital role of measurement in simultaneously evidencing clinical need, therapeutic efficacy, and prudent expenditure. These features are exemplified by IAPT and, while not wholly reducible to the initiative, have become ever more characteristic of other mental healthcare settings. This is in part due to the lauding that IAPT has widely received and its casting as an exemplar programme by bodies such as NICE (the influence of which itself has grown with and through the initiative). As psychological expertise helped to configure IAPT, so too has IAPT reconfigured the psychological complex.

CHAPTER 3

Producing Treatability

Reconfiguring the Subjects of Therapy through Entwinements of Clinical Practice and Mental Health Law

Within initiatives to enhance access to therapy, psychological care is generally presented as something that many people want and who are too often denied access to it (e.g. due to long waiting lists). Yet, there can also be other governmental considerations for enhancing the accessibility of psychological care. In this chapter, I focus on something that the psychological complex (Rose, 1985) itself often configures as a 'matter of concern' (Latour, 2004), namely the diagnostic category 'personality disorder'. The diagnosis is commonly subject to reflexive consideration about its ontological coherence, its legitimacy as a clinical target, and the affective and practical responses of healthcare professionals to people living with it (Bendelow, 2010; Eastman Starling, 2006). Individuals diagnosed with variants of personality disorder associated with antisocial actions have often been involuntarily detained within the NHS and the criminal justice system. There, the disciplinary logics that always infuse psychological care are particularly visible and impactful, with therapy framed partly as a mechanism for addressing antisociality. In the case of personality disorder and its treatment, then, the affordances of an ethic of access can be rather different to those enjoined by initiatives like IAPT.

Ruminations on personality disorder – or personality disorder*s*, given the various subcategories that exist – date back to at least the 19th century (Berrios, 1993; Werlinder, 1978). They are commonly framed as global personality dysfunctions rather than discrete forms of mental illness (such as schizophrenia or depression). Accordingly, personality disorders have long attracted much interest from psychologists as well as psychiatrists. In the United Kingdom, the constructs of antisocial personality disorder (ASPD) and psychopathic personality disorder (psychopathy) have been particularly important within debates about the intersections between criminal justice and mental health (Manning, 2000, 2002, 2006; Pickersgill, 2009a, 2009b; Pilgrim, 2007). Individuals regarded as 'personality disordered' who have committed criminal offences transgress a range of boundaries: between normality and pathology, victim and perpetrator, and patient and criminal. There are enduring concerns about the medicalising circularity of associating violence or 'criminality' more generally with personality disorders (Wootton, 1959). Still, legal and policy innovations have often underscored rather than dissolved that association.

In the early 21st century, the revision of mental health legislation for England and Wales focused significant attention on personality disorders (Pilgrim, 2007). In 1999, the UK government began to formulate plans for rewriting the 1983 Mental Health Act (MHA) of England and Wales (with Northern Ireland and Scotland having separate legislation). These plans captured the attention of psychiatrists and psychologists, who were keenly aware of the potential for revised policy to reshape practice. However, the possible effects of such governance on framings of pathology per se were less widely appreciated. For decades, ASPD and psychopathy had been widely thought to be resistant to clinical intervention. Yet, as increasingly fractious discussions about the MHA played out, personality disorders came gradually but profoundly to be positioned as plastic rather than more obdurate constructs. In other words, they became treatable.

This chapter tells the story of how that happened. First, I introduce some of the legal and clinical context from which debates about a refreshed MHA emerged. I move then to reflect on key mental health policy developments over the late 1990s and early 2000s, and discuss the associated perspectives of clinicians. I then describe how the policy machinery itself shifted gear to accommodate some professional concerns. The rapprochement between political/policy and clinical goals came to be materially visible in four 'Dangerous and Severe Personality Disorder (DSPD) Units' at existing NHS hospitals and prisons. These sought to treat individuals meeting the criteria for DSPD while at the same time managing the risks they were understood to present to others. Finally, I analyse the culmination of these interconnected debates: a 2007 revision to the MHA, and the growing (though still not universal) belief that personality disorders are indeed treatable. The result was a reconfiguration of the role and accessibility of (predominantly psychological) care for people previously deemed 'untreatable', perhaps most notably within forensic settings. In sum, I demonstrate how the intensions underlying initiatives to enhance access to therapy are not always benign and can transform ideas about the subjects upon which they seek to intervene.

The 1983 MHA and Therapeutic Pessimism

In 1983, the first major revision to the MHA of England and Wales in more than 20 years was unveiled. Refining and extending much of the content of a 1959 predecessor, the Act was largely steered by the recommendations of an expert committee chaired by Lord Butler of Saffron Walden. Seen by many to be liberal and forward-thinking, the Act they helped to constitute was in turn largely well received (Moncrieff, 2003; Simpson, 1976; Wootton, 1980). This is not to say, though, that the 1983 MHA was appreciated by all and in full. Importantly, it continued a long tradition of allowing courts to order the compulsory detention of offenders with 'mental impairment' or 'psychopathic disorder'. This was to the frustration of some clinicians given their acute awareness of the potential for the punitive practice arising from the ability to detain people in this way. As clinical psychologist Steve Pilling (who went on to become a major figure in UK mental health) reflected, given its 'tautological definition [. . .] it seems quite possible that patients classified as psychopathic could continue to be detained under the terms of the new act as they were under the old' (Pilling, 1983, p. 93).

Nevertheless, the 1983 MHA did technically increase restrictions on the involuntary hospitalisation of convicted criminals (as well as non-offenders). This was well received by many, and Pilling himself noted that that the legislations would reduce 'some of the potential for abuse of powers to compulsorily admit people' (Pilling, 1983, p. 95). Specifically, it introduced what came to be known as the 'treatability test'. This mandated that an offender could only be held in NHS settings subject to the availability of treatment that was 'likely to alleviate or prevent a deterioration of his [sic] condition'. The 'test' thus sought to ensure that a diagnosis of psychopathy was not by itself sufficient for involuntary hospital detention: the disorder also had to be regarded as treatable. Accordingly, the treatability test came to direct the gaze of mental health professionals working with criminal offenders to the ontology of psychopathy, inviting the question: Could 'psychopaths' be treated?

In the United Kingdom, as in many other national contexts, the treatability of psychopathy had been a matter of enduring contention. A minority position, which maintained that therapy was both possible and potentially efficacious, was an established element of clinical discourse. Still, most clinicians seemed pessimistic. Following the 1983 MHA, forensic psychiatrist Adrian T. Grounds succinctly expressed such pessimism:

> The detention of offenders in the legal category 'psychopathic disorder' in special hospitals for treatment raises a number of critical issues. There are doubts about the nature of the disorder; what constitutes treatment; who is 'treatable'; the effectiveness of treatment; and whether evidence of psychological change implies reduced risk of reoffending. (Grounds, 1987, p. 474)

The treatability test in the Act invited reflection on these issues, as did the influential third edition of the US nosology, the *Diagnostic and Statistical Manual of Mental Disorders* (*DSM-III*), published in 1980. *DSM-III* devoted a major section to personality disorders, and the significance this accorded to them was not lost on UK-based health professionals. Its introduction of the category of antisocial personality disorder (ASPD) was particularly interesting to forensic practitioners due to its apparent overlap with the older category of psychopathy. Furthermore, it had a more specific definition than the opaque construct of psychopathic disorder in the 1983 MHA (and of previous DSM articulations of disorders of sociality; Pickersgill, 2012a). Over time, ASPD came to have increasing traction within the United Kingdom.

Previously, many mental health professionals appeared to have regarded individuals configured as personality disordered as a nuisance – people who were far from being proper subjects of the clinical gaze, even as they remained at its margins. Rather, people with personality disorder were often framed as an impediment to the 'real work' of treating people with discrete mental illnesses (as discussed by Cavadino, 1989). Individuals living under the label of personality disorder were frequently excluded from health services and were often explicitly disliked by practitioners. Such disdain was exemplified in an influential 1988 paper, 'Personality disorder: The patients psychiatrists dislike' (Lewis and Appleby, 1988). This was a particular issue for people characterised with ASPD or psychopathy, given the overarching significance of perceived social deviancy in making such a diagnosis. For clinical psychologist Ronald Blackburn (1988), characterising someone with one of those personality disorders was 'little more than a moral judgement masquerading as a clinical diagnosis' (Blackburn, 1988, p. 511).

Still, as noted, personality disorders remained articulable as conditions that could and should be treated. An influential proponent of this view was community psychiatrist Peter Tyrer, a frequent writer on personality disorders. In 1991, Tyrer and colleagues argued:

> One of the important consequences of better classification and awareness of personality problems is the recognition that people with personality disorders suffer considerably and merit help, even if it cannot always be given

> in a reliable and effective form. In the past, many therapeutic disciplines have tended to regard personality disorders as not really part of psychiatry's province and that they should therefore be separated from 'real' mental illness. This view is often implicit and rarely finds its way into print but is unfortunately common in practice. Views of treatment are now changing. Psychotherapy in particular, which has always maintained that personality disorders are part of its territory, has persevered in attempts to understand and modify the harmful attitudes that dominate the personal lives and relationships of people with personality disorders, and has helped to transfer this awareness to others. (Tyrer et al., 1991, p. 468)

The preceding quote emphasises both the subjective distress suffered by people diagnosed with a personality disorder and the extent to which this could be ameliorated through psychological therapy. These assertions can be read as simultaneously seeking to de-stigmatise personality disorders and advocate for their treatment. Nevertheless, therapy could be 'long, arduous and difficult to complete' (Tyrer et al., p. 468; see also Stein, 1992; Stone, 1993; Yorston, 1999).

As inspiring as Tyrer's comments might have been to some, other mental health professionals were concerned about the evidence for such claims. In the 1990s, the concept of evidence-based medicine was making its presence felt within clinical communities, and the production of 'hard data' to substantiate claims of treatability was enjoined. As a 1998 editorial in the *British Journal of Psychiatry* asserted, 'There is a need for claims of therapeutic success within the field of personality disorder to be rigorously appraised' (Cawthra and Gibb, 1998, p. 8). These comments echoed psychologist Bridget Dolan and psychiatrist Jeremy Coid in their influential 1993 review of treatments for personality disorders commissioned by the UK Department of Health and the Home Office. While Dolan and Coid (1993) expressed cautious optimism about treatability, they also underscored a need for statistically robust trials to provide firm evidence for the effects of interventions. These long-standing, if relatively subdued, tensions regarding the treatability of personality disorders were revitalised at the close of the 20th century as the UK government moved to reconfigure its mental health policy.

The Advent of Dangerous and Severe Personality Disorder

On 15 February 1999, Home Secretary Jack Straw asserted in the House of Commons (1999) that there was

> a group of dangerous and severely personality disordered individuals from whom the public at present are not properly protected, and who are

> restrained effectively neither by the criminal law, nor by the provisions of the Mental Health Act [. . .] the government proposes that there should be new legislative powers for the indeterminate, but reviewable detention of dangerously personality disordered individuals [. . .] The individuals concerned must have the best possible chance of becoming safe, so as to be returned to the community, whenever that is possible. (House of Commons, 1999)

Soon after, the concept of 'Dangerous and Severe Personality Disorder' (DSPD) began to circulate widely, leading to a wholesale DSPD Programme imbricating mental health and criminal justice.

Emerging from Whitehall, DSPD was, to be clear, not a formal diagnosis. Rather, it was an emergent administrative category for risky individuals. It was widely regarded as having been animated, at least in part, by the July 1996 murder of Lin and Megan Russell by Michael Stone. A prior offender diagnosed with a personality disorder, Stone was involuntarily admitted into De La Pole Hospital, Hull, in November 1994. He was subsequently discharged in January 1995, following a decision that he was no longer eligible for compulsory detention under the MHA (South East Coast Strategic Health Authority, 2006). Media constructions of a dangerous individual abandoned by mental health professionals as a consequence of legal constraints sat alongside broader public fears about violent crime (Freestone, 2005; Manning, 2002; Prins, 2007; White, 2002). Politicians appeared keen to respond to these concerns.

Sitting under the umbrella of DSPD were people regarded as psychopaths and others meeting criteria for ASPD who were also believed to present a clear and long-term danger to the wider public. Some mental health professionals were highly sceptical about the introduction of this category; clinical psychologist Ronald Blackburn, for instance, argued that the 'idea of a clearly demarcated category of 'dangerous psychopaths' or 'severe personality disorders' represents a disease entity approach which is at best a gross oversimplication and at worst a demonic stereotype' (Blackburn, 2000, p. 2). The political aspect to DSPD was signalled by psychiatrist Peter Tyrer (2001) in his renaming of the category as Jack Straw Syndrome.

Of course, the law has long sought to configure and govern 'risky' or 'dangerous' individuals (Bartlett, 2003). What is pertinent here is that the already broad mandate of the State for defining and managing dangerousness was nevertheless considered too narrow by Straw. He argued that powers for indeterminate detention should be extended, regardless of whether the individual to be detained was currently before the courts. The DSPD proposals therefore represented a radical and controversial step by the UK government in the administration of offenders understood to be living with a personality disorder. As such, it also represented a reconfiguration of the activities of mental health professionals themselves.

In July 1999, a consultation paper was released that advanced the possibility of a legislative change that would enable individuals categorised with DSPD to be subject to indeterminate confinement in a special unit within a prison or NHS hospital (Home Office and the Department of Health, 1999). As sociologist Mark Freestone put it, these 'DSPD Units' were intended to be 'a 'third way' between the prison service and the special hospital and as such a unique environment' (Freestone, 2005, p. 450). The Units were to be a place to detain individuals considered to be threats to the wider public while at the same time providing therapy to reduce the risk they purportedly presented.

As an instrument of governance, the DSPD proposals were closely related to the Dutch *Ter Beschikking Stelling* system (de Boer et al., 2008). This was (and remains) an institutional arrangement aimed at managing criminal offenders deemed to be living with particular kinds of mental ill-health, with the aim of decreasing the risk associated with them. The proposed DSPD Units also echoed earlier suggestions made in 1975 by the Butler Committee (McCallum, 2001), and bore a striking resemblance to a recommendation advanced in the so-called Fallon Report (Fallon et al., 1999). Released in January 1999, this detailed the results of an inquiry into drug use, pornography, and possible paedophile activity at Ashworth Hospital (a high-security mental health facility near Liverpool). The report proposed the establishment of special units for individuals with severe personality disorder within prisons and NHS facilities – similar, therefore, to Straw's DSPD Units, and perhaps an inspiration for them (Bartlett, 2003).

Straw's plans were unveiled at a time when significant doubts remained about the treatability of personality disorders. In light of these and with the Stone case in mind, the DSPD Programme was an attempt to remedy the social and clinical problems surrounding individuals configured as severely personality disordered. However, as indicated earlier, the DSPD proposals were widely resented and resisted by mental health professionals (Chiswick, 1999; Eastman, 1999; Haddock et al., 2001; Mullen, 1999; White 2002). Serious concerns were raised by clinicians who were keenly aware of and anxious about their role as agents of social control about a profound shift in professional focus toward public protection. The DSPD Programme was not, however, the only change to mental health policy and practice the government sought to introduce. As the century closed, plans were put in place to create what was initially presented as an entirely new MHA for England and Wales – and clinical contestation grew with these.

Changing the Terrain of Mental Health

Toward the end of the 1990s, it was increasingly felt by the UK government that the 1983 MHA needed 'updating'. Accordingly, in September 1998 they charged an expert committee to review the Act. Chaired by lawyer Genevra Richardson, the Committee's proposals – published as the Richardson Report in July 1999 – were widely considered humane and progressive and received favourably by clinicians (Department of Health, 1999b). For instance, the Report enjoined the further enhancement of what was commonly understood to be the 'clear therapeutic ethos' of the 1983 MHA by extending the conditions of the treatability test (Glover-Thomas, 2006; Grounds, 2001).

In November 1999, four months after the release of the Richardson Report, the government published a Green Paper: 'Reform of the Mental Health Act 1983: Proposals for consultation' (Secretary of State for Health, 1999). A key point of agreement between it, the Richardson Report, the DSPD consultation paper, and the Fallon Report was that psychopathy should be removed from the MHA and replaced with the more general category of personality disorder. This was deemed by many to be 'long overdue' (Laing, 2000, p. 223), given that the legal definition of psychopathic disorder was in practice applied to a range of subcategories of personality disorder (like ASPD).

Unlike the Richardson Report, however, the emphasis of the Green Paper was on compulsion: compulsory treatment and compulsory detention. It also rejected many of the Richardson Committee proposals (Bartlett, 2003). For example, in marked contrast to the extension of the treatability test recommended by Richardson, the Green Paper advocated the removal of that test altogether. Furthermore, under its terms, individuals characterised as personality disordered could be detained involuntarily based on risk, irrespective of whether the specific DSPD proposals came to fruition.

Unsurprisingly, then, the Green Paper was heavily criticised by clinicians, as well as by members of the Richardson Committee (Peay, 2000; Szmukler and Holloway, 2000; Zigmond, 2001). As lawyer Nicola Glover-Thomas (2006, p. 32) put it, within the Green Paper, 'risk management has trumped therapeutic endeavour'. Though the 1983 MHA certainly referred to the risk presented by a patient, the Green Paper placed this theme front and centre (Laing, 2000). The foregrounding of risk – and the controversy it attracted – characterised the debate on the rewriting of the 1983 MHA over subsequent years.

The Danger of Dangerousness

Notwithstanding the negative reaction to the 1999 Green Paper, the UK government continued with its plans to revise the 1983 MHA and implement the DSPD Programme. In 2001, £126 million had been committed to DSPD service development, and the Programme was being piloted at specialised Units at Rampton Hospital (Nottinghamshire) and HM Prison Whitemoor Prison (Cambridgeshire). The DSPD Programme as enacted was a somewhat diluted version of what had originally been proposed and worked within the ambit of existing legislation. The individual DSPD Units were extremely well resourced, with little expense spared in terms of both their construction and function. High costs were justified in the context of the government's longer-term and imbricated plans for mental health and crime control.

DSPD also formed the explicit focus of a 2000 mental health White Paper, which underscored concerns with personality disorders and dangerousness (Department of Health, 2000a, 2000b). Yet again, the UK government found that its plans were very poorly received. One editorial in the *British Journal of Psychiatry*, for instance, argued that the White Paper was a 'profoundly illiberal document' (Grounds, 2001, p. 387), drawing attention to its inclusion of potentially broader criteria under which offenders could be indeterminately detained via mental health law. A *BMJ* editorial expressed the continuing concerns of clinicians with the government's proposals and highlighted the difficult balance between care provision and risk control (Szmukler, 2001; see also Chiswick, 2001; Gunn and Felthous, 2000). Writing in *The Psychologist*, the 'coercive' dimension to therapeutic work in relation to personality disorders was highlighted by clinical psychologist David Pilgrim and solicitor David Hewitt (2001, p. 527). Readers were reminded that DSPD itself was as a 'politically invented notion' (Pilgrim and Hewitt, 2001, p. 527).

The White Paper was thus criticised across the United Kingdom and in a variety of outlets – and by mental health lawyers as well as clinicians (Peay, 2003). Critique focused on the preoccupation with risk and 'dangerousness' that characterised the document (Buchanan and Leese, 2001) and questioned the meanings of these terms: How would dangerousness be measured? How dangerous would an individual have to be to qualify for the DSPD Programme? How did dangerousness relate to treatability and to risk? Representatives from mental health organisations such as the British Psychological Society directly lobbied the government to consider such matters far more carefully (Harper, 2005). However, when in 2002 the government followed up the White Paper with a Draft Mental Health Bill, these persistent (Pfohl, 1978; Wootton, 1959) questions remained largely unanswered.

Curiously, given the government's previous focus on DSPD, the 2002 Draft Bill did not specifically address this category. Still, mental health stakeholders found the Bill to be troubling for a range of other reasons. Not least of these was wording which raised concern that highly antisocial individuals (i.e. individuals who might come under the rubric of DSPD) could more easily be detained involuntarily within mental health services. Significant debate reigned over this point (Pilgrim, 2007). Still, as lawyer Peter Bartlett pointed out, the concept of dangerousness was hardly unprecedented within English and Welsh mental health legislation (or, indeed, to that of many other nations). As such, concerns about social control elided the uncomfortable fact that clinicians had always played a prominent role in configuring and governing deviance. Furthermore, it was 'not obvious' how far the Bill extended existing powers for the detention of individuals who were perceived to be a threat to others (Bartlett, 2003, p. 328). Despite these caveats, Bartlett nevertheless considered the Bill 'badly flawed' (Bartlett, 2003, p. 327) and observed that with it, 'the government managed to achieve a consensus rarely seen in mental health politics. Sadly, the consensus was negative: virtually no one supported the draft bill' (Bartlett, 2003, p. 326; see also Moncrieff, 2003).

Towards Treatability

As debate about the MHA reigned, deliberations regarding the treatability of personality disorders became increasingly apparent. Promissory discourse regarding more efficient and efficacious therapies was instantiated within recently established academic units, such as the Nottingham Personality Disorder Institute, and informal networks and formal associations, such as the British and Irish Group for the Study of Personality Disorder (BIGSPD, formed in 2000). These centres and forums arose from and further animated clinical interest in the aetiology, development, and treatment of personality disorders.

At the same time, public spending on personality disorder services and research significantly increased, supported by bodies such as the UK Medical Research Council, the Department of Health, and the DSPD

Programme. One emergent sponsor was the National Forensic Mental Health R&D Programme, established in April 1999 (three months before the release of the initial joint Home Office/Department of Health proposals for DSPD). The Programme commissioned literature reviews into the aetiology and management of personality disorders, as well as research on behalf of the Department of Health. In so doing, it became a key funder of personality disorder research.

Still, the proliferation of research and the promise of new treatments for personality disorders did not readily foster a unified front of clinical enthusiasm: views remained mixed (e.g. Chiesa et al., 2000; Haddock et al., 2001; Kendell, 2002). Nonetheless, while some expressed doubts about treatability, an increasing number of clinicians wrote articles and produced commentaries that pointed towards effective interventions. The London-based 'therapeutic communities' at Cassel and Henderson hospitals were, for instance, highly regarded for their effective work with individuals diagnosed with a personality disorder (Manning, 2002). In particular, psychological strategies more broadly were viewed with optimism – partly as a consequence of a growing evidence base (e.g. Bateman Fonagy, 1999; Chiesa Fonagy, 2000; Mullen, 1999). Influential Broadmoor-based psychotherapist Gwen Adshead summed up the view of many when she wrote in 2001 that there could be 'no justification for global assertions that personality disorder is untreatable' (Adshead, 2001, p. 412).

Particular faith was placed in the psychological techniques of cognitive analytic therapy (CAT) and dialectical behaviour therapy (DBT, an approach based on CBT). Hopes for these interventions increased during the first few years of the 21st century, even as the number of RCTs remained low. Pharmaceuticals, such as antipsychotics and antidepressants, were also being used as 'adjuncts' to the psychological treatment of personality disorders (Sushovan Tyrer, 2001; Triebwasser Siever, 2007). This mixing of modalities brought into sharp relief the ontological plurality so often evident within mental health (Helén, 2011; Pickersgill, 2010).

Clinicians were urged to forego the notion of a 'fix all' for personality disorder and to concentrate instead on the 'functional assessment' of the condition (Davidson, 2002). The functional approach produced an increasingly modularised view of personality, first by cataloguing an individual's particular 'abnormal' personality features and exploring the distress experienced as consequence of them, second by using those catalogued features as the basis for a complex management plan. This would be 'bespoke' rather than 'off the peg'; individualised but nevertheless drawing on an eclectic array of existing interventions (Hogue et al., 2007; Livesley, 2007).

At the turn of the century, then, a variety of key actors were beginning to configure personality disorders as potentially plastic – capable of responding to the appropriate and skilled application of therapeutic knowledge. This positivity, though, was not without nuance or caveat. For example, Rampton Hospital psychologist Kevin Howells and his colleagues suggested that different models of disorder lay beneath the assorted treatment strategies, raising questions about appropriateness and efficacy (Howells et al., 2007). Concerns also circulated that many of the treatments touted for a broad spectrum of personality disorder had shown evidence of effects only for the category of borderline personality disorder (Crawford, 2007). Furthermore, as Bartlett (2003) wryly observed, predictions about treatability seemed to relate more to the person doing the predicting than the person about whom predictions were made.

While the mental health professions undoubtedly were moving toward an understanding of personality disorders as treatable, there was by no means a consensus. Conflicting feelings and perspectives continued to circulate, even – as noted by psychologist Tony Lavender (2002) – within DSPD services themselves. Indeed, as a British Psychological Society (2006) report reflected, some doubted whether the concept of personality disorder was useful within clinical practice at all. Yet, it was precisely because the tide of opinion on personality disorders was so clearly turning that some commentators felt compelled to advance concerns and to demarcate limits to therapeutic knowledge and the potential for change.

A Policy Push

While clinicians at the coalface of practice were starting to write positively, albeit cautiously, about the treatability of personality disorders, there was markedly less subtlety in some of the proclamations made by the UK Department of Health and associated bodies. For instance, its National Institute for Mental Health in England (NIMHE) published a report, *Personality Disorder: No Longer a Diagnosis of Exclusion* (NIMHE, 2003a), arguing that personality disorders were treatable. Any remaining doubt about this was regarded as lamentable, and something that a future MHA might address. The controversial proposed removal of the 1983 treatability test was characterised as 'highlight[ing] the need for new community and in-patient services for people with personality disorder' (NIMHE, 2003a, p. 28). Mental health professionals were encouraged to be more open-minded to the potential of treatment in light of this.

Ten months later, the NIMHE released the provocatively titled *Breaking the Cycle of Rejection: The Personality Disorder Capabilities Framework* (NIMHE, 2003b). This aimed 'to challenge the discriminatory association between personality disorder and dangerousness by putting in place services aimed at reducing vulnerability and promoting more effective coping by individuals' (NIMHE, 2003b, p. 10). It further promoted a vision of treatability by painting a more sympathetic picture of people with personality disorder than many others – not least the UK government itself – had in the past:

> In recent years, the emphasis on risk and dangerousness associated with a very small number of people with personality disorder, has obscured the fact that very many people with this diagnosis are highly vulnerable to abuse and violence themselves – and to self-harm and suicide. (NIMHE, 2003b, p. 10)

While the NIMHE document alluded to the MHA in its section on 'The broader policy context', it refrained from more explicit articulation of the interconnections between the assumed clinical antipathy towards personality disorders and the proposed MHA (specifically, the provision that would remove the treatability test). The controversial category of DSPD was not even mentioned. Nevertheless, the influence of both DSPD and the 2002 Draft Mental Health Bill was evident in the list of competencies deemed necessary for clinicians working with individuals diagnosed with personality disorder, particularly skills in 'assessing and managing risk to self and others'. Risk – the leitmotif of the proposed reforms to the 1983 MHA – thus structured the NIMHE clinical guidelines, even as the same document made gestures towards destigmatisation.

The year 2003 also saw the publication of a treatment review commissioned by the Home Office and Department of Health through the DSPD Programme (Warren et al., 2003). The review, conducted by a team of psychologists (including Bridget Dolan) and psychiatrists, aimed to provide an evidence base for 'informing the decisions about the development of services for DSPD' (Warren et al., 2003, p. 8). Building on the prior treatment review by Dolan and Coid (1993), the 2003 'update' came to similar conclusions; namely, that personality disorders were (potentially) treatable, especially through the application of therapies such as DBT and therapeutic community models. Among their five recommendations, Warren and colleagues asserted that 'Greater priority should be given to research into the treatment of personality disorder, given the paucity of the evidence currently available' (Warren et al., 2003, p. 7). The review thus contained a message to which both policymakers and many clinicians were receptive: therapy was possible, but more research was needed.

In sum, through 2002 and 2003, the development of policy and clinical discourse on personality disorders brought the treatability of these conditions into sharp focus. Seemingly in recognition of the controversy it had generated, and mindful of its aims to successfully implement DSPD policy, the Department of Health sought to ally itself with practising clinicians. It did this by evoking tropes similar to those that had become increasingly evident within mental health discourse – chiefly those seeking to destigmatise personality disorders and to configure them as treatable – and articulating these within the pages of key policy documents. These texts were aimed, in part, at fostering a more favourable outlook towards the proposed mental health legislation. In the process, the hopes of clinicians were brought more closely into alignment with the aims of policymakers.

How to Treat Dangerousness

The alignment of policy and clinical goals was most markedly apparent in the DSPD Units. By the autumn of 2005, four high-security pilot DSPD Units were running, which contained 'some of the most difficult and challenging individuals in society' (DSPD Programme, 2005, p. 27). Two Units were inside prisons (HMP Frankland and HMP Whitemoor) and two were within NHS hospitals (Broadmoor and Rampton). Generally speaking, the prison Units stressed the correctional aspects of the DSPD Programme, whereas the hospitals focused more on its therapeutic dimensions. However, even within DSPD Units, tensions existed between carceral and clinical approaches (Freestone, 2005; Maltman et al., 2008).

In Broadmoor and Rampton hospitals, treatment was administered by multidisciplinary teams consisting of clinical and forensic psychologists, psychiatrists, nurses (who comprised the bulk of the workforce), and a range of other staff (Ministry of Justice, 2011). At Rampton, a psychologist undertook an initial treatment needs assessment (TNA), which preceded a detailed, multidisciplinary formulation and thereafter an 'agreed set of prioritizations of treatment needs' (Hogue et al., 2007, p. 65). Therapies offered included the aforementioned DBT and CAT, with CBT initially particularly emphasised by Broadmoor (Perkins et al., 2015), alongside therapeutic group work and a range of structured skills programmes.

Multiple professionals worked together to simultaneously implement DSPD policy and treat what was seen as the psychological and social deviancy of people categorised with personality disorder. While treatment was aimed at reducing offending behaviour, many clinicians were concerned to treat 'the person in personality disorder'. In practice, this meant a more expansive therapeutic vision than a clinical focus restricted only to managing those aspects of an individual that were (in the modularised vision of personality) assumed to be associated with criminal antisociality. It also implied everyday patient life as itself having the potential to generate therapeutic effects. As Broadmoor-based clinical and forensic psychologist David Perkins asserted with colleagues in a paper reflecting back on the DSPD Unit there:

> Day-to-day interactions on the wards play out the PD [personality disorder]- linked patterns of relating to others, and therefore these daily interactions in themselves offer opportunities for corrective experiences. Integrating this with more formal psychological therapy enables a more holistic service and one that helps to integrate a sense of self. (Perkins et al., 2015, p. 16)

While, as we have seen, medication might be used as an adjunct, psychological therapies were salient for the treatment of personality disorders. These were later also emphasised in UK clinical practice guidelines as treatments for both ASPD (NICE, 2009) and borderline personality disorder (National Collaborating Centre for Mental Health, 2009). Several years later, guidance to practitioners working with criminal offenders regarded as personality disordered continued to emphasise psychological approaches to treatment and management (National Offender Management Service/NHS England, 2015). Alongside DBT, CBT – which was commonly employed in the probation service and, as noted, used within Broadmoor – also came to be more widely considered as a noteworthy intervention (de Boer et al., 2008; Maden, 2007). As Armstrong (2002) has argued, CBT can readily be made to serve both punitive/carceral and therapeutic/clinical ends: it is retributive (individuals are held accountable for their antisocial behaviour) while also being rehabilitative (antisocial actions decrease following therapy). It is thus particularly well-suited to forensic mental healthcare.

The nature and role of treatment in DSPD Units underline three central issues. First, these were sites where the goals of policymakers and clinicians were closely aligned: policymakers could be satisfied that the risk dangerous offenders represented was being reduced, while psychologists, psychiatrists, and others were given the time and resources to follow a therapeutic imperative to treat individuals diagnosed with a personality disorder. Second, the autonomy of clinicians within DSPD Units complicates the presumption of the unilateral political capture of clinical goals that might be inferred from the previous section. That some psychiatrists and psychologists framed their work as treating personality disorders rather than solely managing risk reveals a more dynamic, though still asymmetric, relationship between the aspirations of policymakers and those of healthcare professionals. Third, the activities of the DSPD Units had subtle yet important implications for wider configurations of personality disorder. With few established conventions regarding the 'correct' way to treat these conditions but with a remit to do so regardless, clinicians in the DSPD Units employed different forms of therapy. The various treatments relied on diverse underlying models of personality disorder, and their juxtaposition thus (re)assembled heterogeneous models of the conditions. In essence, the DSPD Units acted as laboratories within which the ontology of personality disorder could be experimented with, and they played a salient role in configuring the category as treatable.

The Arrival of an Act

Despite these developments, many professionals continued to contest the UK government's evolving plans for mental health law. As we have seen, the 2002 Draft Mental Health Bill did not garner the support the government had hoped. It was, in the end, withdrawn, and another Bill was released in September 2004 (Department of Health, 2004a). Somewhat less controversial than its predecessor, the Bill marginally mollified detractors by reintroducing some treatability criteria for cases where involuntary compulsion was being considered. Despite this move, it was still critiqued for its emphasis on risk. Furthermore, some of its detractors claimed that the Bill ignored, for the most part, the views of mental health institutions. This was interpreted as exemplifying the indifference of the UK government both to the clinicians who would implement the MHA and the individuals who would be under its purview (Brown, 2006).

The government, however, considered that it had 'taken seriously the concerns raised about the first version of the draft Bill' (Department of Health, 2004b, p. 4). Still, it refrained from pushing the second Bill forward. Seemingly in response to the massive criticism levelled against it over the previous seven years, the Department of Health instead made a different move. Specifically, it announced in March 2006 that, rather than completely replacing the 1983 MHA, it would instead amend it (Brown, 2006). Accordingly, on 18 November 2006, a third Mental Health Bill was released (Department of Health, 2006a).

Predictably, the 2006 Bill was hardly uncontentious, not least since, like its predecessors, it forsook the treatability test. According to the Department of Health, this was because the test had led

> to a false presumption that some – particularly those with severe personality disorders – are untreatable. This means that detention is sometimes not used when it ought to be, even though people with severe personality disorders can be – and are – treated compulsorily under the Act. (Department of Health, 2006b, p. 3)

By removing the treatability test, the legislation arising from the 2006 Bill would, clinicians and others were reassured, 'take away some unnecessary obstacles to practitioners' ability to use the Act where it is warranted by the needs of the patient and the degree of risk' (Department of Health, 2006b, p. 3). In essence, the government was arguing that treatment, largely psychological in nature, was being unfairly denied to people who would benefit from it.

The treatability test was not completely abandoned, however. Rather, it was reconfigured into the 'appropriate treatment test'. Similar to the 1983 treatability test, this revised set of criteria for detention included the key qualification that treatment should be readily 'available' rather than merely being a theoretical possibility. The appropriate treatment test would, apparently, call for 'an holistic assessment of whether appropriate treatment is available, not focused only on the likely outcome of treatment' (Department of Health, 2006b, p. 3). Psychological therapies were explicitly highlighted as coming within the purview of what the legislation would define as 'medical treatment', since 'To exclude them would be inconsistent with the reality of mental health care and might inadvertently encourage the use of medication even where there are more appropriate alternatives available' (Department of Health, 2006b, pp. 2–3).

By removing the treatability test and replacing it with the appropriate treatment test, the Department of Health sought to ensure that people who 'should' be involuntarily detained could be legally held, but with safeguards in place: at least some kind of treatment needed to be available. Nevertheless, what, precisely, a 'holistic assessment' entailed was unclear. So, too, was the procedure for establishing – or formally contesting – whether a particular treatment was 'appropriate'. Moreover, many commentators were concerned that the Bill illegitimately conflated 'appropriate' with 'effective' treatment; in other words, that individuals could be detained as a consequence of *some* kind of treatment being available, irrespective of whether it was the *right* kind.

Despite these concerns, the Bill was eventually passed with some modifications. Thus, after almost a decade of political wrangling, a revised MHA for England and Wales was given Royal Assent on 19 July 2007. In marked contrast to the original plan for a radical reconstruction of the 1983 Act, the 2007 legislation was an amended and revised version of its predecessor. The chief detractors of the Department of Health were, for the most part, more or less mollified. Not surprisingly, though, some discontentment continued to be registered (Prins, 2007).

Personality Disorder Is Treatable

On 22 June 2007, one month before the 2007 Act received Royal Assent, the National Forensic Mental Health R&D Programme officially closed. Given the emerging consensus on the treatability of personality disorder, the UK government seemed no longer to feel the need to continue to invest so significantly in research through this dedicated mechanism. As Frankie Pidd of the Department of Health's National Personality Disorders Development Programme commented in an article co-authored with psychologist Janet Feigenbaum:

> The evidence base has emerged over the past two decades to indicate that personality disorders are treatable. A range of psychological therapies has been shown to be the most effective treatment for personality disorders, though medication can have some additional effect in reducing the severity of symptoms. (Pidd and Feigenbaum, 2007, p. 8)

In highlighting this emergent evidence base, the comments above also tell a story of epistemic progress – reflected too in a British Psychological Society report on treatments for personality disorder (BPS, 2006), alongside various other opinion pieces and research articles. Though Pidd and Feigenbaum accepted that some clinicians might disagree, they asserted that this was based on a 'false belief' (Pidd Feigenbaum, 2007, p. 7) and, worse, one that would increase the stigmatisation of individuals diagnosed with a personality disorder. Pidd and Feigenbaum therefore evoked a discourse of destigmatisation, consistent with the trend in the mental health professions since at least the 1990s (Pilgrim Rogers, 2005), which was especially apparent in recent years in discourse centred on personality disorders. In so doing, Pidd and Feigenbaum presented not only a therapeutic imperative to work with individuals labelled thusly but a moral duty as well.

More widely, journals such as *Psychology, Crime and Law* devoted entire issues to contributions on personality disorder, many of which illuminated the treatability of these conditions. As highly regarded psychologist Peter Fonagy noted in the introduction to one special issue, clinicians should 'celebrate the emergence' of 'effective' interventions (Fonagy, 2007, p. 3). For internationally celebrated personality disorders expert John Livesley, the literature was now 'clear that personality disorder can be treated' (Livesley, 2007, p. 28).

Beyond Treatability

If today personality disorder has been authorised as treatable, with psychological therapies underscored as central modalities of intervention, so too has the category come to be increasingly 'psychologised'. In line with the wider trends in clinical psychology discussed in Chapter 1, practitioners increasingly speak through an idiom of 'complex emotional needs' or 'personality difficulties' (Trevillion et al., 2021). This includes within forensic contexts (Moran et al., 2022; NHS England, 2023a). Such talk moves further away from what many see as the more psychiatric language of 'disorder'. However, this de-medicalising shift would have been unimaginable without the efforts made to configure personality disorders (or difficulties) as treatable in the first place (and not least by psychiatrists), and thus as a proper target of psychological intervention.

Over time, services have increased, and the policy focus on personality disorders has expanded even further beyond the criminological considerations that once anchored so much debate (McBride, 2017). Yet, the widespread reconfiguration of these categories as treatable never led to a panacea. The patchy provision of psychological care for people characterised as having a personal disorder remained (Royal College of Psychiatrists, 2020; The Consultation and Advocacy Promotion Service, 2011), and stigma and discrimination endure (Bax et al., 2023; Bonington Rose, 2014). Moreover, there are indications that the appropriate treatment test resulted in an increase in length of involuntary detentions for people diagnosed with a personality disorder who are based within the criminal justice system (O'Loughlin, 2014). The ramifications of an ethic of access, then, are not necessarily always positive or straightforward.

With regards to the DSPD Programme more specifically, this initially continued to expand following the 2007 MHA. By 2008, alongside the original four high-security units, four medium-security units and some community services for DSPD were in operation (de Boer et al., 2008). The costs, though, were significant. Following the 2008 financial crisis and a 2010 general election, the Conservative-led UK government came to reflect on just how much cheaper it was to undertake the treatment of offenders with a personality disorder within prisons rather than hospital-based DSPD Units (Department of Health/NOMS Offender Personality Disorder Team, 2011). The DSPD Programme was thereafter scaled down, before finally coming to an end in 2013 (Tyrer et al., 2015). In its wake, the Offender Personality Disorder (OPD) Pathway was launched (O'Loughlin, 2014). This 'is a set of psychologically-informed services operating across criminal justice and health' (NHS England, 2023a). Upon establishment, the OPD Pathway sought to expand access to treatment while, in the eyes of some, diverting resource away from special hospitals (Player, 2017). It, too, has had subjectifying effects, helping to further circulate psychological and psychiatric concepts within the criminal justice system (McBride, 2017).

As for the MHA, it is – again – being reconsidered. In 2017, an Independent Review of the Mental Health Act was announced, chaired by Professor Sir Simon Wessely of King's College London. A resulting 2018 report highlighted, among other issues, a rise in detentions under the 2007 Act (Wessely, 2018; see also Wessely et al., 2018). Wessely argued that 'looking back we can see that some of the decisions taken by government leading up to the 2007 Act were an overreaction' – with the concept of DSPD implied as an example (Wessely, 2017, p. 7). Subsequently, a further Mental Health Bill was promised (Department of Health and Social Care and The Rt Hon Matt Hancock MP, 2021), although this was acknowledged to have progressed more slowly than expected (Department of Health and Social Care, 2021). A draft Bill was ultimately published in June 2022 (Department of Health and Social Care and Ministry of Justice, 2022), and the following month a Joint Committee on the Draft Mental Health Bill was appointed by the House of Commons and the House of Lords to consider it in more detail. In January 2023, the Committee published a report responding favourably to some elements of the Bill (Joint Committee on the Draft Mental Health Bill, 2023). This included how the Bill had reconfigured the appropriate treatment test in light of the critique it had attracted: to underscore therapeutic benefit rather than merely the availability of therapy. However, despite high hopes, the year 2023 concluded with no announcement that the Bill would make its way into law. This was to the considerable chagrin of many clinicians and people with lived experience of mental ill-health (BPS Communications, 2023; Mind, 2023).

With the arrival of another (Labour) government in 2024, a revised Mental Health Bill was produced in November of that year (Department of Health and Social Care, 2024). This was generally met with optimism, after several years of frustration. One of the actions that the Bill aimed to achieve, and perhaps a legacy of the political and legal debates discussed earlier, was 'supporting offenders with severe mental health problems to access the care they need' (Prime Minister's Office, 2004, p. 84). As a news item in the *BMJ* remarked, mental health charities, on balance, 'hailed' the Bill, yet nevertheless 'emphasised the need for investment in services and buildings' (Dyer, 2024, p. 1). These concerns were mirrored by clinicians (Goddard, 2024), who – like Roman Raczka, President of the British Psychological Society – highlighted the need to invest specifically in the therapeutic workforce as part of programme of funding (BPS Communications, 2024). At the time of writing, the Bill has not yet progressed to law. Accordingly, its ramifications for access to care and the ontology of personality disorder remain ambiguous.

Configuring Law and Practice

Reported inside journal pages, argued through presentations in large conferences and small seminars, and attested to by healthcare professionals, claims about the treatability of personality disorder resound powerfully through clinical discourse. This chapter has explored how personality disorders came to be broadly deemed legitimate sites of effective therapeutic action – how they became 'treatable'. In doing so, I have sought to highlight how in some cases access to therapy can be shaped by interlocking penal and clinical concerns in the context of disquieting political demands.

While law is a powerful tool for ordering the social, debates over legislative changes cast into sharp relief the ambiguities legislative mandates and processes are designed to manage. They also illustrate how law participates in configuring the ontologies of the entities upon which it acts (Cloatre, 2013; Seear, 2020). Attempts to rewrite the 1983 MHA directed attention to long-standing problems associated with the category of personality disorder and those characterised with it, animating clinical discourse. Moves to remove the treatability test from the Act to facilitate detentions were particularly controversial, resulting in backlash against successive bills. Yet, revised legislation seemed more palatable after those plans were diluted and individuals labelled with personality disorder were reconfigured as patients who could – and should – access therapy. While the government profited from this revised understanding, so too did clinicians who had long held that belief – including through professional acceptance and direct support in terms of funding and employment opportunities (Manning, 2002).

Professional perspectives can, at times, have significant influence on mental health policies (Grob, 2008; Prior, 1991; Schatzman Strauss, 1966), and in the United Kingdom practitioners mobilised alongside others to contest and eventually influence the 2007 update to the 1983 MHA. In so doing, they shaped the law that would govern their practice. This underscores the capacity of clinicians to purposefully torque the psychological matrix (Rose, 1985) wherein they operate, and which itself subjectifies them and configures the nature of their professional work. We can see too that while mental health law, policy, and practice sometimes operate antagonistically (Greig, 2002), they are also reciprocally configured, with potentially significant effects on the persons acted upon by these (Pickersgill, 2013).

Access to therapy is not just about providing more services or enhancing throughput within these of people seeking psychological care. It also entails the classification and subjectification of particular people as in need of therapy (Hacking 1995, 2002), with the disorder to which they are ascribed configured as malleable through the application of therapeutic expertise. The significant shift vis-à-vis treatability that occurred for personality disorders has been a direct consequence of the interactions between, and reciprocal contouring of, professional and policy debates, moral and epistemic discourse, and law and clinical action. Attention to these reveals how regimes of normativity (Pickersgill, 2012b), mental health praxis, and the psychological per se can be (re)configured together. This, in turn, implies urgency for even deeper consideration of what kinds of legislative and therapeutic futures we want.

PART II

Configuring Care

CHAPTER 4

Prefacing Care

The Reciprocal Configuration of Patients, Services, and Professionals during Referral and Assessment

Within the United Kingdom, IAPT/NHS Talking Therapies is surely the most visible example of attempts to enhance the accessibility of psychological care (Pickersgill, 2019b; Pilgrim and Carey, 2012). Beyond this well-resourced initiative, however, there have been funding changes for mental healthcare more broadly. These have resulted in cost-cutting measures and created workforce challenges, with claims made that patient care has been compromised as a consequence (Gilburt, 2015). There are various effects of this on whether someone can access therapy (and if so, what kind and for how long). Even if a service is technically available, for instance, and a GP has referred someone to it, the referral might still be declined by a busy psychological practitioner.

This chapter examines how clinical psychologists manage, and make decisions around, patient referrals – the prefaces of care per se, which can either enable or preclude access to therapy. Such negotiations involve a rather different type of boundary work to that seen in the previous chapters: the negotiation of the boundary between certainty and uncertainty, and the subsequent substantiation of the decisions that follow from this. Following a referral, clinical psychologists must resolve an uncertain situation: Should they accept this, and continue forward to an assessment? Thereafter, they must decide whether the person referred is suitable for their service – and, indeed, for therapy more generally – and find ways to justify whatever happens next. These decision-making practices involve a form of morally inflected professional judgement (Styhre, 2013) that involves configuring different kinds of ontologies which entail their own set of boundaries.

One interpretation of uncertainty is as an affective state of individuals acting within specific sociopolitical and clinico-epistemic infrastructures. It can also be viewed as a constitutive characteristic of biomedical practice in which clinicians and researchers variously both live with and set about clarifying different kinds of ambiguity (Calnan, 1984; Fox, 1980;

Timmermans and Angell, 2001). Uncertainty is not necessarily something that practitioners refrain from acknowledging (Gerrity et al., 1992). Still, it is often – but not exclusively – 'worked upon in medical settings to effect its elimination' (Ross, 2017, p. 90), with certainty 'a moral ideal to be achieved' (Adamson, 1997, p. 135). In conditions of uncertainty, expert knowledge can act as a key resource within decision-making (Sulik, 2009), serving to reinforce the autonomy and power of practitioners within clinical interactions (Broom and Woodward, 1996).

The practices of clinicians might not be directly or primarily experienced and self-categorised as being carried in a state of 'uncertainty', while nevertheless the tasks being undertaken are precisely aimed at clarifying a hitherto undefined plan of action. Such manufacturing of certainty requires engagement with a range of epistemological and normative ambiguities: What do we know? How should we act? What will come to pass as a result of (in)action? Uncertainty is thus, in a sense, productive (Moreira et al., 2009; Reed et al., 2016; Thompson-Lastad and Rubin, 2020). Moving towards its resolution can involve epistemic development and the production of sociality through the imagining of different subjectivities and futures, and the animation of affects and actions to realise or avoid them. Importantly, however, the risk remains that none of this will result in a situation regarded as satisfactory by healthcare professionals working the boundaries between certainty and uncertainty – or those seeking therapy who are subject to its effects.

Within clinical psychology specifically, practitioners must decide what patients to work with, and to what ends. This can be tricky, not least given the indeterminacy of therapy: what should be done about a referral is not clear in part because what will happen as a result of an intervention cannot be known in advance (cf. Halpin, 2022; Hayes et al., 2020; Hollin, 2017). Decision-making around referrals – as with so much else – further involves assumptions about persons that can invoke gendered, raced, and classed imaginaries and which might ultimately be deleterious to potential service users (Kugelmass, 2016). Alongside these issues are the configuring and navigation of less obviously fraught yet nevertheless charged matters, such as particular framings of a service and of the expertise of therapists. Configuring these can also result in potentially iniquitous forms of professional action; for instance, when a service might have an informal policy of declining to accept for referral people who live with certain psychiatric diagnoses (such as borderline personality disorder) (King, 2001).

In navigating uncertainty, clinical psychologists – like other health professionals (Kuiper et al., 2023; McEvoy and Richards, 2007) – juggle service demands and pressures, patient requests and concerns, and their personal ethical and epistemic frameworks for considering who should receive therapy and why. This juggling is itself a social process: ultimately, decisions rest with individuals, but choices are shaped through imagined socialities and actual engagements. The uncertainty work (Moreira et al., 2009; Pickersgill, 2011) of adjudicating access to psychological therapy can consequently itself be characterised as a social process, as well as the affective state noted previously.

In considering the prefacing practices of psychological care, I focus my analysis on clinical psychologists' accounts of how decisions are made – that is, how certainty is synthesised – about what to do with people following processes of referral and assessment. Decision-making, I argue, requires configuring at least three kinds of ontologies: the ontology of a potential patient, the ontology of the service in which they work, and the ontology of their profession. Their configuration does not occur in isolation; rather, to different extents and in varying ways, these processes happen in concert. Moreover, it is important to stress that potential service users might strategically configure their own self-presentation in ways that can contribute to securing access to care and particular kinds of treatment (Hillman, 2014; Stivers and McCabe, 2021; Wamsiedel, 2020). Hence, my emphasis on professionals should not be taken to suggest that their power in defining situations or selves is anything like absolute. What sociologists have called the 'candidacy' of people for therapy necessarily involves particular presentations of the self by those seeking it (Dixon-Woods et al., 2006; Liberati et al., 2022; Mackenzie et al., 2013), which are likely to articulate with the ontologies principally under consideration here (Chinn and Abraham, 2016; Kovandžić et al., 2011).

Aside from the insights from the literatures noted earlier, my approach in this chapter and the ones that follow is, as noted in the introduction to this book, shaped by the scholarship of Ian Hacking (1995, 2002) and Nikolas Rose (1985, 1996), among others (e.g. Danziger, 1990, 1997; Foucault, 1988, 1989; Woolgar and Neyland, 2013). More specifically, I take from them as useful the notion that ontologies are brought into being through discursive and practical work, including processes of classification and categorisation (rather than necessarily and straightforwardly pre-existing social interaction). These processes of configuration are also open-ended. While working the boundary between certainty and uncertainty might result in a particular course of action under specific circumstances, decisions can be challenged and revised, and the ontologies of patients, services, and professionals are subject to reconfiguration. Another assessment, a patient complaint, staff burnout, and so on can all reposition the boundaries of particular ontologies, and thus – at the same time – the boundary between certainty and uncertainty. A formal revision to service criteria, for instance, might reconfigure multiple ontologies, involving the re-specification of various boundaries as a result – triggering, perhaps, the making of different clinical decisions. The ontologies that form the focus of this chapter, then, are very much works in progress: processes of configuration have products that can always be unsettled and remade.

In what follows, I articulate the (overlapping) ways through which ontologies are configured in interviews with clinical psychologists based in a range of services, from highly urban to very rural, in England and Scotland (data which will also ground the two chapters that follow this one). To begin with, though, I summarise how processes of referral and psychological assessment play out at a general level. Within my analysis I respond critically to my interlocutors' accounts while also taking seriously the notion of psychological expertise and their expressions of frustration – and sometime despair – that therapy was not better accessible (Matza, 2018; Zhang, 2020).

The Process of Referral

Unlike seeing an IAPT therapist, most people must be referred by another health professional before they can access a clinical psychologist, for example a GP or even another psychological practitioner. This referral may be in the form of a letter to a relevant clinical psychologist or can be sent to a service as a whole for consideration by a team. That team could either be comprised primarily of clinical psychologists or include a range of practitioners such as community psychiatric nurses, social workers, and occupational therapists. Despite the concerns of some clinical psychologists about psychiatry (discussed in Chapter 1), the service team could in fact involve a psychiatrist as well: despite disputes between the *professions* of clinical psychology and psychiatry, individual *professionals* often collaborate well together. In multidisciplinary teams, decisions must be made not only whether to accept a referral but also whether the person seeking access to therapy should see a clinical psychologist specifically. Emma, who worked in a multidisciplinary team in rural England, described how 'we have a team meeting every Wednesday morning, where we look through the new referrals, and then decide who is going to go and do the assessment'. This entails a set of assumptions about potential patients, as well as the negotiations of boundaries between professionals: Whose expertise is best suited for the subject that has been produced through the process of referral and the referral meeting itself?

Services vary with regard to which parts of the NHS referrals come from as well as who issued them. Services admitting, for instance, 'people with *serious* mental health difficulties, or quite *complex* difficulties' (Brenda) might largely take referrals from a Community Mental Health Team (CMHT) (emphasis in the original; same for the quotes that follow throughout the chapter). Referrals for people experiencing distress relating to a physical complaint, such as cancer, could be from a nurse. In these instances, the referrer might speak to a clinical psychologist prior to a formal referral to get a sense of fit for service. As Felicity (who worked in the same NHS organisation as Emma) told me, a cancer nurse might 'ring me up or email me about someone, and we'd have a discussion with them'. Hence, and as will be unpacked later, decision-making around referrals can take place prior to their instantiation.

Referrals can also come from beyond the NHS altogether. Susannah, a senior practitioner in Scotland, told me that referrals to her child and adolescent mental health service (CAMHS) could come from schools and social work. This practice is less common outside of CAMHS, and we might speculate about how in those setting referrals from beyond statutory services are considered compared to those from well-known and trusted NHS referrers – given the extent to which the perceived expertise of referrers is salient to clinical psychologists (as we will see later here and in the next chapter). At the same time, however, clinical psychologists can sometimes have very close relationships with third-sector bodies, with this positively influencing their considerations of referrals from such organisations. This is in contrast to, for instance, unknown GPs based in large practices in big cities, whose propositions might perhaps be subject to more rather than less scrutiny.

It can also be possible – as has been championed by IAPT/NHS Talking Therapies – for people to refer themselves for psychological therapy. Nevertheless, this remains relatively rare beyond primary care settings. Anita, a senior manager who worked in such a setting in a large city, was one of the few clinical psychologists I spoke with whose service accepted self-referrals. She described her and her team's hard work at seeking to grow self-referral despite capacity constraints and concerns: 'We market materials in different languages, you know, bus stops, on stations, newspapers, we leaflet every household, we publicise ourselves in the newspaper or any magazine that might be going out.' However, even when a clinical psychologist might in principle be 'happy to accept self-referral' (Harriet), this is, as mentioned, uncommon. Indeed, my interviewees on occasion expressed overt scepticism or disquiet about it, with Ivor (a senior practitioner in rural Scotland), for instance, cautioning that 'the danger is you get a lot of worried well people coming forward'. On the one hand, some clinical psychologists can be alarmed at the need that lies outside their existing waiting list, with further lowering of barriers to access having the potential to make a challenging job even harder. On the other, practitioners can be alert to the possibility of a kind of 'false need' and its potential to distract from those regarded as truly requiring their care.

Regardless of the mechanism by which someone comes to be referred to a clinical psychologist, what happens afterwards depends sometimes on its urgency, but also – as in other healthcare settings (Buchbinder, 2017) – on what professionals judge to be the nature of the service. This includes who it is targeted towards, staff capacity, and its position vis-à-vis other services. In some cases, a single person will screen all referrals, refusing and accepting different patients and taking some to a team meeting for further consideration. Within other settings, in the words of senior psychologist Esther (based in a rural Scottish service): '*every* referral has to be *considered* at a team meeting before they get allocated'. Having introduced the seldom simple process of referral, I next turn briefly to consider what generally happens if someone is considered potentially appropriate for the service to which they have been referred.

The Process of Assessment

Following what is often termed a 'successful' referral, people seeking treatment will commonly be 'assessed' by a service team member. Assessment seeks to ascertain the nature of the presenting problem and whether psychological therapy (and that particular service) is the best means of addressing it. If it is a multidisciplinary service, assessment will not necessarily be undertaken by a clinical psychologist; instead, another clinician with psychological expertise might work with the referred person to jointly articulate their requirement (or not) for therapy. The time taken to see someone for an assessment varies – this reflects, for example, the service size, location, and focus. It can, on occasion, proceed at pace; Arthur, who worked in an early intervention service for psychosis in rural England, told me: 'What we try to do as a team is, get hold of people, preferably on the same day that we get a referral at least by phone and arrange to see them within a week.' Others, however, might wait much, much longer. Time from referral to assessment is also shaped by varied waiting list targets. For example, Irene, a senior clinical psychologist practising in adult mental health in the north of England, described to me how targets drove 'how quickly you have to respond to those referrals'. Waiting lists, targets, and their roles in configuring access to therapy will be considered more closely in the next chapter.

Assessment is sometimes framed as the beginning of therapeutic work itself. This might be in terms of building what clinical psychologists regard as an alliance and collaboration with a patient that will provide a good basis for therapy. It could also entail the recommendation of psycho-educational resources through which people seeking care can 'skill themselves up and inform themselves' about the nature and purpose of psychological treatment, as described by Harriet, a mid-career psychologist who worked in adult mental health in rural Scotland. Some clinical psychologists described the boundaries between 'assessment' and 'treatment' as blurrier still, imbricating the prefacing of care with therapy per se. One interviewee working in secondary care, Grant (based in the north of England), reflected candidly on this: 'To be honest, I struggle to distinguish assessment from treatment.' For him, 'as soon as you start hearing somebody's story and you start listening to somebody's story you're giving them space to do something that can create change'.

Yet, assessment and treatment were clearly and sharply bounded by other clinical psychologists with whom I spoke: Irene – quoted earlier, and part of the same NHS organisation as Grant – very explicitly accounted for assessment and treatment as distinct. This was part of a longer answer to a question I asked about how she preferred to manage her waiting lists. She reflected regretfully how she might say to someone at the point of assessment that 'unfortunately this isn't, this isn't us beginning therapy', before telling them that they will 'be waiting for possibly two years' for treatment – when that estimate was itself 'sugaring the pill'. Such a sweetener was needed because 'I can't bear to look someone in the eye and say, "you'll be waiting three years"'. Consequently, we can see that the boundaries between assessment and treatment might be understood as more necessary to retain in situations where resources were tight and waiting lists long.

The process of assessment also enables the assessing clinician to form an understanding of what they see as the 'suitability' (sometimes described as 'readiness') of someone for psychological therapy. As will be illustrated in the following sections, appraising suitability requires the resolution of an array of uncertainties. Will the individual referred for care engage sufficiently with the therapeutic process such that enough gains are made to justify seeing them over and above another on a waiting list? Are there any predisposing factors that might interfere with therapy? Are they the kind of person the service should be seeing? An assessment thus involves not only configuring the presenting issue but also the subjectification of the person being assessed.

Configuring Patients

Towards the end of my interview with Ivor, a senior clinician working with older adults, I asked what complaints would be made 'when psychologists get together'. His answer: 'probably the workload, number of referrals that come in'. This refrain is common. Lots of referrals make for long waiting lists, and these can sometimes be felt to be endless – with associated targets something that, as senior CMHT psychologist Liam described to me, 'dominates my daily life, my nightly life'. Decisions around prioritisation are always a challenge within healthcare (Allen et al., 2004; Berg, 1997; Dew et al., 2010; Hoeyer et al., 2015; Vassy, 2001) and can be difficult to make and to defend. The following is a lengthy extract from my interview with Irene, whose comments illustrate how moral and procedural uncertainties around prioritisation can be rendered explicit and subject to reflexive work:

> We try to think about it from a perspective of, 'These are our clients, aren't they? These are our patients and we have all these needs, don't we? What's the best way to use our time really? What do you think?' And to try and think about that. So sometimes generally people just wait chronologically on that list, but sometimes people will be prioritised. And it feels to *me*, that as the lead, part of my role is to, probably, be somebody that people look to, to say, 'What do you think, Irene? Should we be prioritising this person?' That always feels to me like a really important decision, because on the one hand it's easy to sit down with somebody in a room and think, 'Oh, bless, you know, really damaged, really ready to work, what I wouldn't give to start doing therapy with this person right now'. But they're the person that you're in a room with, whereas the other people on the list might just be names. They might just be names because you saw them six months ago and you've forgotten them. They might be names because your colleague saw them and you didn't make that personal connection with them. So making that decision to prioritise somebody, we try to think of that, well, I think of it as an *incredibly* important decision.

The problems of workload and waiting lists are compounded – and rhetorically managed – when referrals are framed as 'inappropriate'.

As Briony, an early-career clinical psychologist in an urban Scottish service, told me, 'sometimes you'll get referrals and you'll think, "that's definitely not for us"'. A referral might, for instance, be configured as inappropriate if someone was drinking alcohol or consuming illegal pharmaceuticals in a fashion that clinical psychologists considered excessive and in ways regarded as contraindicative to therapeutic success. Consequently, illegal substance use is not an uncommon exclusion criterion for a service; senior practitioner Esther noted that if someone had not 'stopped' drinking they would be sent 'back to another service'.

Dierdre, who worked with children in Scotland, described an inappropriate referral as follows:

> A referral that doesn't meet the complexity for a specialist to a free mental health service but there are lots of other services out there. There's social work for, I mean there are referrals that still come to us where it turns out children are just in an abusive situation and they are presenting with mental health problems, but we're not the first line agency.

Another senior clinical psychologist in an urban English service, Ursula, reflected that she might not accept a referral into her service as a consequence of 'social' issues:

> [I]f people have got a lot of kind of *social* type difficulties, they've got housing difficulties, no fixed abode, that kind of issue, we would tend to want them to be in a position where they've dealt with the social issues before they come and try and look at the psychological issues.

Key, then, to the work of determining whether to accept a referral is a requirement to configure a perceived need for (a certain style of) treatment within someone seeking care. This process is contoured by understandings and experiences of wider service pressures, resource challenges, and forms of priority setting (Allen et al., 2004; Vassy, 2001), which are themselves politically shaped (Joyce, 2001; Moreira, 2011; Syrett, 2003). However, need itself is not enough, and configuring the patient exceeds the configuring of need per se. Important as ontologies of distress are, so too are the wider psychosocial dimensions of a person that are deemed to modulate distress and the possibilities of intervening in it.

This configuring might initially be undertaken in the absence of the very individual seeking or referred for therapy. In this respect, decision-making is made actionable through inscriptions of people found within referrers' letters, any additional locally available information, and perhaps an informal conversation with the referrer. Leanne's reflections illustrate this point:

> [I]t would be easier if things were much more clearcut. But I just don't think, I think you've got to accept there's always going to be a bit of occasional grey areas somewhere. So, sometimes, I phone a GP and ask for a bit more information about a referral, to try and help make that decision as to whether the referral is appropriate

Such conversations can place uncertainty work upstream of the actual referral. As Leanne said,

> [I]f we're referring within the mental health directorate, so that's referrals from other psychiatrists, or the community mental health team, we're supposed to sort of really, instead of just sending in referral, have a conversation with someone before we do that. So we don't end up knocking referrals back

Naturally, practices vary. For instance, Grace, a senior clinical psychologist working in physical health in the same NHS organisation as Leanne, said she would undertake an assessment even in the case of an ostensibly inappropriate referral:

> Even if somebody's quite *extreme*, you know, maybe there are issues with alcohol, there might be issues with suicidality, I think there's still a duty of *care* to do an assessment of that *person* rather than saying, 'oh well I can't see them'. I would do an assessment and then link up with whoever I thought more appropriate agencies, or try to with the person's permission as well!

However, Grace also stated that she was sent inappropriate referrals only '*Very very rarely*'. Hence, the extent to which the ontology of a patient is configured at a distance seems, to an extent, to be a function of a wider workload that itself relates to how the service is construed both by the psychologists working in it and by those referring to it (see, relatedly, King, 2001).

A mid-career clinical psychologist working in adult mental health in Scotland, Harriet, also emphasised the importance of meeting with everyone who passes an initial referral screening 'to determine if psychology's for *them*'. This determination is a key point during a process of ontological configuring: it is where a psychologist makes certain that the patient is the kind of person who not only fits with the service but will benefit from therapy. Such a framing of assessment implicitly configures psychologists as having specific expertise not only in the administration of psychological therapy but also in ascertaining its likely success. This notion of the expert psychologist will be explored more fully later in this chapter.

The attribution of 'readiness for therapy' is a salient aspect of the uncertainty work of determining if psychological therapy should progress, and clinical psychologists tend to strongly emphasise its import.

Ascertaining 'readiness' might involve configuring someone as being suitably 'psychologically minded'. This is a term that has circulated within the psy-professions for more than 50 years now (e.g. Appelbaum, 1973). Epistemic authority for ascertaining this can, to an extent, be delegated to various technical instruments. One of these is the Psychological Mindedness Scale (Shill and Lumley, 2002), which was used by Brenda, a clinical psychologist working in secondary care in the south of England. However, not all practitioners use this kind of tool; most I have spoken with instead deploy clinical experience and judgement to configure and perceive psychological mindedness within someone.

The determination of psychological mindedness can have significant effects: it subjectifies a person *as* psychologically minded, itself hardly a morally neutral ontology within the context of (potential) psychological care. The concept also reaffirms the expertise of clinical psychologists, since they can often claim to have the best skills among an interdisciplinary team to recognise psychological mindedness. This does not necessarily afford benefit to specific patients, however, since an expert (and hence hard to challenge) declaration of the absence of psychological mindedness can contribute to the preclusion of therapy.

One senior clinical psychologist, Esther, spoke of the importance of psychological mindedness while simultaneously reflecting about its lack of conceptual clarity: 'I don't think anyone's come up with the definitive idea on that.' Esther described how she would often be asked to do assessments for 'difficult' cases, with a particular view of ascertaining whether someone would benefit from psychological therapy. I asked her, 'How do you make those calls?' She answered:

> We would look at, what, what, what they're being referred to us as, first of all, and we're trying to move towards when the referral comes in there's a triage system and someone is triaged as suitable, or not, at the first point of call. So are they keen to be seen? Is it *their* choice to be seen by us or are they being pushed into it? Will they *work* in therapy, and will they attend sessions? Then we also look at what therapies are available for them. And our biggest problem has been junior doctors getting rid of mixed bag personality disorders, who don't want to work [at therapy], who've been in the service for years and actually there is no known evidence-based therapy to work with them. And they're the ones that everyone thinks, 'oh, I can't bear seeing that person again', and sometimes we have to be fairly brutal and say, 'well, what *can* we do?'

Esther's concluding question relates to the professional skill of clinical psychologists in appraising a person's capacity to benefit from therapy.

Other sociological scholarship on mental health has underscored the continued moral dimensions of the psychological complex and the varied ontological, epistemological, and practical exclusions that can occur within it (Brossard and Chandler, 2022; Lane, 2020; Mladovsky, 2023). We might, then, take the position that there are good reasons to assume that the synthesis of certainty in this respect will be far from free of bias (Kugelmass, 2016). As the final substantive section of this chapter will elaborate, navigating the question of whether to work with an individual deemed unable to benefit from therapy itself contributes to configuring clinical psychologists' professional ontologies.

In summary, referral and assessment generally entail the configuring a patient as being like 'X', where 'X' is a multifaceted biopsychosocial matrix. 'X' might, for instance, encompass (1) someone's demographic categories like age and ethnicity; (2) psychological identifiers such as the nature of the presenting issue and 'readiness' or 'motivation' for therapy; and (3) social and personal indicators including employment status, and the existence of networks of support beyond the NHS. Importantly, 'X' might also be defined in the negative, and more clearly enact ontological boundaries, as in 'not like A, B, or C' (e.g. not a regular user of illegal substances, such as heroin). The subjectification that results from such uncertainty work produces typifications that make professional work more straightforward to undertake. At the same time, people seeking therapy are also situated within a larger moral order of value in relation to how viable they are as successful therapeutic subjects, and what factors are taken to impact on such viability (Latimer, 1997). While patient ontologies were often concretised in person, through the aforementioned accounts we can see that certitude about the (in)appropriateness of a referral can also be synthesised in the absence of the very person subject to such adjudication. In these instances, inscriptions of them within the text and talk of other professionals are framed as more valuable in limited-capacity services than time spent assessing someone face-to-face. (Pre-)Assessment in the absence of the individual referred for psychological care can thus act as a kind of implicit or even explicit healthcare rationing. A provisional configuration of a patient as like 'X' can be later substantiated, or further clarified, through actual discussion with them. Aside from the dimension of readiness for therapy, the centrality of certifying whether a someone is like 'X' is to ensure compatibility with an ostensibly predefined service ontology, legitimising initial decisions made about the acceptance or denial of a referral. However, as we will see, service ontologies are also often configured through the prefacing practices of clinical psychologists.

Configuring Services

During my fieldwork, I was occasionally informed that the establishment of IAPT had resulted in disinvestment in other services and/or longer waiting lists. Some respondents who were involved in the development of IAPT itself hotly contested such claims of disinvestment. Still, the lived experience of many clinicians – at least as narrated to me – was one within which IAPT had impacted the wider mental health ecosystem in a range of ways, including some that were overtly negative. As Kent, a senior clinical psychologist in urban England, put it: 'commissioners feel that they're already funding services to take care of patients' needing psychological therapy, 'but then the services that are being funded don't really feel that they have the *capacity*, or the skills' for particular individuals. Ursula, who worked in an English service geared towards 'complex' forms of psychological ill-health, asserted that 'we're getting more referrals that IAPT won't see', which 'increases the demand on our service, whereas actual resources aren't getting any bigger'. Some practitioners – like Dana, a clinical psychologist working in physical health in rural England – were concerned that there was 'such a gap in service between primary and secondary mental health care that lots of people are falling in that'. Similar reflections are often made by people seeking access to psychological care, who can experience being too unwell for entry into some kinds of services at the same time as being not unwell enough for others.

The impact of the mental health and social care ecosystem on specific services is not just restricted to the ramifications of IAPT, however. Rather, wider shifts in the landscape of formal services and the finances of third-sector organisations in light of the politics and economics of austerity in the United Kingdom have shaped what is possible for patients and what is doable by clinicians. This creates circumstances within which psychologists are confronted with uncertainties that might not otherwise be encountered. Dana foregrounded this through an example of being referred a patient – such as someone with a head injury – on the basis that the referrer did not 'know how or what to do with that person'. She reflected that 'if there were local [third-sector] services for them', then 'they would be doing those things in the community'. Accordingly, an absence of wider health and social services can coerce clinical psychologists into ontological negotiations they would rather leave for someone else.

Clinical psychologists often told me that waiting lists placed them under a great deal of pressure. As noted above, this will be unpacked more in the next chapter; here, it suffices to say that such experiences of pressure shape decision-making about referrals. Partly to manage demand, some services – like the CAMHS service mid-career clinician Verity worked in – had 'very detailed referral criteria' and inclusion/exclusion criteria for what kinds of people should be seen. Some clinical psychologists were critical of these: as one senior secondary mental healthcare practitioner put it, 'I *hate* services that are precious' (Louise). Nonetheless, inclusion/exclusion criteria and tightly defined service remits are common.

Such criteria are not, however, necessarily immutable. Senior clinical psychologist Arthur, for instance, framed his rural English service remit as feasible to flex to accommodate people judged to be most in need; in his words, there could be 'a kind of *stretching* of the services'. In a resonant account, Carl – another senior practitioner in the same NHS organisation – discussed how he managed a service focusing on 'the severe and complex part of, of psychology, related to adults'. Sometimes, however, individuals were accepted who were regarded as belonging to 'a group who are, if you like, severe and not complex'. This was, as Carl admitted, 'probably quite a small number'. Still, it is clear that some clinical psychologists are, on occasion, able to reconfigure the boundaries of their service to accept patients who they perhaps formally should not. This is suggestive of a kind of moral economy, participation in which itself implies a resistance to bureaucratised forms of care that has the potential to stifle compassion and empathy (Matza, 2018). At the same time, it also raises questions about equity of access in relation to potential patients who are *not* accepted following a referral – in other words, the people for whom services do not 'stretch'.

Less commonly, some interviewees were explicit about the boundaries of their service, reporting a lack of facility to stretch it. Leanne, a clinical psychologist in Scotland early in her career, underscored how the presence rather than absence of other services impacted how she saw her own service and those referred to it. She indicated how the existence of other options for people seeking care enabled her to reify service boundaries, as part of a process of what sociologist Mara Buchbinder (2017) terms 'facilitative' gatekeeping. In a discussion about referral processes, Leanne simultaneously described both limits for her service and a kind of person who would not necessarily benefit from it, and noted that exclusion could feasibly be beneficial:

> [M]aybe [a referred patient is] not even appropriate for this service, it might be a case of writing back to the GP and suggesting that the problem seems to be mainly about relationship issues, and they don't seem too severe, maybe they could benefit from, perhaps, from being sooner, from

> Relationships Scotland, for example. You know, there's agencies that we might think are more suitable.

Resource restrictions and allocations were also sometimes deployed within the interviews as devices through which to configure and legitimate service boundaries. Leanne configured an identity for her service in relation to the funds that were available to support its operations:

> [W]e had this kind of awkwardness of referrals come in, and it's to do with stress around chronic pain. We've had to be really strict with that, and I mean, that's felt really difficult, because obviously people are struggling. But it's been health related, we've had to sort of explain to the referrer that we can't take them because there's no funding for a post.

Limits to capacity were alluded to by Esther while discussing assessment:

> It may not be that psychological *therapy's* needed, it's maybe that they need support and that's what we're *very* clear about, the service doesn't offer support. We *have* to do psychological therapy. We're a small service offering, sort of, a specialist component to the mental health unit and *that's* what we really have to do. With no workforce that's important that we stick to the psychological therapies

Clinical psychologists working in services where they managed the psychological issues relating to physical ill-health generally appeared to have less difficulty in clarifying service ontologies and making decisions about access. In essence, choices were made largely in relation to the physical issue for which a service was specifically funded to provide care. When I asked Felicity, a relatively recently qualified practitioner, whether there would ever be instances where a decision would be reached that a referral was in some sense not quite right for her service, she replied:

> Yeah, yeah. And I think there are some referrers, and I suppose in our referral criteria, it's, kind of, that the psychological difficulty's meant to come about as a facet of their physical health problem. So, and we do get some people referred who've had a severe injury or a mental health problem, and then have got diabetes, and so we get sent them. And so we do try to pass those back to kind of the mental health teams. Or if it's something that can be managed by primary care mental health, if it's, kind of, panic attacks, even if it is about panic attacks during treatment, then we might, you know, see if they could, they could offer some input. So we do do signposting at that time.

However, even for ostensibly closely characterised services aimed at addressing the psychological dimensions of physical ill-health, ontological stretching could still occur when, for instance, 'clinical judgement' (Amy) suggested this was necessary. As Felicity continued,

> [T]here's also issues about unmet need, I suppose, and things like, pain services. There isn't any, service at the moment for kind of a pain management programme where I'm based, and so I get sent quite a lot of referrals for that. And that's not always been a consistent thing. Sometimes I have kind of had a couple of people on my caseload who are from that route, but as our service has developed and as the lead from my service is trying to think about developing a, a pain service, but asking for more money for that, we've kind of said we're not going to take those referrals but we're going to log how many that come through to us.

These comments demonstrate that the stretchiness of a service is itself a property that can shift and change over time. Again, this is accounted for as a consequence of the wider ecology of services. In Felicity's case, a decision was reflexively made to exclude people seeking care to galvanise support to develop an additional service. Hence, denial of access can be presented as a rational course of action that reflects the clinical and economic realpolitik of the NHS. In so doing, the pain of specific individuals becomes reconfigured as a resource to support the expansion of psychological therapy for a larger population.

To recap, formalised service boundaries were often in place to manage waiting lists, yet clinical psychologists could sometimes renegotiate inclusion/exclusion criteria to accept particular people into therapy. Reconfiguration of a service ontology might be in response to wider resource challenges and the risks of patients falling between the cracks of different services. Resources were similarly introduced by respondents to account for why they might not take on particular individuals, ossifying service ontologies. Likewise, the presence rather than absence of alternative services could be invoked to concretise service boundaries. The discursive processes through which clinical psychologists configured service ontologies, then, was in part a function of the wider economic and organisational context within which those clinicians were embedded. At the same time, clinicians also exercised individual agency in how they engaged with this context in the resolution of 'uncertainty moments' through implicit and sometimes explicit judgements about who is most in need of access to psychological care. Sometimes, this will mean accepting people for therapy even though they do not quite seem to align with the formal service remit. Others who are referred for different reasons or whose presenting issues are constructed differently by a clinical psychologist will not, however, be accepted into a service. Service ontologies are consequently negotiable, yet not infinitely so, further complicating the algebra of healthcare rationing, and (dis)advantaging some patients over others.

Configuring Clinical Psychologists

Through talk of referrals and assessments, the clinical psychologists with whom I spoke tended to configure their own ontologies as professionals alongside those of patients and services. During my fieldwork, two key moral and epistemic constructions commonly emerged: the good clinical psychologist and the expert clinical psychologist. Within these, practitioners as individuals and as a professional group can be regarded as synecdochical.

Earlier I described how the prefacing practices involved in accepting a referral often entail a requirement for a given clinical psychologist to configure a potential patient as being compatible with a particular NHS service. I also showed how a seemingly settled service ontology can sometimes be reflexively reconfigured to accommodate a particular (kind of) person. This can even include someone characterised as 'unready' for therapy. Arthur reflected on this as follows:

> [L]ocally there hasn't been a high percentage of people who are being told that they're, they're not ready for a service. Actually I suspect there might be a lot of people who are *not* ready actually, but who are offered a service. I think partly that's been produced by the fact that often they're not in touch with anything else, so there's pressure on the person assessing to say well we need to provide-they clearly need something.

This account appears to be framed critically, on two counts. First, Arthur seemed to imply that clinical psychologists should not take on people who were 'unready' for therapy. Second, he critiqued the 'pressure' placed on professionals to nevertheless do, thus exonerating clinical psychologists for acting in ways that might otherwise be undesirable. In this respect, Arthur paints a complex picture, one in which the challenges of delivering care for many results in it being apportioned to some specific individuals who otherwise might and – according to the epistemologies of practice performed by a variety of clinical psychologists – perhaps even *should* go without. While morally ambiguous, the professional figures painted here are nevertheless, ultimately, good: they are clinical psychologists who do what they can to help in difficult circumstances.

Notions of readiness and psychological mindedness were leveraged in some interviews in discussions that presented exclusion from therapy as a form of care, and which consequently preserved the clinical and moral identity of a psychologist as 'good'. Brenda explained that it was important to ascertain that someone was 'ready' for therapy before accepting a referral, reflecting:

> [I]t's kind of, making sure that person's actually ready and motivated for treatment, so they don't come in and come out too quickly in terms of that they're not ready, and they've often . . . kind of research of that, you know, are treatment failures at this stage as often people go through an awful lot of, interviews and assessments, and they'll end up not being able to manage the therapy and then dropping out and then feeling quite a failure about it.

Yet, through the course of the interview it appeared that Brenda's default position was in fact to accept someone into therapy. She described how she would undertake psycho-educational activities with a patient to increase 'psychological mindedness so that they really are open and ready' for therapy. Consequently, Brenda's talk configures her as a good clinical psychologist who exercises evidence-based clinical judgement (Timmermans and Angell, 2001) in three ways: first, by describing work with patients to actively configure them as subjects amenable to therapy; second, by implying that not accepting someone for therapy is a form of care, since it would prevent them 'feeling quite a failure' if not ready for a psychological intervention; and third, by alluding to research that grants epistemic legitimacy to her account.

Similar sentiments were expressed by Chloe, an early-career psychologist working in Scotland:

> [I]f you take on someone at the wrong time the chances are they might have a negative experience of therapy, so they'll have an experience where therapy hasn't worked and then that makes them *much* less likely to come forward again, so you've got to be very mindful of that.

An account of readiness was not always essential in constructing a clinical psychologist as 'good' when not accepting someone for therapy, however. For instance, Clarisa, a senior clinical psychologist in urban England, noted that 'if the person doesn't really sit with us', then 'I think it's our responsibility to really help the person to be signposted' to another service. Through underscoring the assistance that would be provided to a person in absence of psychological treatment, Clarisa (and several other interviewees) configured themselves within their talk as caring practitioners even while describing a context in which they would refuse access to their services.

Closely relating to the good clinical psychologist was the figure of the expert clinical psychologist, who was, for instance, skilled in making judgements about readiness in the first place. Issues of expertise were commonly raised in discussions about access to services, with respondents sometimes foregrounding the different kinds of understanding, knowledge, and experience clinical psychologists brought to bear in practices such as multidisciplinary assessment (or discharge) meetings, as well as in treatment itself. Regarding assessment, Anita, a senior practitioner working in primary care, reflected that some CBT therapists are 'not able to really *fully* assess or formulate and think about engagement' whereas clinical psychologists 'are able to do that. And I think that skill is quite unique, which really enables engagement.' In relation to treatment, Leanne described how in her service 'the slightly, I suppose, less complex cases, would go with the CBT therapist, and the clinical psychologist would take the more complex ones'. These comments are a reminder of some of the points underlined in the first part of this book: that in times of strained resources, where clinical psychologists are an expensive professional group and waiting lists threaten to grow and grow, configuring the boundaries of expertise can be a well-rehearsed and strategically enacted process.

Configurations of expertise were also supported by a discourse of scarcity (Frank, 2013); in Leanne's words, psychology was a 'really limited resource'. One dilemma relating to this was reflected on by Carl, who talked about the challenges of undertaking some kind of 'stop-gap' work with people on long waiting lists in his rural English service, for example 'bibliotherapy with occasional meetings'. However, a consequent 'conundrum' is that '*every* time you do that, you take away from, you're using the same resource that's been used to do the end-point therapy'. Carl did not think 'psychologists should be doing that, actually'; rather, 'someone else should be doing it!' – presumably someone less well paid. Akin to the notion of therapeutic wastage discussed in Chapter 2, clinical psychologists can thus configure themselves as having highly specialist, uniquely important, and very valuable skills subject to selective apportionment between different patients and purposes.

Expertise and a discourse of scarcity also figured in Carl's account and that of some other senior clinical psychologists when discussing who they might themselves see for assessments and/or therapy (e.g. Esther in Scotland, and Irene in England). Since the capacity of clinicians in senior management roles to work with patients directly was limited, they or their team might carefully select individuals who would be deemed to benefit from their particular constellation of experience and expertise. As Carl described, his team 'would ask me to see particular people who they thought it would be a good idea if I saw them'. Carl went on to configure himself as follows: '[My team] know that I'm a reasonably flexible, integrative sort of therapist, and that I can form working alliances with, with difficult people.' For senior clinical psychologists, then, the uncertainty work regarding not just whether someone should be seen but also who should see them enjoined a reflexive process of configuring their own identity in relation to skillset, experience, and indeed disposition. Of course, central to this was also a configuring of patient ontologies prior to therapy itself: Were they the sort of person who required the costly resource of senior staff time – for example, were they sufficiently 'complex' (Irene)?

In this section, I have illustrated how the ontologies of both the good clinical psychologist and the expert clinical psychologist come into play within practices of referral and assessment, and the work of making certain that a particular patient should be seen for therapy. These ontologies are, again, also a function of the wider healthcare and political circumstances within which clinical psychologists are situated. For instance, claims to (greater) expertise are strategically useful in an economically orientated mental health policy context that positions other professionals, like CBT therapists, as the answer to the problem of restricted access to services. Constructions of the good clinical psychologist also legitimate difficult decisions made by practitioners when not taking on a person for therapy, or when contravening professional and epistemic norms to do so. Finally, the realisation of professional ontologies and the praxis of working the boundary between acceptance into and preclusion from therapy are reciprocally constituted. In other words, it is in part through ascertaining whether to take on someone for therapy that professional ontologies emerge and are validated and sustained, shaping future engagements with potential service users.

Reciprocal Configuration

Following a referral, decision-making about whom to accept for therapy (and how long to continue it) entails the (partial) resolution of uncertainty. In essence, clinical psychologists must address a question that has an answer which is only ever legible within particular epistemic, economic, and moral contexts: What, practically speaking, should happen next to the patient? This procedural uncertainty relates to the matter of therapeutic indeterminacy (cf., Hayes et al, 2020; Hollin, 2017): there are multiple possible outcomes of therapy, including null or even negative effects. The work of responding to procedural uncertainty entails a form of skilled judgement (Styhre, 2013) involving the configuring of three key ontologies: that of the patient, the service, and the clinical psychologist (as both an individual and a professional group). In this respect, movement through uncertainty moments is (psycho)socially productive: action, affects, and ontologies are realised through the synthesis of certitude (Kuiper et al., 2023; Moreira et al., 2009; Reed et al., 2016) as part of the prefacing of (potential) care.

Rather than merely reflecting realities, the processes of configuration clinical psychologists engage in can be regarded as helping to bring them into being (Hacking, 1995, 2002). While patients, professionals, and services obviously pre-exist uncertainty work, ontologies are clearly configured and sometimes reconfigured through this, as opposed to necessarily patterning outcomes in a straightforward fashion (Moreira et al., 2009; Pickersgill, 2011). Those seeking therapy – and, to an extent, those who might provide it – can be marked deeply, for better or for worse, by the certainties clinical psychologists produce at the point of referral or assessment, perhaps especially if a decision is reached to offer no treatment at all.

Even if accepted for therapy, working the boundary between certainty and uncertainty configures patients (and providers) in particular ways; given the intersubjective nature of psychological practice, this can be expected to have implications for future care. The configuring of ontologies within clinical psychology consequently has normative dimensions, beyond barriers to access per se. These further include the role of bias (Kugelmass, 2016): not as some kind of exogenous entity introduced into a dispassionate and objective professional appraisal, but as a constitutive element of clinical experience that shapes and directs the management of uncertainty and therapeutic (in)action. Clinical psychologists, it seems, are able to exert power to configure patients and services – even within limits imposed by wider economic and organisational factors – in a fashion that can stretch or shrink a service remit and facilitate or deny access to it to particular people. An epiphenomenon of this autonomy will likely sometimes be the reproduction of forms of structural discrimination within the micro-sociology of the assessment.

Navigating procedural uncertainties further participates in the configuring of clinical psychologists as both expert and good: synthesising certainties enjoins invocations and practices of the resourceful application of credentialed knowledge towards enabling or enhancing care. What is important to note, however, is that clinical psychologists can produce different modes of care that are moulded by context (Pols, 2003;

Schwennesen and Koch, 2012). For instance, both seeing someone who is deemed unready for therapy *and* not seeing them can be configured as worthy acts. In effect, the denial of access to care can in some cases affirm professional identity as a good psychologist. As we will see in the chapters that follow, resonant issues can play out in the management of waiting lists and with regards to the sometimes involuntary discharge of individuals from therapy.

CHAPTER 5

Performing Autonomy

Working with and against Healthcare Structures to Configure Access and Exclusion

Healthcare professionals, for the most part, tend to like their autonomy (Abbott, 1988; Freidson, 1988). They do not especially enjoy being told what to do by agents and institutions beyond their sphere of expertise and practice. This is not least when such instructions are issued from sites perceived as being underpinned by logics and concerns orthogonal to the operant values of the clinic. Policy edicts from politicians whose understandings of the needs of clinicians and patients are regarded as somewhat lacking can be especially poorly received.

Nevertheless, professionals must operate within such environments, and sometimes enjoin others to adapt to situations about which they themselves have doubts (Harrison and Dowswell, 2002; McGivern et al., 2015; Waring, 2007). Few domains are more politically charged than healthcare, and – as a public body – the NHS must be responsive to the shifting priorities of governments and ministers. This includes changes in funding, and particularly limits on it. Since 2010, the UK government has created considerable challenges for the NHS through financial under-resourcing (Ham, 2023). Commissioners, managers, clinicians, administrators, and other NHS staff have consequently had to torque their activities to suit a sociotechnical context within which many feel more is being demanded for less (Liberati et al., 2023). While initiatives such as NHS Talking Therapies have promoted certain kinds of practices and interventions, even these operate within a wider ecosystem. Comparatively well-resourced services never exist within their own hermetically sealed bubble, untroubled by bad weather and the choppy waters upon which they float.

In the case of clinical psychology, while individual practitioners might not like certain changes occurring within the psychological complex (Rose, 1985), their practice can nevertheless sometimes be reconfigured in response. We have seen in previous chapters how professional developments and discourses can shape wider contexts, yet specific clinicians might still find themselves practising in circumstances within which they experience practical challenges and frustrations. Consequently, clinical psychologists make do and mend as best they can; like all healthcare professionals, they configure their labours in relation to the organisational constraints and affordances to which they are subject (Scheid, 2004; Strauss et al., 1985), as well as, to a greater or lesser degree, seeking to contour these. They can, like other professionals (Bezes et al., 2012; Waring, 2007), also come to accommodate challenges. One means through which this occurs is via forms of ontological respecification (Schneider et al., 2022; Woolgar and Neyland, 2013). For instance, as we will see, clinical psychologists sometimes reframe – and thus transform – economic restrictions into useful encouragements towards good clinical practice.

In the previous chapter, I analysed the reciprocal configuration of patients, services, and professionals. This was part – and a result – of the process of working the boundary between certainty and uncertainty in relation to whether a clinical psychologist should work with someone following a referral (and, potentially, assessment). In what follows, I inspect these issues in greater depth, specifically to better comprehend how autonomy is imagined, negotiated, and performed in practice. The chapter will also go further in examining how targets, most strikingly in relation to waiting times for therapy, manifest within the accounts of clinical psychologists. I consider their role in (re)configuring the nature of psychological care and highlight the implications of this for access and exclusion.

Over the last two decades or so, NHS targets have come to focus not so much on the total numbers of patients on a waiting list as on the length of time from referral to treatment. It is, then, waiting *times* rather than lists per se that are key to governmental consideration (Sheard, 2018). While many clinicians will speak of challenges with waiting lists, the specific concern is how the length of those lists impact the time it takes for a person who is accepted into a service to receive therapy. Waiting time targets have commonly come to represent the metrics by which the accessibility of care is measured; accordingly, they often serve as the focus of attempts to 'improve access'. How long are patients waiting for therapy, how many of those 'breach' the target, and how can waiting times be improved?

Notable examples of these technologies of government (Rose, 1999) are targets relating to the Commissioning for Quality and Innovation (CQUIN) framework in England and the Local Delivery Plan (LDP) Standards – formerly the Hospital Efficiency and Access Targets (HEAT) – in Scotland. Launched in 2009 by the UK Department of Health, CQUIN provides financial incentives for actions such as reducing waiting times. As indicated earlier and as other sociologists have shown, these have fixed clinical attention on enacting initiatives that sometimes relate narrowly to an isolated target, rather than on good care more broadly (Bailey et al., 2019; Montgomery et al., 2020; cf. Bevan and Hood, 2006). Operating between 2011 and 2015, the Scottish HEAT targets stated that no one should wait longer than 18 weeks from referral for psychological therapy to treatment, and this continues to be required through the LDP Standards. The HEAT targets LDP Standards likewise can be read as seeking to improve healthcare and encourage accountability for positive results. Just like they do in England, targets steer and shape Scottish clinical practice as a consequence (Greer et al., 2016; Schang and Morton, 2017; Steel and Cylus, 2012).

Here, I am less concerned with the specificities of these targets than with their ambiguous role in practice, and their practical and affective ramifications. This includes analysing how clinical psychologists rework processes of entry into therapy, and the aims and character of care, to meet targets. Doing so illuminates how, despite – and indeed as one direct effect of – the disciplinary power (Foucault, 1989) of targets, practitioners find ways to perform autonomy within practice. In other words, clinical psychologists sometimes exercise their discretion precisely to address external demands, as opposed to meeting targets through practising in fixed, standardised ways. Attending to these matters indicates how shifts in psychological care in response to targets reconfigure clinical psychologists' relationships to their work and their patients. Targets can thus be understood as contributing to 'making up' (Hacking, 1995, 2002) the subjects configured through therapy – as well as those excluded from it.

I regard autonomy as a kind of enacted, negotiated, and relational practice (Gauthier-Mamaril, 2022) rather than one that is fixed or predetermined – hence my use of the term 'perform'. In this respect, I draw on sociological scholarship that indicates how autonomy is experienced and performed, in part, through negotiating and reconfiguring its always ambiguous boundaries (McDermott et al., 2023; Shuster and Lubben, 2022; Waring, 2014). To be sure, healthcare is often highly structured through national governance and a range of local tools (Berg, 1997; Harrison and Ahmad, 2000). Yet, clinicians of different kinds demonstrate a marked capacity to improvise in the face of challenges (Kamp et al., 2023; Kuijper et al., 2022). That includes through measures introduced with the aim of standardising clinical praxis (Jensen and Vabø, 2023; Timmermans and Berg, 1997). Autonomy might often be regarded by health professionals as being curtailed or limited, but it seldom seems to disappear completely.

My approach perhaps stands in slight tension with clinical accounts of care which contend that autonomy has concretely reduced. My choice of words here – 'slight tension' rather than 'opposed' – is deliberate. I do not want to refute the claims of professionals who are practising in a financially challenged NHS. That being said, my relational understanding of autonomy likewise precludes me from wholeheartedly endorsing the statements of concern I have encountered. Some styles of autonomous practice are indeed possible to perform, even if the act of doing so is itself enjoined by the same targets regarded as reducing it. The normative corollary of this is that practitioners' claims around (a lack of) clinical autonomy need to be treated with respect but also require their own close inspection.

Waiting Lists

Let's start with waiting lists. As we have seen, these can be challenging to work with and were a problem for a clear majority of my interlocutors in clinical psychology. Such issues were systemic rather than simply affecting certain teams; although Grace, for example, had not traditionally had a waiting list for her rural Scottish service, other clinical psychologists had started referring to her to manage their own workloads. This created fresh demands that might be ameliorated within a better-resourced system. Practitioners sometimes expressed deep disquiet at just how bad things were and often continued to be. Senior clinical psychologist Carl, for instance, told me how he was '*grossly* unhappy about the fact that people have to wait' (emphasis in the original; same for all the quotes that follow). Louise, a more recent entrant into the profession working in an English city, described how 'it can feel quite heart-breaking after an assessment to then say, "well, it looks like the service that's best for you is an 18 month wait"'. Mid-career clinical psychologist Molly, who worked in the same NHS organisation as Louise, reflected:

> I guess every day, I probably have a moment where I feel really bad when I meet somebody that I *know* I could offer an effective intervention to, but I haven't got the capacity to do that. So, every day, my colleagues will come to me and ask my advice about patients and I know what they *need*, but I can't offer it.

Dealing with waiting lists, not least when confronted by the 'postcode lottery' (Ursula) of access to psychological therapy, consequently entailed an affective toll. This was in addition to the practical, cognitive, and moral labours inherent to the uncertainty work (Moreira et al., 2009; Pickersgill,

2011) of ascertaining who should get an intervention, what sort, and why. As Molly vividly described, she felt she had to 'ration' her 'compassion':

> I *like* to think that, more compassionate people who genuinely want to help people who are drawn to this sort of profession, but then I think the practicalities and the daily grind of the resource limitations, mean that you have to kind of ration your compassion. Gosh, that sounds awful saying that aloud, but you do find that you are kind of limited in what you can offer people, you can't offer them this never-ending kind of access to what they want and they don't always take it up anyway do they, so you do have to have some limits on what you can offer people.

A range of emotions seemed to bubble below my interviews with clinical psychologists and sometimes surfaced starkly, such as when Grant, who worked in rural England, told me that 'the whole NHS ethos . . . of more for less' was 'bullshit'. Such bluntly stated views were more commonly expressed once my recorder was turned off. Salient among the affects channelled were frustration with limited resources through which waiting lists might be reduced, sadness and even anger that patients had to wait so long, and on occasion guilt that more could not be offered.

Managing Demand

To deal with busy workloads, demands for accountability, and emotionally laden moral and clinical decision-making, psychologists sometimes elect to use social and procedural technologies to manage waiting lists and referrals. These configure the referral process without necessarily or linearly determining it, and are examples of certain performances of autonomy that also create space for more. This might be through the discretionary classification – and hence subjectification (Hacking, 1995, 2002) – of people seeking care in particular ways that have implications for the temporalities of care (which can also be expected to have subjectifying effects). Amy, for instance, described how, in response to 'ridiculous' waiting lists, her service developed a process whereby (potential) patients were 'split' into 'priority' and 'routine' groups, with the latter 'only' receiving 30-minute assessment meetings. This agentic configuring of the service, and of the patient themselves, apparently 'massively helped' with the waiting list.

Other mechanisms for managing waiting lists and times are the delegation of decision-making to pre-packaged delivery models. Nonetheless, these are sometimes modified to better suit the contexts wherein they operate, and their operations can configure professional autonomy in turn. The Choice and Partnership Approach (CAPA) was an example of this noted in several interviews and conversations I had with clinical psychologists. CAPA is a model of engaging and assessing people for therapy, particularly in child and adolescent mental health (CAMHS) services, which centres an initial 'choice appointment'. This is an initial appointment at a time of the patient or their carer's choosing, as opposed to one that is decided in advance by the service team (Robotham et al., 2010). Dierdre summarised her use of this approach:

> I don't know if you've heard about the CAPA model? We used, I wouldn't say we did CAPA as it was designed but we did a choice appointment where we aim to have somebody seen within eight weeks and basically we do the assessment. Unless it was completely obvious that the referral was rubbish and it shouldn't be us, it was far better and better use of our time to get somebody in for an hour to have a discussion about what needs to be different, what is it that we're hoping to be different, why would it be us, and working out whether there's a mental health need that we are best placed to meet than trying to do that dialogue back and forth with their GP who doesn't *get it*. And who ultimately is not a mental health professional so that hour of time for that referral was often better spent on face-to-face assessment, and then a discharge, than it would have been back and forth to the GP trying to work out if it was for us or not.

In this example, we can see how CAPA was reconfigured to become 'doable' (Fujimura, 1987) in relation to the assemblage of personnel, demands, and concerns of Dierdre's service. This is itself a performance of autonomy, and the operations of CAPA – even while creating space for patient autonomy – also enact a particular configuration of professional autonomy. Part of this is that the expert – or not – contribution of GPs is rendered less relevant. Accounted for in terms of timesaving, it also squarely positions the clinical psychologist as the principal agent in the process of referral and assessment. Such an elision of physicians implicitly contributes to a bigger project of professional autonomy within a medically dominated NHS.

As we saw in the previous chapter, some of the uncertainties associated with managing waiting lists and referrals can be tamed through a careful configuration of services as having their entry determined by referral criteria. Referral criteria – or commissioning criteria more generally – can be framed as restraining the autonomy of clinicians (Mladovky, 2023). Still, there can be room for manoeuvre. Even in cases where there were 'very detailed referral criteria', clinical psychologists '*might*', as mid-career professional

Verity told me, see people who would not meet these (in this instance, from a different geographical region). The 'might' here is significant: it gives space for the performance and configuration of autonomy.

Brenda, who worked in secondary care in the south of England, told me that despite quite specific commissioning criteria 'sometimes we plug gaps maybe, where we should . . . you know, *ethically*, it feels we need to plug the gap, we need to provide the service'. Yet as capacity became ever more restricted, things had to change: 'It's come to a point now where we have just too many referrals.' Consequently, Brenda felt that she and her colleagues were no longer able to carry on in this way – an unofficial pathway into her service for individuals who did not meet its strict criteria was now 'closed'. This was framed as an affectively and normatively challenging decision, but also one that was in some senses inevitable; as Brenda put it, 'what else can you do?' She went on: 'If we carried on. . .with. . .we're *hiding* a need that needs to be addressed.' Within this account we can see that autonomy is not so much straightforwardly present or absent as it is reconfigured and enacted in different ways over time.

Despite a reflexive understanding of the necessity of finding creative ways to access services, clinical psychologists can also express frustration with referrals they regard as misaligning with their expertise and service. This was palpable in an interview with Louise, which underscored her autonomy over whether to accept particular people into her urban English service (and where the moral aspects of patienthood seemed also to emerge through talk of 'worth'):

> I look at them [a patient referral] carefully to say, 'is this really appropriate?' The vast majority are, in some way or other, worthy of an assessment from my service at least, for me to determine whether I'm the right person, but it's the initial phase of looking at the referral when you usually don't have a huge amount of information, and I will often go back to the referring agency and just *double-check*, 'oh, so you've said, this, this, and this, what else might be going on? Am I really the right service?' And I ask that person to think about, and try and ask them to think about it in context, 'well, look, I'm very busy, I may have to prioritise this case over another one if you're telling me it's an urgent referral, and I need you to think carefully with me if this you know if this is an appropriate referral'.

Esther, in rural Scotland, likewise appeared frustrated when describing how 'psychiatry make referrals for people they don't know what to do with', in the hope that clinical psychologists might be able to help – yet, unfortunately, 'it doesn't necessarily mean we can do anything either'. Rory, a senior clinical psychologist working in CAMHS, implied that 'inappropriate' referral could act as a strategy to absolve clinical responsibility while nevertheless ostensibly 'doing something':

> I mean, the elephant in the room is that very often people make referrals to mental health services because they've run out of ideas of what they can do themselves, and it's a way of getting it off their desk and onto somebody else's.

We can see that an unwillingness or inability to actively configure someone as suitable for a given service can result in another clear performance of professional autonomy: an intentional, rather than protocol-derived, denial of psychological care.

Technologies of Exclusion and Forms of Strategic Inaction

Informal techniques for managing waiting lists and referrals can be regarded as what sociologists like Claire Laurier Decoteau (2013) consider to be technologies of exclusion within healthcare. As we saw in the previous chapter, building walls around a service in the form of rigid exclusion and inclusion criteria can assist clinical psychologists in managing their personal or team's resource through forms of healthcare rationing that privilege some patients while disadvantaging others. Take the CAPA approach, for instance. Verity described having 'adapted' this for her urban service and liked that it meant 'people have to opt into it'. This was helpful because 'it kind of gets rid of all the people who DNA [did not attend] their first appointment, and who actually were not really on board with coming along'. Verity noted that she and colleagues would always 'contact referrers before we discharge people' – for example, if there are 'concerns about vulnerability for the family'. Nevertheless, clinical and normative concerns clearly interact to configure a space of autonomy within which psychologists ultimately have the discretion to continue to see or exclude someone from their service.

On occasion, the disadvantages for patients of high walls around services were explicitly discussed by my interlocutors. Ivor, a senior clinical psychologist working with older adults, was one example:

> I think, you don't want to be in a position where you're excluding a whole group from accessing any part of the psychology service, *unless* there's a good reason for that. Sometimes patients can find themselves falling through the cracks in between the sub specialisms and that's not great if it's unintended

The lack of a clear conclusion about what should be done to prevent patients 'falling through the cracks' implies another approach available to clinical psychologists to take to manage an overwhelming workload: what organisational studies scholars call 'strategic inaction' (Whittle et al., 2016). In this respect, autonomy is performed via decision-making *not* to do something. Arthur, who worked in an early intervention service for psychosis, articulated how waiting lists themselves could be regarded as a technology of strategic inaction:

> [These] tend to be self-serving in the sense that the longer people have been on the waiting list the more likely that either there's been spontaneous change or they've found other means or they *give up*.

In some cases, inaction was itself configured as a form of action: a purposeful refusal to take on more patients to manage a waiting list. In a similar way, inaction can manifest as a strategy of generating low expectations (Gardner et al., 2015); Rory, for instance, noted that for some time his team had 'made a point' of 'not overselling ourselves':

> We knew there was a massive demand that wasn't being met, but we didn't want to go out and just get swamped by referrals, which we then couldn't meet the need of.

Autonomous inaction could nevertheless have affective implications for interprofessional work, which were clear from senior clinical psychologist Irene's reflections:

> I can remember being shown the waiting list when I arrived [in this service] and it filled a room sort of thing. So, we shut the doors, worked through [the] waiting list, offered everybody a time limited piece of work and then when we opened the doors again we had a very *limited* criteria and we did that, and the GPs just hated it

The affective and practical aspects of in/action were also baldly stated by Louise: 'I don't accept self-referrals, as a gatekeeping mechanism. I just think I would be in danger of being overwhelmed if that was the case.' This assertion is striking because there is, unusually, no attempt made to position the decision as clinically necessary, epistemically warranted, or morally just. Rather, Louise's comments simply and straightforwardly underscored the considerable pressures practitioners are under and the mechanisms they must (not) put in place to make it through the day.

Prioritising Patients

Long waiting lists generate normative dilemmas around prioritisation (Allen et al., 2004; Vassy, 2001), contributing to wider practices of local 'micro-rationing' of care (Hughes and Griffiths, 1997). As Sylvia (a mid-career clinical psychologist working in an English city) told me, while external pressures meant that 'we have to prioritise', an almost unanswerable question emerged from this: 'How do you prioritise people who technically are all struggling?!' The intractability of such dilemmas could be interpreted as generating what philosopher Andrew Jameton (1984) termed 'moral distress'. This manifests through contexts of economic and symbolic restraint within healthcare, inflecting professional understandings of their potential to enact desirable therapeutic action (Molinaro et al., 2023). Dealing with ongoing challenges around resourcing, waiting lists, and targets clearly generated different kinds of distress in some of my interlocutors. In the words of Anita, a senior clinical psychologist working in primary care in a large English city,

> I think my kind of experience is that there's something quite punitive that comes with delivering an IAPT service, there's something quite punitive and punishing about what's required in terms of its expectations. And I think you can *really* lose sight of quality and burnout . . . And how you do that as a service head, and you protect your staff, is very, very stressful. And as a result of that I don't sleep. So it's taken a toll on my health, it takes a toll on your family.

Dierdre, working in a more rural location in Scotland, also contemplated how pressures and challenges configured practices of prioritisation and their normative dimensions:

> (With a sigh) Actually the bit that concerns me is that people that aren't being seen that need to be seen and we try and prioritise our waiting list clinically rather than by referral dates, so if somebody's urgent, they sit near the top of the waiting list than somebody that's routine but have been waiting for eight months. But *that* begins to really rub at this point when we've got managers saying, 'right, here are your people that are breaching [the waiting time target], when are they going to be seen?' But you know that the person that's really sitting at the top isn't breaching because she's got another 20 weeks to go before she breaches, but that she's urgently needing an intervention.

The economic context of concerns like those above was often made apparent. Echoing social scientific work into the effects of targets on professional practice (Bevan and Hood, 2006), Arthur noted that 'when money is very tight there can be quite a pressure on managers to organise the service in order to meet, to meet the target'. He elaborated as follows:

> There's a target which is coming up next year, well this year actually, for secondary care psychology services about waiting times. Now, the commissioners locally have agreed the target of trying to increase the percentage of

> people who are seen within 18 weeks. That produces a dilemma because we could organise the service to make sure that 50 per cent of people are seen within 18 weeks, which would meet that target, but the way we'd do it is to make sure the other 50 per cent are waiting even longer. So it, it introduces a real ethical dilemma there, because the consequences of not meeting that target that is a CQUIN target is that we have money withdrawn, which means that we end up with less therapists and everybody waits longer.

In some cases, prioritising patients when also dealing with targets did not necessarily generate normative dilemmas, since the appropriate clinical response might be deemed clear. Yet, it nevertheless generated additional accountability work (Neyland and Coopmans, 2014; O'Reilly et al., 2009) as actions needed to be substantiated. This is indicated in comments made by Susannah, a clinical psychologist working in CAMHS in Scotland:

> So, obviously if we're trying to meet the HEAT target to see people within 18 weeks from referral to treatment, we've got to kind of keep on top of erm the waiting list. And, you know, we may have had to say, for example, if you know somebody's got a problem that they have to be seen more quickly for, like a severe anorexia or something like that, that can take up a huge amount of a clinician's time and it maybe then that some of the other ones that are waiting for a more routine appointment start to breach the 18 weeks, but, you know, that, that is not acceptable to, you know, the powers that be.

Technologies of exclusion, strategic inaction, and their dynamic relationship with practices of prioritisation must then all be interpreted against the background of increasingly stretched services and governmental initiatives aimed at enhancing access despite the constraints experienced by clinicians.

Targeting Therapy

Clinical psychologists are often deeply concerned about the wider context of healthcare and its shaping of their practical circumstances. While targets themselves were not necessarily framed by my interviewees as radically new – 'there has always been targets' – the germane issue was that 'now there is more of a pressure to meet them' (Verity). Senior practitioner Olivia, for instance, spoke of 'an increasing, sort of *push* towards seeing a certain number of people a week', while Dana – a clinical psychologist working in physical health – reflected 'that the numbers and things that we are expected to see aren't really realistic'. Frank, another psychologist with many years of experience, judged targets to be 'destroying clinician, individuality, clinician led thinking'; in other words, targets were judged to compromise professional autonomy.

An exchange with senior clinical psychologist Ursula is illustrative of the operations of governmental power exerted with and through targets, and the normativities entangled with them. She noted that 'our service level agreement for our bit of the service is eight weeks from referral to assessment, and then a further eight weeks from assessment to being in therapy'. This SLA was 'imposed on us'. When asked whether it was easy to work, Ursula responded:

> No. (laughs) We don't hit that, we don't hit that at all. We don't hit it at all. I mean when the service level agreement came in with the new commissioning structure in 2012, April 2012, we had pre-existing waiting lists, and we had no extra resource to deal with that pre-existing waiting list. So, basically, we actually felt that we couldn't offer a different service to people referred from the 1st of April as the ones who got referred on the 31st of March. So we continued to operate a waiting list, which varies from about hmmm two months, sort of, within target to somewhere around ten. Ten months.

In Scotland, the aforementioned HEAT targets included clear waiting time targets, and these played a big role in the work of many, though not all, of the clinical psychologists I spoke with. Amy, for instance, noted that 'the scrutiny that we are under now . . . in terms of our waiting lists and who we see, when and why is *huge*'. She went on:

> I have to say, I let the managers worry about that and I just do, you know, I take the option of I can only work, I can only see a certain number of people and I will work *really* hard for those people, but I-I don't worry about it, there's nothing I can do about it, you know. We've cleared this big backlog of patients, that's my contribution!

The burden of scrutiny, then, was not necessarily carried by all clinical psychologists in the same way. However, even Amy's comments noting that the 'worry' over meeting targets was apportioned to managers rather than herself ambivalently reposition responsibility to her also: Amy notes how hard she has worked, and how her 'contribution' to the team meeting targets was through having 'cleared this big backlog'. Despite the somewhat humorous tone through which Amy narrated her experiences, a sense of pride also came through. At the same time, patients themselves – individuals in distress and seeking care – are aggregated and depersonalised as a problem to be solved. Targets can thus be viewed as disciplining and configuring the subjective relations clinical psychologists have with their labour, and well as subjectifying those with whom they work.

Amy's comments also hint at the efforts that had to be made to monitor a service, specifically in relation to data collection, for it to be accountable to targets:

> But it is the level of scrutiny is huge now, compared to how it was, you know, when I started in the profession or even just a couple of years ago, yeah, the level of detail *exactly* how many people have been waiting, *exactly* how many days and *for what*, what are they waiting for? There's a lot more detail going into that now.

Natasha, a senior clinical psychologist in a Scottish city, underscored that such data work (Bossen et al., 2019) was an issue even when targets were being comfortably met: any data input errors generated alerts and concerns that had to be swiftly addressed to demonstrate that her service was, in fact, delivering according to the priorities set and demanded by the government.

Some clinical psychologists advanced concerns about the quality of care that could be provided for people in the context of target-focused services. Indeed, Ivor, in his relatively rural service, felt that the pressure of targets 'sometimes leads to discharging people where you think they could make more progress with more sessions'. Sylvia, from the perspective of working in a highly urban service, similarly reflected that targets in the absence of substantive additional resource meant 'a dilution in terms of what we're offering to clients':

> I *notice* the type of care in the crisis team that we were providing when *I* first started four years ago, for example, to what we're providing now. And I know, and I can say confidently, my personal opinion is that we're not providing the type of care that we were providing four years ago. What we're doing now is very *much* firefighting, very much trying to get people sort of discharged as quickly as possible, and get people *seen* according to certain *targets* and standards that we should, comply by to make sure that we just basically, it's just like a conveyor belt processing, sort of factory.

This 'firefighting' was also presented as having affective ramifications for staff – stress, sickness, and burnout – which, given the intersubjective nature of psychological therapy, means implications for patients in turn:

> Because we've had a reduction in terms of funding, we've not been able to sort of fill positions, um. And people are, you know, even more pressured to provide more with sort of less, and so we've got staff sickness and burn-out and all that sort of stuff. So they go off and the pool of people to manage this increasing workload is, is reducing. So, it's very pressured, it's very stressful, and you are just not able to give that same level of *care* that we've been able to.

The affective impacts of targets (Liberati et al., 2023), and the kinds of service organisation these enjoined, were also mentioned by some other respondents: Ivor spoke of the 'stressful' nature of being confronted by people who 'might benefit from long-term therapy' without being 'in a position to provide that'. For her part, Susannah described an 'incredible *pressure* on professionals to meet the HEAT targets' and underscored the 'scrutiny' of waiting lists from 'senior management'. She went on:

> [Y]ou've got more people coming in and it means you've got to have . . . a more rapid throughput and there's a sort of pressure on you, I suppose, to, discharge, so you can take the next people on. So I think it's actually put professionals under quite a lot of pressure.

Such pressures can be regarded as reconfiguring, rather than always and simply reducing, the autonomy of clinicians as they act to actively remake their work to meet targets.

'Pressure' and 'Focus'

For a smaller number of clinical psychologists, targets lacked salience; they were, rather, a problem for someone else. Their accounts emphasised, for instance, performances of temporal autonomy (cf. Goodin et al., 2008; Bailey and Madden, 2017), as in remarks from Tina, an early-career clinical psychologist based in an English city:

> I also can have sessions that are 20 minutes long or . . . two hours, if the person's going to be away or something like that, so you do have the luxury of . . . meeting the clients' needs, which is really nice, really. And that's when they need it most, really, when they're in crisis, they want someone to listen . . . So it is nice, I think, that we can do that, . . . and you don't feel the pressure – or I don't – in having my supervisor or manager saying, 'You have to see this many people. It's got to be this, this, and this.' It's not like that.

Still, the spectre of the comparator loomed large: Tina framed 'meeting the clients' needs' as being afforded a particular 'luxury', while colleagues felt the 'pressure' of managerial demands. Accordingly, the configuring of her own psychological work seemed dependent on the wider role played by targets. Not only one form of content within the wider terrain of mental healthcare, targets have become the context through which the psychological is configured.

While the clinical psychologists I interviewed and engaged with more widely were generally critical of targets, resonant forms of the ambivalence that threaded though Tina's reflections above were sometimes expressed by, particularly, clinicians working in Scotland (connecting, perhaps, to a wider rhetoric of progressiveness within Scottish health politics and policy; Greer et al., 2016; Stewart, 2013). Liam, for example, was a senior clinical psychologist in a community mental health team (CMHT) whose role was presented as requiring an unremitting focus on targets. Yet, these were nevertheless regarded as 'hugely beneficial' in terms of raising the visibility of clinical psychology within the NHS and affirming that 'it's just not acceptable that people should wait that long, for such an important service'. Based in a far more rural setting than Liam's urban Scottish practice, mid-career practitioner Megan likewise spoke about some of the pros and cons of the HEAT targets:

> I can see the reason why they're there, to try and, keep services ticking along, so people aren't waiting years and years to be seen. Because obviously, that's not helpful either. But I think there seems to be a feeling that if you don't meet the HEAT targets, you're going to get penalised in some way.

For her part, early-career clinical psychologist Briony spoke both of a 'pressure on services' as well as about their 'concern' that 'you can maybe meet the target, but how are you ensuring' the provision of 'quality therapy' alongside 'decent outcomes for people as well?' However, she too felt that targets also had some benefits:

> [The HEAT targets are] focusing the mind quite a lot, and services very much so. And in a way I think it's fantastic that we have targets that are about psychological therapies, you know? For so long we've often delivered good services but people have had to wait a year for them or people have had a really tricky path to that and might not have been able to access psychological therapy. So, I think that we have a target that's sort of putting that on you know the agenda is really good.

Esther similarly deployed an idiom of 'focus', noting that the HEAT targets had contributed to having 'really modernised us' and 'actually kind of responsibly demonstrating what we do' – albeit with challenges for clinical psychologists themselves:

> HEAT targets, painful as they are, has *focused* [our locality] on *this* is what we need to do. ... I think the HEAT has been in one way a *blessing*, because it's focused on us, and got quite a lot of work going on about the staff that we need to deliver the service. But for the staff at the front line, it's quite hard work.

Verity illustrated some of the labour involved in configuring services to meet targets, but also enrolled them into a mode of 'doing good care' (Pols, 2003, 2006). Adhering to targets – and discharging patients to meet them – thus became part of how Verity configured herself as a good psychologist:

> [E]very Wednesday, we sit and we go through, and we work out how long people have waited on a waiting list, and, you know, if anyone ever looks

> like they get close to breaching then we're, we're quick to get them picked up. I mean [the HEAT waiting time target] has a big impact on the way that we all work, because we all have to think more about discharging people, you know, and not holding on to people, I think psychologists are terrible for holding onto people forever

Another clinical psychologist, Chloe, working in primary care and part of the same overarching NHS organisation as Verity, Liam, and Briony, spoke of similar themes:

> I think for a while psychologists were quite guilty of seeing people for ages and ages and ages and not really getting anywhere, so it is about maintaining a short-term structured approach, and that will you know facilitate picking up more people because you're going to have faster rates of discharge and things

Despite, as we have seen, Arthur's concerns about targets, he likewise framed these as having some advantages: 'I actually think that without those targets the [early intervention] services [in my locality] wouldn't exist at all!' Accordingly, targets can 'have their benefit[s]'. Nevertheless, 'there can be problems' with targets: they can, for instance, 'start to distort the service'. To illustrate this point, Arthur gave the example of an IAPT service where a conversation with a potential patient following referral was conducted by telephone; classifying this as 'assessment' rather than simply a 'screening' 'had a *massive impact*' on whether the service met its targets. For Arthur, this was 'an example of how you can design the service to meet the targets, not necessarily to meet the needs of the people who are accessing the service'. Some clinical psychologists are, clearly, well aware of the 'gaming' effects of targets that social scientists such as Bevan and Hood (2006) have highlighted.

These reflections underscore the professional autonomy clinical psychologists can have to reconfigure their work to address targets, with implications for the ontologies of psychological care – and, of course, for patient access and experience. Performances of professional autonomy intrinsic to such reconfigurations of therapeutic temporalities and practices were not, however, necessarily straightforward. Rather, the clinical innovation of individual practitioners was sometimes presented less as an agentic and knowingly strategic move and more as an almost inevitable response to a kind of structural coercion. Similar to some other interlocutors, Anita highlighted how group therapy had become one answer to the question of how to manage waiting lists:

> [W]e have to create more capacity in treatment. So we're always balancing that out, *every single month*, how many have come in, where's the capacity

> for treatment. And the shift that has come about is that we are *forced* to deliver more group work.

Despite the discourse of inevitability (Leonardi, 2008; Pickersgill, 2024) threading through such accounts, professional autonomy and creativity are evident in terms of how clinical psychologists meet the very significant challenges they face, in a manner that might not be feasible for others imbricated within the psychological complex (e.g. CBT therapists).

In sum, certain clinical psychologists seemed to find mechanisms of accommodating targets, including through framing them as enjoinments to good therapeutic practice. Such ontological respecification (Schneider et al., 2022; Woolgar and Neyland, 2013) in turn foregrounded particular configurations of the good psychologist. At the same time, performances of autonomy were also commonly cast as responses to economic, political, and institutional structures. In this respect, autonomy can itself be considered as a kind of local 'workaround' (Clarke and Casper, 1996) to adapt to structural impositions that reconfigured the content of psychological care.

Limiting Therapy?

Sometimes, services operate with limits on the number of times a clinical psychologist can meet with someone for therapy. Before concluding this chapter, I will talk briefly about the management of those limits, since they serve as an additional example of how waiting lists and associated targets shape psychological care. Their negotiation again demonstrates both the challenges and potential for performances of professional autonomy.

When discussing session limits in interviews and elsewhere, I was generally given figures ranging from 6 to 20 sessions, depending on the nature and complexity of the service and the cases seen. Session limits can align clinical and bureaucratic rationales; they might appear 'in a lot of clinical guidelines' while also being 'management based' (Grant), and psychologists commonly recognise that there are 'really big political, economic, resource reason[s]' (Irene) for their existence. Consequently, practitioners can explicitly seek to emphasise the limits to therapy at the very start of seeing a patient. By not doing so – and instead, for instance, 'at the beginning you say, "we're here to solve your problems"' – some psychologists were cautious of 'inviting a sort of an eternal therapy' (Carl).

Session limits affirm the need for patient prioritisation and extend the normative challenges related to those processes; as Will (a senior clinical psychologist in urban Scotland) reflected, difficult decisions sometimes had to be made in services 'where you can only have 10 sessions or something, or whatever random number gets picked out'. Specifically, should 'I continue to work with this person until I feel they've got the optimum benefit from it' if 'it means other people are having to wait' as a consequence? Dana, in rural England, reflected:

> I think they're [session limits] more difficult if you don't necessarily feel like the person is ready for that ending [of therapy], and it is more about, this is what I can provide, this is the system around me, this is as much as I can do. So it's splitting apart – endings being difficult just because you're a human being, and endings being difficult because a service is specified, a way of working with someone for a certain amount of time, and it doesn't feel like it fits, or has been long enough, or appropriate.

My interview with Brenda was also illustrative of how session limits relate to waiting lists and the wider healthcare context. When I asked how long she might work with someone, she replied:

> Ah! (laughs) Well, before, before the sort of accountability stuff came along, I think . . . I don't think that it was particularly right for that, people would, you know, clinicians would see people for some reason they kind of thought they needed to be seen, which had its advantages, but also disadvantages of actually not being able to do endings, and we don't have that, that luxury anymore. We've got too many . . . less resources, and too many referrals. We have big waiting lists so, we've had to come up with some ideas about how long we see people, and what's the purpose of seeing them. So, it's no bad thing. You know, much more accountable, do a lot more outcome results.

Like targets more generally, then, session limits can be reconfigured as beneficial to public and individual mental health. In the preceding extract, 'luxury' is deployed with some irony, but also almost pejoratively, in ways that attribute the benefit to longer-term therapy to psychologists themselves rather than those with whom they work. In so doing, Brenda, similar to other interviewees mentioned in this chapter, undertakes moral boundary work (Lamont, 2000; Pryma, 2017) between different kinds of clinicians.

Similarly, while not 'totally set in stone', the idea of session limits appeared to discipline early career clinical psychologist Leanne's practice, in that if the number of therapeutic sessions with a specific patient was 'creeping up', she would discuss it with a supervisor. Adhering broadly to them was one means by which she configured herself as a good psychologist through drawing implicit boundaries between herself and others:

> I'm sure that people do go over [the suggested session limit]. I haven't, too much, but maybe that's just me. So I tend to try and, I like things being quite focused. I try not to let cases drag on too much.

More generally, just as waiting time targets per se could be respecified to substantiate some forms of psychological praxis, so too could session limits – at least in principle. Arthur, who, as noted earlier, accounted for the positives in waiting time targets, described how session limits could act as 'a kind of stimulus to be more creative' within therapy. He gave the example of brief interventions delivered in groups, asserting that these were 'actually *better*' in terms of 'the amounts of clinical change' for patients than 'longer individual therapies'. While this was not a common claim, its utterance demonstrates how autonomy can be performed in ways that enable clinical psychologists to adapt to the pressures upon them with patients configured as potential – even likely – beneficiaries of these adaptations.

Further, again similar to targets, session limits are not always an issue for individual practitioners. This is despite considerations of their wider significance. For instance, while mid-career clinical psychologist Natalie (based in physical health in an English city) was aware that other colleagues 'have got to have capped sessions', she was 'generally able to offer patients the number of sessions I feel that they need'. Still, sometimes she might meet with some individuals 'maybe sometimes less frequently than you might be, might be desirable, to fit in the people that you need to see'. Megan, who also worked in physical health, was likewise not overtly troubled by session limits, although she noted: 'I think my manager would be a bit peeved if every person I saw for, like, six months', given the ramifications of this for staff and service capacity and patient throughput.

Unlike waiting list targets, however, session limits are more negotiable as a consequence of the credentialed expertise clinical psychologists can claim and leverage. One mechanism for performing autonomy in this regard is through the reinterpretation of such policy as 'guidance' (Grey and Silbey, 2014). When I asked Grant, who worked in rural Scotland, if he had session limits, his reply was:

> No, I would say it's a *guideline* . . . the psychologists and the psychological therapists that work into community mental health teams, I would say have a *guideline* of around 20 sessions . . . however, it is on the basis of need and if, if there is a good rationale for working longer with somebody then we would continue to work with them, and I've got several people on my caseload that I've been seeing for a couple of years. So it's not unusual for people to go over that 20 sessions.

As with some others I interviewed, Molly framed herself as 'lucky' in relation to the governance of session limits, in this case because her manager 'trusts us to monitor that'. Patricia, working in a CMHT in the same metropolitan area, also invoked the language of luck. When responding to a query about session limits, she described how her team was 'kind of lucky at the moment' because 'it hasn't got that far yet'. However, she also noted wryly: 'It will, it's coming to me, I know it is!' Patricia described how she would 'try and utilise my self-discretion' in relation to how long she would see people for therapy, but 'unfortunately I'm inheriting this big waiting list so probably I will have to be tighter'. She reflected that it was important to consider how to go about 'balancing that and thinking about what's appropriate for each person'. Her mechanisms for doing so appeared to meet with wider approval – or at least did not seem to have caused any alarm: 'I've not been told off yet.'

These extracts illustrate how autonomy can be performed while also indicating how the spectre of harder limits on the number of sessions within which psychological care can be delivered haunts accounts of therapeutic practice. Adjacent services can provide worrying contrasts against which professionals frame themselves – despite wider challenges – as 'lucky'. Further, while clinical judgement can be exercised, supported by assertions of expertise, this may nevertheless require the data work of reporting and/or living with the possibility of being 'told off'. One clinical psychologist early in her career, Chloe, spoke of how she was 'very anxious' about the possibility that if 'somebody' looked at her records, they would see that she regularly exceeded session limits. In sum, session limits are shaped through waiting list and time targets and, like them, contribute to configuring psychological work.

The Constraints of Care

In this chapter, I have underscored some of the salient challenges and concerns that clinical psychologists have with waiting lists and times, and especially targets in relation to these. Over the 21st century, healthcare targets have proliferated (Bevan and Hood, 2006; Sheard, 2018) alongside the intensification of financial challenges to the NHS across the United Kingdom (Ham, 2023; Liberati et al., 2023). Here, I have explored how targets function as a technology of government (Rose, 1999). I examined how clinical psychologists describe the nature and ramifications of targets, and leveraged their accounts to generate further understanding of how professional autonomy is performed through conditions of 'targeted' care.

Waiting lists and targets operate as both circumstantial issues for healthcare professionals and more systemic matters shaped by harsh economic realities. Clinical psychologists, for instance, lament their effects on the care they provide, or they anxiously anticipate deleterious impacts in the future. Accordingly, targets can be considered as, in a Foucauldian sense, 'productive' (Foucault, 1989). This includes through channelling affects of anger, frustration, and sadness, and stimulating or recasting professionals' epistemic, practical, and accountability work (Neyland and Coopmans, 2014; O'Reilly et al., 2009). Consequently, targets can be regarded as (re)configuring the subjectivities of the individuals – clinicians and, I suggest, people seeking or undertaking therapy – that are embroiled within the psychological complex (Rose, 1985).

The intensification of professionals' work in response to policy shifts can enjoin styles of practice that result in reduced support for those whom they ostensibly labour (Watkins-Hayes, 2009). In the case of clinical psychology, resolving the problems of waiting lists and associated waiting time targets often involves processes of prioritisation that can employ implicit – and at times explicit – strategies of exclusion and even inaction. These techniques result in various kinds of informal categorisations of people seeking psychological care, which contribute to how people are 'made up' prior to and during therapy (Hacking, 1995, 2002). In turn, we might expect these processes of subjectification to become imbricated with how clinical psychologists practice with particular patients (e.g. those classified as unlikely to be 'appropriate' for a given service), contouring the nature and outcomes of therapeutic praxis. The social and organisational technologies employed within healthcare can thus be understood as having the potential to participate in the constitution of the psychological itself.

There are also more tangible implications for people seeking care. We have seen, for instance, how some clinical psychologists account for themselves and their acts as being configured through a kind of externally imposed pressure (Mladovky, 2023) that can encourage discharge. In that respect, decisions can be framed as active and autonomous. This is as opposed to an unreflexive failure to 'let go' of patients who are judged as unlikely to benefit further from the additional application of psychological expertise, or who were unlikely to benefit in the first place. Despite the challenges of healthcare targets, then, some clinical psychologists find ways to accommodate these and align them with pre-existing and reworked therapeutic rationalities (cf. Harrison and Dowswell, 2002; McGivern et al., 2015; Waring, 2007). Doing so folds the kinds of practice targets enjoin into ideals of good care (Pols, 2003, 2006).

On occasion, clinical psychologists narrate their tribulations through a discourse of inevitability (Leonardi, 2008; Pickersgill, 2024), explaining actions as logical consequences of wider contexts and individual circumstances. Still, practitioners are able to perform autonomy in certain ways, even if only to adapt to the pressures they experience. Such performances simultaneously advantage and disadvantage different patient groups, resulting in a kind of 'exclusionary inclusion' (Decoteau, 2013). Referral criteria, for instance, are a mechanism for ensuring that clinical resource is, ostensibly, apportioned to those deemed most in need, while also serving to address waiting time targets by effectively narrowing the population of potential service users. Understandings of need itself, however, can be regarded as configured by political exigencies around what money is invested and the epistemic politics of clinical psychology. These shape what is known about 'what works' and for whom – and thus who, ultimately, can access care. Often developed by practitioners themselves, referral criteria can consequently act upon others as technologies of exclusion. Given what we know about the imbrications of psychology and society (as discussed in the introductory chapter), the resulting 'micro-rationing' (Hughes and Griffiths, 1997; Vassy, 2001) might serve to benefit some seeking therapy over others. In the next chapter, I will attend further to some of these matters through an analysis of how clinical psychologists involuntarily discharge patients who do not attend appointments (DNA).

CHAPTER 6

Prompting Exclusion
How 'Did Not Attend' Policies Shape the Involuntary Discharge of Patients

Clinical work is always enacted in relation to the organisation of healthcare systems, and the economic and political rationalities shaping these (Scheid, 2004; Strauss et al., 1985). Local policies and routinised bureaucratic practices are key elements of the infrastructures undergirding care (Timmermans and Almeling, 2009). These can be reconfigured in relation to the shifting salience of national matters, such as waiting time targets. In Chapter 5, I analysed the configuration and performance of professional autonomy within clinical psychology against the backdrop of targets and financial constraint. Here, I explore the uncertainty, affective, and moral work inherent to clinical psychologists' adjudications of what should happen to people who do not attend the therapy appointments that have been scheduled for them. I consider in turn how such arbitration can be both enabled by and enabling of autonomous action in ways that have serious implications for potential or ongoing access to psychological care.

Formal and informal patient attendance policies are key infrastructural arrangements supporting professional decision-making in relation to what many term DNAs (people who 'did not attend' appointments). As such, these policies can prompt exclusion from services and contour clinical perspectives around why this might be desirable. Over the last 15 years or more, I have encountered multiple articulations of concern about how psychological services manage non-attendance. These have been advanced by people who have accessed services (or tried to), activists, and advocacy organisations, as well as some health professionals themselves. In my interviews with clinical psychologists, responses to queries about DNAs could be lengthy. They not only described the processes per se but also indicated how they related to DNA policies and to the broader labour of psychological care. I interpret these interview data against the backdrop of more casual conversations I have had with practitioners about 'non-attendance'. Such dialogues often made explicit many of the matters that can be implicit within my structured research encounters, and accordingly have shaped the analysis I present.

While healthcare is powerfully shaped by policies and guidelines (Berg, 1997; Timmermans and Berg, 1997), healthcare professionals are also well known for their improvisation skills (Jensen and Vabø, 2024; Kamp et al., 2023; Kuijper et al., 2022;) and can take a more 'discretionary' (Johannessen, 2017) approach to practice (Dew et al., 2010; Kellogg, 2011). Attendance policies are no exception, with nuanced negotiations of these often apparent within clinical psychology. As we will see, these are underpinned by processes of moral characterisation and configurations of expertise, which both unfold from and are constitutive of accounts of DNAs.

Non-attendance and Healthcare Resource

Patient attendance is an enduring issue for healthcare systems. Often, resource-related arguments about non-attendance inform discourse within political and policy arenas. An illustrative example comes from political reporter William Russell (1984), writing in the *British Medical Journal*, which triggered various letters in response. Russell's article described a discussion in the UK House of Commons around people not attending appointments, and the introduction of computers into the NHS to help monitor this. According to Russell, the then Under Secretary of State for Health, Conservative MP John Patten, asserted 'the need for hospital patients to recognise their moral responsibility to turn up on time for appointments in order not to waste valuable NHS resources' (Russell, 1984, p. 1928). While the politics of the NHS – and the associated responsibilisation of patients (Miller and Rose, 2008) – ebb and flow, such sentiments could still be encountered decades later. As one senior official commented following the rollout of more digital 'solutions' to DNAs within the NHS:

> It's important that people realise that not turning up to appointments can have a big impact on the care and treatment we are able to give other patients. It wastes Doctors' and Nurses' time too, which costs taxpayers money. (NHS England, 2014)

The financial dimensions of patient non-attendance at clinical appointments have also sometimes been made clear with regards to worries about waiting times following the COVID-19 pandemic (which has had significant impacts on how quickly people can be seen by services; Shah et al., 2024). Guidance released by NHS England in February 2023, for instance, included on its list of 'Benefits of reducing DNAs' the claim that reductions would contribute to 'improving the efficiency of resource allocations by systems and therefore improve how providers can use their capacity to deliver care' (NHS England, 2023b). Such coupling of concerns about DNAs and resource allocation is not unavoidable, however: resonant guidance on waiting times produced by the Scottish Government (2023) later that year centred attendance but avoided discussion of financial imperatives in relation to this (placing responsibilities on the NHS and individual clinicians rather than those seeking care). These rhetorical differences matter: rhetoric, after all, configures reality. Still, some in Scotland might argue that NHS England were simply more willing to 'say the quiet part out loud': Scottish health professionals are all too aware of the financial (and political) considerations shaping the policies that govern them.

Clinicians themselves have for decades reflected on who does not attend treatment, why, and what might be done about it (e.g. Baekeland and Lundwall, 1975; Dengrove and Kutash, 1950). This includes considerations and concerns around the economic and practical implications for services, which can also intertwine with worries about patients per se. In relation to the latter, unscheduled missed appointments are often regarded as having adverse impacts such as enhancing 'the risk of further deterioration, relapse and hospital readmission' (Mitchell and Selmes, 2007, p. 423). Apprehensions can also be articulated as worries that health services themselves are not always doing all they can to support people to attend appointments. For example, one *British Medical Journal* article, published a few years after Patten's reported comments, noted in its introduction that missed appointments in 'outpatient departments may lead to inefficient use of facilities and result in unnecessary costs and delays in assessing patients' (Frankel et al., 1989, p. 1343). However, the paper went on to argue that this was not 'a reflection of patients' generalised indifference to the service offered', but more an issue of 'communication and administration' (Frankel et al., 1989, p. 1345). Directly quoting Russell's article, it concluded: 'Before attributing the problem of non-attendance in the United Kingdom' to supposed patient irresponsibility, 'it is important to ensure that the administrative arrangements are likely to facilitate attendance' (Frankel et al., 1989).

Clearly, as a 'matter of concern' (Latour, 2004), different problematisations of non-attendance can operate in concert, with narratives of people not attending healthcare appointments reflecting varied political, normative, and clinical perspectives. Nonetheless, worries about the financial ramifications of non-attendance can be keenly felt, not least within the context of a health service that is widely understood to be underfunded and, relatedly, often short-staffed. Psychological therapy services in particular are often regarded as a 'scarce resource' (Houghton et al., 2010, p. 510), with non-attendance framed as a problem in relation to a logic of efficiency (Veblan, 1983 [1921]) that has come to configure clinical services and practices. These issues interact with and are shaped through health service debates and wider discussions of waiting lists (Pope, 1991), since a missed appointment can contribute to slowing a person's journey through a service. Consequently, tackling DNAs is regularly perceived at the clinical coalface as one means by which waiting time targets can be met (Tweed and Salter, 2000).

Despite ongoing sociotechnical innovation aimed at maximising attendance, DNAs continue to be a feature of clinical life. Accordingly, health professionals repeatedly negotiate (non-)attendance as part of their day-to-day work. In practice, clinical psychologists can experience a missed appointment in varied ways, including as 'rude' (Tweed and Salter, 2000, p. 472). However, this can also be framed as a 'relief' (Tweed and Salter, 2000): the time that would have been spent working with someone for direct therapy is 'freed up' for the clinical psychologist to deal with one of the many other tasks that demand their attention (e.g. writing notes about the last person they saw). Nonetheless, at national and organisational levels there remains a drive to decrease non-attendance, with ensuing responsibilisation (Miller and Rose, 2008; Rose, 1996) and subjectification (Hacking, 1995, 2002) of healthcare professionals and people seeking care. As the following sections will show, how this agenda instantiates within the NHS varies among clinical psychologists and services yet commonly acts to configure practitioners as autonomous experts. This is even as formal policies and procedures can act to prompt or nudge them in the direction of discharge.

What Do 'DNA Policies' Look Like?

DNA policies seek to encourage a particular disposition and set of actions on behalf of individuals referred to or engaging in therapy: most ideally, to be a regular and timely attender of appointments – and so to be a cooperative, 'good' patient (Lorber, 1975). However, DNA policies also configure clinical psychologists themselves. Specifically, professionals are incited through DNA policies to work with people in ways that are regarded as likely to reduce the likelihood – indeed, the organisational 'risk' – of non-attendance, and so decrease the chance of discharge.

In other words, DNA policies act as a technology of government (Rose, 1999) which enjoin clinicians to practise in ways that seek to delimit the conditions of possibility for someone to be configured as a 'problem' (Lorber, 1975) or even 'bad' (Dingwall and Murray, 1983) patient. At the same time, people can be configured as such precisely because of and through such policies.

DNA policies are wide-ranging, although a rule of 'three strikes and you're out' (with three missed appointments leading to exclusion) is not uncommon. However, some services ostensibly permit only one unarranged missed appointment prior to potential discharge. Where I work in Edinburgh, the local Child and Adolescent Mental Health Service (CAMHS) – part of NHS Lothian – includes the following caution on its webpage:

> If you cannot attend an arranged/planned appointment, please contact your local team as soon as you can to reschedule. Please note, **if you do not attend (DNA) an appointment without letting us know, CAMHS will not routinely offer a further outpatient appointment**, and you will be discharged from the service. (NHS Lothian, 2025, bold in the original)

Harriet, a mid-career clinical psychologist, described a similar policy in her adult mental health service elsewhere in Scotland:

> [W]hen it comes to DNA for a *first* appointment like that, [if someone does not attend] then they're discharged. If it's DNA for a *repeat* appointment, we will send them a letter asking them to get in touch within 10 days if they still require an appointment and if they *don't* get in touch in the 10 days, we assume they no longer want psychology and we discharge them. And the GP gets a copy of that letter, so if the GP wants to chase them up, he can, or she can.

Given that the capacity of primary care is notoriously limited, one might wonder how likely it is that a GP would in fact 'chase' someone in this way. However, positioning GPs as having the capacity and expertise to engage a potential patient for psychological services and prepare them for therapy can help to absolve clinical psychologists of the practical and moral responsibility of doing so themselves. In the preceding extract, this absolution is also emphasised through presenting the task of engaging with people as discretionary rather than demanded by clinical judgement: GPs were said by Harriet to sometimes 'want' rather than 'need' to 'chase [patients] up'.

Other clinical psychologists likewise operated with slightly different policies for first as opposed to subsequent appointments, with procedures around discharge sometimes reflecting the patient groups the service was designed to work with. Also important was how long a person might have waited for therapy in the first place. Senior clinical psychologist Irene worked in England with people categorised with personality disorder, and her policy for assessment was similar to Harriet's approach for later appointments:

> We generally have a DNA policy that, well, it depends where you're at in the process but if you're just at the assessment process and you DNA, one DNA and we'd probably write to you and say, you know politely, 'you haven't, you haven't come, we're not sure if you want this. If you do, get in touch with us and if we haven't heard from you in a couple of weeks we'll assume you don't want it right now and discharge you'.

Harriet went on to describe her policy for therapeutic appointments in ways that reciprocally configured the ontology of her service, her patients, and herself:

> If they're in, if we're at the *treatment* stage, so bless them, they might have sat on the waiting list for two and a half years and then they DNA, we have a kinder policy. Particularly if we're cognisant that there are major attachment issues, because engaging someone with a significant personality disorder you kind of have to prove yourself, by putting up with being mucked about a bit in order to show yourself to be a worthy parent, if you like. So you put up with a bit more DNA with some of those. But notwithstanding *that*, we're also allowing for the fact that people have all sorts of difficulties in coming to sessions. And they've waited *two years*. So if they DNA a treatment session early on, at the beginning, we would offer them another session and when they've DNA'd *two*, they get the two week, 'we're not sure, get in touch'.

Much like Irene, senior clinical psychologist Ursula was sensitive to how a missed appointment might relate to particular contexts:

> [I]f somebody doesn't come for an initial assessment then we'll write, and invite them to come to contact us within two weeks, and if they don't contact us within two weeks then we will discharge. If somebody comes and then DNA's a subsequent session then we will send them a further appointment, and invite them back to continue the conversation, and also, you know, when people don't come, and clearly aren't, can't, won't, whatever, come, we will write to the referrer, and say, 'not really', especially if we don't know the client, you know, 'we don't know why they haven't come, please feel free to give us a call if you want to discuss this, have they got particular access problems, or if they've got, if they're very depressed', you know, if someone's very depressed, the motivation to get up and come out on a Wednesday morning at 10 is, probably, not great, and we've got to be aware of all of those factors when you're looking at your DNA rates really.

Through this extract we can, first, see the efforts to which professionals will sometimes go to reduce the likelihood that a person is discharged prior to or at a very early stage of work with a clinical psychologist. Second, it is apparent that, on occasion, other healthcare staff – including non-psychologists – can be configured as having sufficient epistemic authority to contribute to the synthesis of certainty about what to do about 'a DNA'. Third, different strategies to managing non-attendance can be related to and help to solidify particular configurations of patients that might then have implications for therapy.

Structuring Care in Relation to DNAs

Given wide-ranging clinical and health services concerns about patient non-attendance, a variety of techniques are employed by services for clinical psychology – and psychological therapy and mental health more generally – to encourage people to come along to appointments for assessment and treatment. A regularly touted method of enhancing engagement with services is a simple telephone call reminding someone of their upcoming appointment (Pennington and Hodgson, 2012). Over the 15 years or so, SMS messages have become increasingly routine as well (Sanghara et al., 2010). These can even be used as an adjunct to therapy itself (Furber et al., 2014) – reworking long-standing temporalities and sites of therapeutic interventions, and reflecting a wider digitalisation of mental health (Pickersgill, 2019a). For early-career clinical psychologist Emma, reminders had been notably successful as an infrastructure to support patient attendance. As she reflected during a discussion about what she might do in relation to a DNA:

> [I]t's about, if they [patients] do miss a couple [of appointments], saying, 'well what's going wrong with our systems? Why are these reminders not working, or, you know, are you finding these sessions aren't helping you, or, do we need to just call it a day for now, and you can come back at a different time?' So, so yeah, that's usually two, if there are two DNAs in terms of no contact, no cancellation, then I would phone, I would usually phone them. If I can't get through on the phone I'll send a letter, offer them another appointment in the letter, if they don't turn up to that, then I would usually discharge, they might not get a discharge from the whole *team*, but I would say, you know, 'for things to move forward, we need a bit more, kind of, commitment from your end'. I mean, it's never happened! It's never happened in the service I'm in, because there are enough reminders that, you know?

Expectations around attendance could also shape the content of clinical encounters. As Briony, another relatively recently trained clinical psychologist, reflected when discussing DNAs:

> I suppose generally what would happen is if someone did not attend and hadn't phoned or hadn't cancelled then we would send them a 14-day letter saying, you know, 'you didn't attend, please contact us within the next two weeks if you'd like to be seen again, if not, you'll be discharged back to your GP'. Generally, it's generally the usual rule. Certainly, I would discuss at the start sort of expectations of therapy, of attendance, of kind of what engaging in therapy means in terms of the work in between sessions and I think most of my colleagues would.

Arthur, who worked with people who had experienced psychosis, likewise made clear the salience of various material and discursive techniques to enjoin attendance:

> [W]e don't discharge people for missing an appointment. However, we are becoming much more robust in a clear contract with people at the beginning of therapy to say that we . . . expect people to attend a high proportion of appointments, and that if people have missed two or more appointments they will be contacted to ask whether they want to continue. And if we don't receive communication from them we'll assume they don't, so we'll write to them and ask that. But also that, we expect at least 60 per cent attendance at the planned therapy appointments, which we use, you know we put on all our material, and is up on the waiting room, which *means* that if people are missing appointments, even if they're turning up for further ones, it becomes an issue to discuss in therapy, that actually 'you're missing a high proportion of your appointments here, you know our policy says that we may discharge you if you can't attend these appointments, therefore how do we work on making sure that you're coming to your appointments'! It's something that we instigated a while ago to try and help *prompt* those conversations and *therefore* reduce the kind of the rate of dead time that you get with people that are not coming to appointments.

Attendance contracts of the kind mentioned by Arthur appear to be designed to cement expectations, with patients configured as having the facility to exercise the autonomy to sign them freely. In the process, considerations of the relations of power that shape the contents and enactments of such contracts in the first place are elided.

As mentioned in the preceding chapters, individuals seeking therapy might also be able to 'opt-in' to some services and book an appointment at a time convenient to them. 'Opt-in' approaches to service design and delivery are purposefully leveraged to limit non-attendance. They also come with the possibility of excluding people – especially already marginalised groups – who have not, for a range of possible reasons, actively opted in within a particular time-frame. Nonetheless, a requirement to opt-in to a service is a popular social technology configuring access to therapy, and which consequently shapes experiences of psychological care. As Amy, who was employed by a multidisciplinary weight management service, summarised:

> We have lots of opt-in procedures, so somebody has to go to their GP and say 'I'm worried about my weight', the GP then has to have the conversation of 'do you want to go to weight management, here's a leaflet'. If you want to go the GP will make the referral but the referral will not be actioned until the client has phoned us, phoned the call-centre and opted in. Then they get sent an appointment, that they have to opt-in to, so they have to say 'I will come to that', then they come to their appointment and we say 'okay, yeah, you're eligible to come to our service, to join our weight management programme, a psychologist assessment if you *want* it you have to phone again and opt-in'. So you have to then phone and say 'yes, I've had my assessment, I do want to come to a group'. So there's three opt-in points, so that has *massively* reduced the DNA rate

Perhaps mindful of the ways in which the structuring of her service could be cast as potentially exclusionary, such opt-in procedures were framed by Amy as having 'hugely reduced the number of people who were referred' yet who 'never knew they were referred'. Also flagged were people who might 'have just said "yes"' following a suggestion from another clinician that Amy's service might afford them some benefit 'because they don't want to upset the doctor or the practice nurse, or whoever'. These reflections configured patients as rather acquiescent to biomedical power, even as they were assumed to have the autonomy to clearly advocate for their psychological need through an iterative process of opting-in.

The rather lengthy process of ongoing opting-in to Amy's service, which required people seeking care 'to demonstrate quite a lot of commitment to their weight management, before they even get in front of any of us', aligned with other structural interventions:

> [O]n top of that, we've introduced lots of quite firm DNA cancellations, attendance policies basically. So every time a psychology assessment, appointment goes out, it very clearly says 'if you cancel twice you will be discharged and if you DNA you'll be discharged' and the policy's very clear because in the past we've had, you know, waiting lists of months and months and months and a huge DNA rate.

Just as Amy made plain how opt-in procedures were a strategy for managing non-attendance, so too in the preceding comments does she render explicit how DNA policies relate to waiting lists.

In a similar way to Amy, Ursula also underscored the value of individuals actively opting in to services. The importance of this was articulated through configurations of patients who 'don't know' why they have found themselves within a service:

> Our DNA rate hovers around 11, 12 per cent. Which isn't too bad, but I think it used to be a lot higher, and we have done various things over the years, like, getting people to actually opt-in to therapy, getting them to complete a questionnaire, if they don't complete the questionnaire they don't get offered an assessment, well, they do if they, they don't have to complete it, they just have to return it, and say, 'I couldn't do it', or 'I don't want to complete it'. They still get an assessment, but we need to know that they're willing and able to come, because some clients, for a long time, you'd get, people would come and say, 'oh, I was sent, I don't know why I'm here', and there's much less of that now. So we operate an opt-in system around that.

Again, this extract simultaneously presents opt-in procedures as having value through decreasing the service 'DNA rate' while also, in effect, saving patients from seeing a clinical psychologist when they did not 'know why' they had been referred in the first place.

Moralising Non-attendance

People who do not attend scheduled clinical appointments are commonly subject to moral characterisations which cast them as 'irresponsible' or even 'irrational' (Buetow, 2007; Lester et al., 2005). Often ignored or minimised in the process is the wider social and personal context within which non-attendance occurs. There are a whole range of reasons why someone might 'DNA', including poor transport links to clinics, caring responsibilities that necessitate rapid reprioritisation, and homelessness which results in appointment letters never reaching their intended recipients. For mental health services specifically, the stigma and discrimination associated with psychological distress, including from some NHS staff, can discourage people from attending appointments (Rogers et al., 2001). Diagnostic and therapeutic journeys might also involve encounters with a range of different professionals which result in repeated affectively challenging requests to narrate difficult personal experiences (Biringer et al., 2017). Further, people are on occasion dissatisfied with the service they have received to date (Binnie and Boden, 2016) and doubtful about the efficacy of the therapy they are offered (Rogers et al., 2001). Perhaps unsurprisingly given some of the underpinnings of non-attendance, DNA rates are higher for people living in very socio-economically deprived circumstances, compounding the inequities to which they are already subjected (NHS Health Scotland, 2015).

Still, the moralisation (Strong, 1990) – that is, the casting of events and actions in moral terms – of patient attendance is not uncommon within healthcare. Moralised configurations of patients have also been evident within many of my encounters with clinical psychologists and others who provided psychological care. These can interact with wider political projects of health-related responsibilisation (Miller and Rose, 2008; Rose, 1996) – i.e. a normative encouragement to 'take responsibility' for one's health (notwithstanding the plethora of social, political, economic, and commercial determinants of illness). Emma's comments about her previous work in an IAPT service provide one example of such subtle moralisation and responsibilisation:

> [Y]ou've got to set those boundaries [in relation to non-attendance] that early on, because if people know what to expect, I mean, it's quite [psychologically] containing, and then also the demand on the service is so high, it's only fair to the other people who might be waiting. And, you know, it's, again, it's about helping people take responsibility for their own recovery, as well. You know, if they can't turn up to sessions, how on earth are they going to do [CBT] homework in between?

Moralising discourses can prompt exclusion from services before someone has even been seen by a psychological practitioner, as is clear in the following extract from an interview with senior clinical psychologist Esther. In this, she notes the problem of 'bad attenders' – some of whom are judged to be outright lying to healthcare professionals:

> Some of us are harder than others, and if we're working from people who've been on the waiting list a long time, then it's just one, one appointment offered and you're off. If they're really annoyed about it, they'll go back to the GP and get reinstated. Some of the GPs will know who are the bad attenders and we get quite a lot of letters now saying, 'they say they didn't get the letter. I don't believe them'. So we're getting some support from the GPs about, 'okay, if they don't turn up, we're quite happy with you not following it through'. People probably get two chances at it. And the other thing we count as DNAs are also cancellations on the day, because we cannot rearrange an appointment in that time.

Within my encounters with clinical psychologists, I did not find overt moral ascriptions to be as typical as more implicit forms of moralisation.

For instance, when I asked Leanne, a clinical psychologist quite early in her career, whether she had a DNA policy, she replied:

> Yeah. And that, I think, most recently, that is with trying to be a bit tougher on that, in terms of first appointments, if they DNA. So the letter that goes out for the appointment mentions that if you don't, essentially, if you don't turn up without telling us, you'll be discharged. So, people, if they don't turn up get discharged, on their first appointment. It's slightly up to us, if it's during therapy. So, someone misses an appointment, we'd probably send them a letter, saying, 'sorry you missed your appointment, please phone in if you'd like another'. We wouldn't necessarily, we wouldn't just automatically send out an appointment. And if it seems like there's a bit of difficulty attending, we'd discuss that with the patient next time.

The language of 'toughness' is important here. To be 'tough' can be a valorous, sometimes moralised position, and in the preceding extract it is explicitly aspirational: Leanne and colleagues are purposefully 'trying' to be 'tougher', presumably in the face of experiences – of patients – which are found challenging. Leanne further reflected on what she 'should' do more of in the face of non-attendance:

> [T]here are actually contracts, which I really should, yeah, I should do - some people are probably better than others. Really, what we are encouraged to do is sort of sign a kind of attendance contract at the first appointment to say that we're, both of us [i.e., the clinical psychologist and their patient], aim to attend the appointment, and if, on their side, if there's maybe a couple of appointments that are cancelled at short notice, or missed, then they could be discharged. You know, so they realise that aspect of it. So, yeah, I should do that.

Natalie was, among my interviews, uncommonly straightforward in her description of how she made use of involuntary patient discharge to manage non-attendance:

> [I]f someone DNAs once then I just send them a letter saying, 'sorry you missed your appointment, if you would like another, then give me a call'. And, you know, they get two weeks to do that and if they haven't called then we discharge them.

I asked her whether, following this, there were instances where someone might try to regain access to her service. She replied as follows:

> Yeah, that's quite frustrating! You know, you'll just have discharged their file and then a few weeks later they say, 'oh, yes, could I get seen?' I'm quite soft I suppose, I don't make them, I probably would just see them then.

> I wouldn't, you know, go back to the GP and say 'write another referral letter' or something like that.

Natalie cast people seeking therapy following non-attendance as creating work, and she configured herself as 'soft'. An implication of such a framing is the possibility that she could instead act in 'hard' ways (or perhaps 'tougher' ways). The term 'soft', then, and the assertation of what she would not do – specifically, 'go back to the GP' – suggest that requiring a patient seek another referral could be interpreted as a kind of administrative punishment for not attending an appointment. In these comments, it was precisely through providing an example of an alternative course of action in relation to non-attendance that Natalie underscored how unscheduled missed appointments can be moralised.

Sometimes, clinical psychologists explicitly or implicitly relate non-attendance to psychological 'readiness' for therapy. For instance, Roisin, who worked within a Community Mental Health Team (CMHT) in urban England, reflected:

> [I]t's good to have [a DNA policy] sometimes, because sometimes people just aren't ready, or aren't able to attend regularly to, to make use of therapy. So we do have a policy. I think, it's, I think it's something about if there are two non-attendances then you have to [discuss] with the person, but, generally if it is two consecutive then I would, but if it's just two spaced apart then I don't, I don't bring it up. It's just if it becomes a recurring thing.

As noted in Chapter 4, readiness is not only an epistemically loaded notion but a morally laden one as well; after all, in everyday life it is generally considered that 'being ready' for something is better than being unprepared. One example of how configurations of readiness operate in relation to (non-)attendance comes from a lengthy conversation with Leanne. During this, she further reflected on what might happen with a patient who frequently does not attend appointments:

> [I]t's always tricky, because, you know, especially ones that you sort of know, if people have got anxiety, or, you know, it can affect them getting to appointments. I mean, sometimes, I've sent back to the GP, if it's said in the letter that they're anxious, you know, and they've not come to their first appointment, and you think, well maybe it's because they're struggling to leave the house. But if that is the case, and they're not ready to come to our service, but I would maybe send – there's now an NHS telephone CBT service, and I'd maybe suggest to the GP they could maybe try that for now. But it is tricky, when you know that their poor attendance is probably to do with their problems, anyway. But there comes a point when you can't sort

> of keep making allowances for that, that that's an example of them not being appropriate for the service yet, that maybe there's something else they could try and work on in the meantime.

Leanne clearly attempted to engage with people who do not attend therapy, and in the preceding extract reflected on an example of an apparently justifiable reason why this might happen, namely if someone was 'anxious'. However, this framing of the challenge experienced by a patient nevertheless participates in configuring them as not being 'appropriate' or 'ready' for the service. Despite the mutability of service ontologies discussed in previous chapters, it is the patient here who is deemed to need to change for the service, rather than vice versa. The moral dimensions of both non-attendance and readiness itself are strikingly clear within Leanne's suggestion that 'there comes a point where you can't keep making allowances' – a phrase which is colloquially associated with 'bad behaviour'.

Mental health policy and practice within the United Kingdom has long evinced forms of circular logic that can result in adverse outcomes for potential patients (such as those diagnosed with a personality disorder; Wootton, 1959). In the preceding extracts, we can see how this occurs through the articulation of psychological notions of readiness with institutional policies of exclusion. The former legitimates the latter, and the latter contributes to the veracity of the former: non-attendance is taken to signify a lack of psychological readiness, which is reified as a justification for terminating someone's therapeutic journey. As such, the 'fault' of non-attendance is configured as sitting with – indeed within – the patient. This is as opposed to, for instance, a framing of the clinical psychologist themselves as ill-suited to working with a particular person. In the process, the morality and expertise of the clinician come to be implicitly reaffirmed by discharge itself.

Negotiating DNA Policies

As the previous sections have indicated, formalised DNA policies do not necessarily remove the potential for clinical judgement and discretion. Rather, they can create spaces for the performance of professional autonomy. Senior clinical psychologist Esther, for instance, told me that if a person had 'accepted an appointment and then DNA'd, it's up to the clinician to decide whether they want to give them another one or not'. Another senior interlocutor, Susannah (based in CAMHS), likewise underscored the formal role of clinical autonomy in relation to discharge:

> [Patients] get two DNA's they can have, and then, if they're a vulnerable family we would have to sort of you know read the notes, but they would be given what we call, 'a two-week letter', so that's, 'sorry that you've not come for these two appointments, if you'd like to come, get back in contact with us' and the GP or the referrer would also get a copy . . . The GP would always get a copy sorry. So it would flag it up to them, so if they wanted to contact the family as well they could, or if they have any concerns they could contact us to see, you know, we think you should still try and see them. So they would give that two-week letter, and then if they still didn't respond to that, it goes back through the referral screening group, and the clinician, senior clinicians in the referral screening group will review the case note and just make a decision about whether to discharge or not.

Similar to other cases discussed earlier, we can see how Susannah and her team actively worked to ensure that discharge was not a predetermined outcome of a missed appointment, despite the presence of infrastructure which might prompt that. I queried what factors would come into the final decision to discharge someone and was told the following:

> Well, we would take into account the kind of type of problem that they're presenting with. So obviously if it's a more high-risk thing we wouldn't necessarily discharge. We would take into account the social factors. You know, for example, if we know that the family, the parents got mental health problems or whatever, we might not discharge them, because we would maybe want to contact, you know, the referrer or social worker or whatever, to see if we needed them to facilitate attendance. If you know if there had been a history of poor attendance that might sort of raise the possibility of neglect and, you know, maybe the family not being able to kind of meet the child's health needs. So we consider the kind of factors really.

The inclusion of a wider social context within Susannah's account is notable and illuminates the extent to which many clinical psychologists are keenly aware of and can closely consider the wider circumstances in which their patients live, and which can shape the possibilities of their attendance at therapy appointments. At the same time, expert judgement – sometimes based on various assumptions, as well as the considered view of other professionals – is central to configuring a patient who is either in need of more support or who should be discharged from psychological care.

Sometimes, clinical psychologists seek to ascertain 'the meaning of the DNA', in the words of Charles, a senior practitioner in a large English city working with people 'who have a long-term condition' alongside 'a psychological difficulty'. He reflected:

> I think we try and respond within a framework of knowing that when people have long-term conditions some days are okay and then some days are utter shit and actually expecting somebody to think 'I need to go and talk to that nice guy' is probably very very unrealistic because I am way down the list of things that need to be done today including 'will I eat, will I shower, how will I get to the loo?' So, we, you know, if people DNA we enquire about what is the meaning of the DNA. You know, 'was it that it was a bad day? How can we help you remember if that was not the reason?'. We are happy to do telephone consultations if people said, 'look, I'm really sorry, I can't come in because I'm just in pain'. We, we kind of try and throw a sort of a net around somebody and give them the sense that they are in our heads, even when they're not here, because when you've got a long-term condition people feel utterly isolated and that no-one understands

Charles clearly associated his adjudication of what should happen following 'the DNA' with the kinds of patients he saw, which was also apparent in my interviews and conversations with other clinical psychologists. Clarisa, for instance, was likewise a very established practitioner in the same city as Charles and explicitly related her approach to managing non-attendance to the nature of the patient group she worked with. She also, more implicitly, associated her mode of practice in relation to non-attendance with her expertise in being able to make a 'clinical judgement' about what should happen following a missed appointment:

> [W]e know that people with borderline personality disorders are likely to be quite chaotic. They would really struggle in forming attachments. Intentionally we have tried not to say that 'if you don't attend two or three sessions you're out', there's more flexibility there. I mean in other teams we have to really specify that 'if you DNA this many sessions and you're not engaging at all, we may have to discharge you', but when somebody *is* in therapy then I think there's a clinical judgement which a clinical [psychologist] needs to make, and work with the person to actually [understand] what's going on.

Importantly, DNA policies can also be more purposefully elided. Some of their flexibility and interpretability – and how those entwine with configurations of psychological expertise – are apparent within CMHT psychologist Roisin's observations:

> [W]e do have a DNA and cancellation policy that's sent out to people when they receive an initial appointment, and, it, it really depends on the individual service-user, and my work with that person, how I use that. Sometimes . . . (pauses) You can get some people who attend really regularly, and engage really well, and then they won't attend, and that will keep happening, but because they engage and they attend a number of times you

sort of think, 'oh, yeah, we won't pay too much attention to the DNA and cancellation policy'! But then you get other people who will cancel a number of times, consecutively, or DNA and cancel, and then ring up, and then you need to sort of start saying, 'well, we need to maybe have some sort of contract, and you need to attend, but if you don't we need to discuss it, and see if there's anything else we can do. If there's not, we'll need to think about discharge.'

Patricia, who also worked within a CMHT in the same city region as Roisin, was unusually frank about occasionally evading her service DNA policy:

MARTYN: [Do] you have a formal DNA policy?

PATRICIA: Yes. Do I use it properly? No ... Sometimes some people I use it properly, other times, I think it just depends what you know about someone. If you know someone's really struggling because of this real valid reason, you might be a bit more kind of lenient, or go to their care coordinator and say 'they haven't turned up again, I really should be discharging them but I know they've got this problem and that problem, can you really encourage them to come along this week because this will be the last time?' So I probably give people a little bit more leeway. I stick that [i.e., the DNA policy] up [on the wall] to make myself do it but it's just become part of the wallpaper so I even forgot it was there! So yeah, there is a formal policy that I should be adhering to, a lot more rigidly than I do.

MARTYN: And is that, and do you feel much pressure to do that or is that part of the freedom [you spoke about before]?

PATRICIA: I probably should feel the pressure and I probably don't.

This extract speaks to the moral configurations that come with a DNA policy – Patricia casts herself in a moral role by describing her disposition as 'lenient' – while also underscoring one way through which autonomy can be performed in clinical psychology. Yes, there is a policy; no, it does not have to be followed. The conversation continued:

MARTYN: But you feel it [i.e. not following the policy] enables you to care for patients better?

PATRICIA: Yeah, yeah, exactly, be a little bit more empathic and it seems a bit hard if you know the reasons, the problems someone's got and actually what's playing out in therapy and yet you kind of say, 'sorry, you've got this problem, you can't come'. 'That's what I needed therapy for!' You know? Then I try and give people a bit more of what I think is a fair chance, and that might mean for some people, well, yeah I do insist on the policy because I know they know, or I know there's something else going on, but for some people I might think this is part of the problem and if I can just get them back in this time and *talk about* the reason that they didn't come, rather than just say, 'I'm sorry, you didn't adhere to my rules so you're not coming back'

Subtle moral adjudications can thus come into play in decisions about whether to continue with therapy: Patricia draws boundaries between people who have been given 'a fair chance' and who perhaps begin to attend appointments more regularly and those for whom it is deemed right to 'insist on the policy'. These different and patient-specific responses to non-attendance act in concert to configure Patricia as a good clinical psychologist: first by being compassionate; second by providing quality care; and third by being able to leverage expert knowledge to determine what might be 'going on' with a patient – and what the psychological ramifications of this might be – to chart a morally and epistemically legitimate course of action.

When There Is No Policy

While the consideration of non-attendance is almost ubiquitous within psychological care, not every service has a formal DNA policy. Such an absence could provide additional opportunities for the performance of professional autonomy, including positive discretion, as in comments made by Jason (who was based in secondary care in a rural English county):

> I've got clients that have DNA'd quite a lot. I work with quite difficult to engage clients, and DNAs and late cancellations are part and parcel of that work, so no I've got no set, set maximums or three strikes and you're out, there's nothing of that nature. I'm free to make my own clinical decision on whether or not the DNAs are hampering the *process* and therefore, *further* input may not be beneficial or whether the level of DNAs are actually reflective of the person's social and, emotional difficulties, and-and need to be thought of in that way.

Accounts of an absence of an attendance policy could also serve as vehicles for conveying the morality of clinical psychologists, as well as illuminating their facility and authority to control patient access on a case-by-case basis. As Olivia, another CMHT psychologist, described to me,

> We don't have a formal DNA policy, although we may be coming to that. We may be kind of setting out kind of leaflets and things about that. I think, because of the people that we work with, then often people do have medical appointments, they have family things that happen. They're often in quite sort of complex kind of social networks, if you like. So I think, you know, we do try and be flexible, so that if people are kind of cancelling for good reason, because they're ill, like I said, they've got hospital appointments, or their husband or wife is ill, or they've got to go to a funeral, that

> happens more often than you'd want it to really! Or you know or there's some kind of huge, family crisis, involving the grandchild usually. Then again, we would try and be kind of flexible with that.

In these comments, Olivia articulated both how understanding she was of the challenges that some of her patients lived with while also undertaking the moral boundary work (Lamont, 2000; Pryma, 2017) of sketching out some of the circumstances in which she would 'try and be kind of flexible'.

Less 'flexible' was Kent, a senior clinical psychologist working with people with physical health conditions. He also described a somewhat moralised informal process for managing non-attendance in the absence of a formal service DNA policy:

> I don't have one [a DNA policy], no. No, I don't. I tend to have a fairly intolerant approach if someone doesn't turn up for their first appointment in that I will immediately discharge if they've been sent a letter with an appointment and contact details to get in touch if that doesn't suit, then I will normally discharge and won't bother trying to contact them, unless, and quite often I will also speak to the nurse who may have made the referral and double-check, 'well, is there a reason why this person hasn't come?'

Molly worked with people around the psychological ramifications of physical ill-health, and provided an even more explicitly moral account of the management of patient non-attendance:

> [M]y physio colleagues, for example, and nursing colleagues, will have a, 'if you cancel without a good reason you will just be discharged' [policy]. Whereas we work, I work with much *riskier* patients, where there are safeguarding issues, and I don't think I could, morally, just discharge those people for non-attending, so I'm probably softer with my DNA policy.

At this point in the interview, I felt that Molly looked somewhat uncomfortable. When I asked her about that, she paused before reflecting:

> I can see, I put two heads on, and I can think from a service level point of view, it would be ridiculous if a patient was only attending 50 per cent of their appointments, but then if you needed that link with a professional was a thing that was helping them stabilising, being able to look after their children, and remain in contact with the services and manage their pain better . . . So, from a service point of view it's ridiculous to be wasting, underutilisation of slots I think it's the way it's recorded. However, from a *human* point of view, I think, if someone uses 50 per cent of the slots you offer them, but makes good use of it when they're there, then *clinically* it kind of feels effective.

This extract entwines different rationalities for determining what do in the event of an unarranged missed appointment. Economic, moral, and epistemic modes of approaching non-attendance 'interfere' (Pols, 2003) with each other, resulting in ambiguity and, indeed, ambivalence. Notably, the 'human' perspective is validated in terms of what seems 'clinically . . . effective'. In other words, the exercising of everyday morality is configured as professionally appropriate in ways resonant with other domains of healthcare (Dingwall and Murray, 1983; Roth, 1972; Shuster, 2019). In doing so, the humanity of Molly's clinical work is underscored at the same time. This also defends against perceived attacks that refusing to discharge is economically wasteful. Molly was thus a good clinical psychologist in more ways than one.

Clinical Discretion and Exclusionary Inclusion

Unarranged missed appointments by patients occur across healthcare, with debates ensuing about the implications of this for resourcing and waiting lists. Local policy relating to (non-) attendance – commonly called 'DNA policies' – are one mechanism through which NHS organisations and services navigate this challenge. These act as a technology of government (Rose, 1999), aimed at shaping the expectations and experiences of clinicians and patients. DNA policies bind these parties together in a kind of transactional relationship (cf. Davis, 2013). In effect, access to care becomes dependent on the realisation of certain circumstances – most obviously and importantly that a patient attends a pre-arranged appointment – which can sometimes be reduced to the assumed dispositional and agentive actions of individuals seeking therapy. Where someone 'fails' to attend a scheduled therapy appointment, the possibility of care can be withdrawn. Indeed, some DNA policies mean that (potential) patients might never get to meet with a clinical psychologist in the first place. This could be due to automatic discharge following an initial missed appointment.

Through the infrastructure of DNA policies, clinical psychologists are supported to engage in 'negative discretion' (Barnard, 2023). In other words, practitioners can say 'no' – to actively elect to discharge people from therapy. Entailing uncertainty, affective, and moral work, decisions reached around discharge can be narrated through a discourse of inevitability (Leonardi, 2008; Pickersgill, 2024). Within this, exclusion comes to be configured as a principal mechanism to deal with non-attendance.

Processes of moralisation play a part here. For instance, a 'tough' approach to dealing with non-attendance is sometimes valourised by clinicians. Individuals can also be judged not to have a 'good reason' for being unable to make an appointment. When clinical psychologists classify people as, for instance, 'bad attenders', this action does not sit adjacent to and separate from psychological work. Subjectification occurs through categorisation (Hacking, 1995, 2002), and the informal categories that healthcare professions identify patients through (e.g. as 'a DNA') are well known to have implications for the scope and limits of the care provided (Latimer, 1997; Vassy, 2001). We might expect, then, that morally laden categorisations of patients contribute to the dynamics of psychological care that people who are not ultimately discharged come to experience.

Clearly, DNA polices can be regarded as a form of gatekeeping and a mechanism for modes of subjectification that might have adverse implications. Yet, they can also on occasion be facilitative of care (cf. Buchbinder, 2017). This is when their existence serves not to prompt exclusion, but rather to stimulate therapeutic work precisely to preclude this. An example is when DNA policies stimulate collaborative considerations of whether there are psychological dimensions to non-attendance that could be addressed by clinical psychologists. Alternatively, policies might catalyse a deeper exploration of the social conditions shaping 'the DNA'. An unscheduled missed appointment can be configured by clinical psychologists as a signal of other issues that might form the foci of therapy. This means that non-attendance and discharge are not always and quintessentially coupled.

When making a decision about discharging a person who 'DNA'd', clinical psychologists necessarily produce or affirm a particular ontology of their patient. Elements of this might be acquired from a range of sources, precisely to resolve an uncertainty similar in nature to that considered in Chapter 4 regarding referral. Specifically: Should someone be enabled – in fact, be permitted – to continue with therapy? Determining this enfolds psychological and sometimes even psychologistic characterisations of patients. Accordingly, decision-making about discharge can act as well to channel and reify the expertise of the clinical psychologist exercising their discretion. However, by defining a situation in principally psychological – as opposed to, for example, social – terms, it is hard to conclude that anyone other than a clinical psychologist should make discharge decisions. Potentially, those decisions are consequently more difficult for others, including people seeking therapy, to contest. This might be a particular issue when non-attendance is configured as evidence of someone not being 'ready' for therapy.

In sum, DNA policies connect therapeutic experience to the wider epistemic and economic dimensions of healthcare. Amid challenging waiting time targets and capacity constraints, they can prompt clinical psychologists towards the exclusion of some individuals to improve access to therapy for others. Indeed, DNA policies can compound pre-existing forms of disadvantage and marginalisation by excluding individuals living within circumstances that limit the possibilities of regular or timely attendance at clinical appointments. Accordingly, they underscore the logic of 'exclusionary inclusion' (Decoteau, 2013) that contributes to configuring psychological care. The existence, operationalisation, and negotiation of DNA policies thus represent a striking example of how an ethic of access can also have problematic effects.

Coda
Psychological Therapy and the Ambivalence of Access

An ethic of access circulates internationally, underpinning global and local strategies aimed at proliferating the availability of care and treatment (Biehl, 2007; Cloatre, 2013; Fassin, 2012; Greene, 2011). In the United Kingdom, this ethic has driven forward policies and practices orientated to improving access to psychological therapies – not least the iconic IAPT programme itself. These have been widely heralded, served as international exemplars, and catalysed research and innovations on therapeutic interventions and in relation to notions of the psychological per se. Crucially, many more people have experienced therapy as a result. Challenges, however, remain. An imperative to get through increasingly long waiting lists within tight time-frames, for instance, can result in care being enabled for some patients by restricting it for others.

Over the preceding chapters I have examined some of the social dimensions and ontological implications of endeavours to enhance the availability of psychological care, and of their ramifications for clinical psychology in particular. My analysis has been grounded in a range of texts (journal articles, policy documents, clinical guidelines, and more) and interviews (predominantly with clinical psychologists, as well as policymakers, advisers, and others who hold power to shape the contexts of psychological care). It was also situated against a backdrop of wider work I have undertaken exploring what Rose (1985) calls the psychological complex. This includes research and dialogue with patients and campaign groups, and increasingly as a direct collaborator with clinical psychologists and psychiatrists.

In part given these assorted engagements, I had various potential readers in mind when writing this book. First were sociologists like myself, and colleagues in adjacent fields. For them I have illustrated how a seemingly progressive and widely shared ethic can imbricate political, legal, epistemic, and affective operations across scales in ways which reconfigure professional praxis such that a range of issues and ontologies are also constituted as a consequence. There are, I suggest, relevant insights here for researchers working in different contexts and jurisdictions that are trying to understand better how ostensibly valorous initiatives can sometimes lead to unfortunate results.

Second, I thought this book might find its way into the hands of some mental healthcare professionals themselves, especially clinical psychologists. To these readers I want to be clear that I respect psychological expertise, and am cognisant of the considerable benefits that people can be afforded by a positive therapeutic relationship with a thoughtful, compassionate clinician. I am optimistic that any practitioner who reads this work will agree with me that close yet supportive scrutiny of clinical contexts and norms is always important for enhancing practice. Hopefully, then, this at times critical account of psychological work will further contribute to the necessary reflexivity of professionals that is overall a hallmark of healthcare.

Third, I imagine some readers will be drawn by their own experiences of psychological therapy, not least if these have been difficult or adverse. I know very well that exposure to psychological services can be detrimental as well as beneficial. Negative experiences of therapy – and of particular therapists – can and do occur. Many people are also structurally or interpersonally prevented from accessing care in the first place. By showing, for instance, how processes of entry into and involuntary exit from services are adjudicated, I hope to have provided additional evidentiary support to all those campaigning to improve the accessibility and operations of psychological therapy.

Condensing Configurations

Politics, policies, and everyday exigencies reciprocally configure the contexts of therapy, the care practitioners provide, and the identities of therapeutic professionals. Take, for instance, professional claims-making about what clinical psychology is and should be, particularly in relation to psychiatry (e.g. formulation focused, non-diagnostic, and so on). Claims about the profession do not merely reflect the nature of clinical psychology; they actively configure it. The tactics and processes of boundary work clinical psychology performs in relation to other professions have helped to stabilise it within the NHS as a key provider of psychological care. Accordingly, debates within, assertions about, and the practices of clinical psychology play a role in setting agendas about the nature and delivery of psychological therapy more broadly. Ultimately, these inform the kinds of expertise that people seeking care find themselves with access to, and thus how their subjectivities are configured through therapy (cf. Hacking, 1995, 2002).

As such boundary-work underscores, clinical psychology is but one facet of a larger psychological complex, even as it is among the most salient within that. Understanding the instantiation and ramifications of an ethic access to psychological care in the United Kingdom thus also requires consideration of other activities and initiatives, which themselves shape the work of clinical psychology. IAPT/NHS Talking Therapies is, as noted, a signature example of how access to psychological interventions has proliferated, with clinical psychologists' roles within it emphasising leadership and management more than therapy directly. At the same time, that initiative has also pushed clinical psychology towards a far more metricised form of practice. This is in part via the significant political support that the data and cost-orientated approach to IAPT attracted.

IAPT is certainly not alone, however, in shaping the wider experiences of clinical psychologists and other psychological practitioners, and the ways in which therapy is accessed. The changing understandings of personality disorders documented in Chapter 3 are particularly noteworthy in this regard. Through the discourse and activities propelled by the updating of the 1983 Mental Health Act of England and Wales, personality disorders became configured as treatable – with psychological interventions commonly foregrounded. People detained in prisons and forensic mental healthcare settings consequently found psychological therapy more accessible, albeit constituted through overtly disciplinary logics. Beyond these contexts, psychological care also became somewhat more available to other individuals living with a label of personality disorder. This was due to those reworked understandings of treatment efficacy and of treatability per se. As 'personality disorders' have become increasingly framed as dimensional 'personality difficulties', the focus of clinical psychologists and other psychological therapists on these has intensified. Such shifts illustrate how legal innovation participates in configuring the focus and availability of therapy, the spatial dimensions of its accessibility and administration, and the psychologies of those to whom clinical (and penal) intervention is directed.

While initiatives to improve access to therapy are often portrayed as laudable, they nevertheless clearly have inherent normativities that demand consideration. Psychological practitioners are themselves often all too aware of these: of how economic restraint in some areas – and largesse in others – configure the contexts in which they work, and of how political and professional machinations impact their therapeutic foci. For these practitioners, the metrics that have come to govern psychological care (e.g. how many patients does a service see, and how quickly) are a significant concern. Worries circulate about what happens as a result. This includes anxiety that CBT is over-emphasised in UK mental health, given its suitability for the time-limited approaches favoured to facilitate greater movement of people into and out of services. This centring of CBT is widely understood to have implications for the innovation, evidence production, and implementation of other forms of psychological therapy which could improve population and individual mental health.

As indicated earlier, one consequence of an ethic of access is that psychological care has become subject to a range of (ac)counting practices. In outpatient settings, where most treatment is delivered, these direct the attention of clinicians not only to the person in the room with them but also to all the people waiting to be so. The temporalities and possibilities of care are often closely defined, metricised as a more or less prescribed number of 'sessions' with a patient (even as clinical psychologists can sometimes evade the limits they are encouraged to adopt). This brings the end of treatment into its beginnings, with projections about the duration of therapy shaping practitioner engagements with those whom they treat, including as part of patient assessment and even decisions about whether to accept a referral. Within these processes, the clinical gaze is also now commonly orientated to a person's 'readiness' for treatment, and thereafter their attendance at therapy appointments is a key object of governance.

If psychological therapy has become ever more configured through bureaucratic, economic, and sometimes directly political considerations, experiences of delivering care also appear to have shifted. Many clinical psychologists, for instance, speak of being under intense pressure. One corollary of this can be an affective disposition to those with whom they work that itself generates feelings of concern. As Molly described in Chapter 5, clinicians are implicitly enjoined to 'ration' their 'compassion': moral distress (Jameton, 1984) appears to be increasingly characteristic of psychological care. A logic of 'exclusionary inclusion' (Decoteau, 2013) consequently permeates psychological services, allowing practitioners at least to try to manage growing demands and to make it through the day while preserving their professional, epistemic, and moral identities.

Psychological Manoeuvres

The need to improve access is thus experienced not simply as a straightforward matter of fact by therapists but also as a matter of quintessential concern (Latour, 2004). Clinical psychologists, among others, widely believe that there is considerable unmet need for psychological care. This sentiment aligns with that of policymakers who have introduced healthcare targets as one attempt to stimulate the increased accessibility of care. Yet, the capacity of psychologists to provide this is not unlimited. Given the financial challenges imposed on the NHS across the United Kingdom (and, indeed, health systems in many other countries), targets are ever more challenging to meet.

Within this context, local policies and actions which aim to enhance patient throughput and reduce waiting lists can flourish. Service-level opt-in procedures and attendance/DNA policies are key examples. As a result, processes of referrals and discharge become embroiled with an ethic of access in ways that generate or intensify practical uncertainties with moral and affective valences. Should someone be accepted into a busy service, for example, if they do not quite 'fit'? Under what conditions should a person who misses a therapy appointment be involuntarily discharged? To what extent does – or should – the length of a waiting list matter in relation to managing the uncertainty work of who should be granted access therapy? These are not easy questions to answer, and clinicians are generally not well supported to grapple with them.

Despite wider challenges, clinical psychologists continue to have opportunities for enacting their professional autonomy. This includes the performance of negative discretion (Barnard, 2023), such that practitioners can say 'no' to referrals and 'no' to someone continuing with therapy. The discretion of clinical psychologists is shaped by infrastructures like DNA policies, which might ostensibly define whether a patient should be involuntarily discharged. However, autonomy is also channelled precisely through these, such as when policy ambiguity configures a therapist as central in deciding whether to discharge someone based on their 'poor' attendance. The exercise of negative discretion can also generate positive effects for someone else seeking care: through the release of clinical capacity, it affords a therapist the opportunity to say 'yes' to them. As devices which help to enact and configure the disciplinary power of therapists (Foucault, 1988), waiting times targets and DNA policies are thus intrinsically ambivalent. Specifically, they operate simultaneously as what we might refer to as engines of access alongside what Decoteau (2013) calls technologies of exclusion.

Sometimes, as we have seen, a person who might prima facie be an 'inappropriate' referral can still gain entry to a service. Doing so entails a certain set of ontological alignments between (shifting) understandings of a patient's subjectivity, of the nature of a service, and of the professional identity of the practitioner adjudicating the referral. Other people might not obtain access in this way, however. Clinical psychologists are adept at justifying their decisions, leveraging different epistemic, moral, and professional registers to do so. But if all choices that practitioners might make can easily be accounted for as 'correct', this leaves individuals who are denied therapy little room for contesting professional power and accessing care. Decision-making around access to therapy that is based on ostensibly psychological grounds (e.g. unreadiness for therapy) might be especially hard to challenge given the epistemic and administrative authority of clinical psychology within the NHS. As discussed in Chapter 1, there are, to be sure, other psychologies circulating in this ecosystem. Still, clinical psychology holds considerable power and has worked extremely hard to achieve and maintain that. If a clinical psychologist configures a person as not really 'ready' for therapy, or simply a 'bad attender', then an ontological respecification (Woolgar and Neyland, 2013) that enables their care to continue is not straightforward to achieve.

It is obviously essential that clinical psychologists employ their expertise when deciding who should access their care, as well as regarding the possible cessation of therapy. A healthy degree of clinical autonomy is vital to this. Nonetheless, potentially significant space remains for personal prejudices to unintentionally become inscribed within decision-making. In the introduction to this book, I underscored how the social is constitutive of psychological praxis; accordingly, expert judgements cannot be assumed to exist in hygienic isolation from, for instance, raced, gendered, and classed perspectives on persons seeking therapy. It is entirely possible to imagine a situation in which an overwhelmed clinical psychologist unreflexively attributes a person as insufficiently psychologically minded and not 'ready' or 'suitable' for therapy. Such a scenario could be more likely in stretched services with long waiting lists, wherein practitioners are expected to deliver results increasingly quickly, and limits are placed on opportunities for self-interrogation of clinical decisions. Even within contexts where autonomy is experienced as severely impacted by systematic underinvestment in healthcare, the accountabilities of clinical psychologists thus cannot and should not be elided. When autonomy is presented as being so curtailed that providing care to some people necessarily requires others to go without, close consideration is still needed of what forms of autonomous action remain, what it does and does not afford, and who it (dis)advantages.

Moving Forward

We need to think more collectively and creatively about how clinical psychologists are enabled by healthcare infrastructures to make the best – most clinically appropriate, most ethical, most equitable – decisions they can within often very difficult circumstances. Currently, the degree to which there are checks and balances in place regarding decisions about access to or curtailment of therapy across different services is not always clear. More constructive challenge as part of team-based referral or involuntary discharge discussions could help, notwithstanding the issues about epistemic hierarchies I raised earlier. Returning to the example of someone not being 'ready' for therapy, the fact that this characterisation is so hard to refute is precisely why its deployment within decision-making demands reflection. When the enactment of decisions that can prevent or curtail therapy requires consultation between colleagues, we might expect an even more robust consideration of potential exclusions to result.

Further, despite the problems with DNA policies, these can at least provide a route by which patients might, potentially, contest professional decision-making (e.g. through presenting the circumstances of a missed appointment in ways that configure these as recognisably 'legitimate'). However, I am somewhat ambivalent about the utility of more policy to address access. National policies can overlook the needs of local contexts, and service-level polices can sometimes be transplanted to other psychological settings without sufficient consideration of their applicability and utility. Policy is accordingly – and as many clinicians rightly attest – far from the answer to everything (Kellogg, 2011; Watkins-Hayes, 2009). It at once ameliorates some concerns and generates others.

IAPT has shown us that ambition and purpose can have profound effects on the provision of therapy; equally, it has illustrated that prescribing too rigidly what a service is and how it should operate causes its own issues. Over time, the initiative – and now NHS Talking Therapies – has grown in ways that grant increased flexibility to providers. There are, however, notable limits to this, configured in part by policy that dictates the large volume of data clinicians are required to collect. I maintain that there must be scope for services – within and definitely beyond NHS Talking Therapies – to evolve over time. This should be explicitly via ongoing, dynamic engagement with those they seek serve.

Rather than finite policy recommendations, then, what I instead propose here is that a companion to an ethic of access is required; namely, an ethos of reconfiguration. This can be characterised as a programmatic willingness to be operationally flexible, to embrace community-driven service (re)development, and to further animate and support healthcare professionals to actively seek out opportunities for this. An ethos of reconfiguration would emphasise variability and malleability, within mental healthcare in general and the provision of psychological therapy in particular. Services should be enabled to reconfigure themselves in light of ongoing user and community feedback and changing needs. Instead of being seen as a failure to get it right in the first place, ongoing processual revision could be championed as evidence of substantive community engagement, responsiveness to changing needs, and critical clinical reflection.

As part of this ethos, different NHS organisations, and individual services and clinicians within them, must be granted the dedicated time and resources to work in partnership with communities to ascertain how best to deliver enhanced access to care, for whom, and what that care should look like. In some cases, this could result in the development of 'simple', bespoke solutions. For one service, it might be that therapy appointments shift to take place in the evenings; in another, it could entail practitioners moving to a new building with better public transport links. In some contexts, it might mean doing away with appointment letters altogether and instead discussing arrangements for care directly over the phone. Elsewhere, it could be that online therapy sessions become the norm. Perhaps some services should avoid diagnostic terms; maybe in others counselling psychologists rather than clinical psychologists should comprise the majority of the team. The point is that there is no one-size-fits-all model for the provision of psychological therapy; this is highly contextualised not only by the economic and professional considerations of NHS bodies but also – and more importantly – by the material and psychosocial circumstances within which these operate.

If these examples look like nothing more than tinkering around the edges, this only underscores the gravity of the situation. When I have discussed these matters with clinicians, the response is often the same: even seemingly limited changes can feel impossible to make given the pervasive lack of funding for mental healthcare. X, Y, and Z might help, but where will the resources to make those modifications come from? Every little change in the NHS takes time, and therefore costs money. Healthcare professionals are too often unable to manage even their current work under existing funding arrangements, without taking on extra labour to find better ways of delivering care.

Money, Money, Money

For at least two decades now, reports by advocacy groups and activist collectives (Mad Youth Organise, 2025; Mental Health Foundation et al., 2006; Mind, 2024; Mind et al., 2013) have provided personal testimonies and quantitative figures about the difficulties many people face in accessing psychological care, with long waiting times commonly underscored. Recommendations about how to address this issue sometimes emphasise the need for waiting time targets and almost always the requirement of greater financial resource. I worry how the former can be used by politicians as a means of responsibilising the NHS without granting them the ability to deliver. However, I agree wholeheartedly with the latter point. It remains entirely apparent to me that NHS services are significantly underfunded, and clinicians alarmingly overstretched.

The impact resources have on the instantiation of an ethic of access cannot be overstated. These are intrinsic to the structural conditions that configure care, and they need to be vastly improved. It is a lot easier to support someone to undertake therapy within a healthcare system where clinicians are not constantly being urged to consider all the other people waiting to see them – sometimes for years. If this book is, among other things, a critique of how professional discretion within psychological services can at times be problematic, it is also a demonstration of how the politics and economics of austerity contribute to configuring those circumstances and, indeed, the psychological itself. The possibilities of subjectification I have highlighted would obviously be textured differently in a less impoverished NHS.

Healthcare professionals across disciplines are doing difficult jobs in challenging circumstances, and clinical psychologists are no exception. During my fieldwork and after, I have also consistently encountered what I experienced as genuine concerns for individuals and for populations. Despite my critique, I align with an ethic of access. This is even as I insist on the necessity of problematising some of its specificities and ramifications. Such criticality absolutely does not confute the proposition that so many activists, academics, clinicians, and policymakers have advanced in the past, and still widely articulate; specifically, that more, much more investment in mental healthcare is needed – locally, nationally, and internationally. Without it, services will continue to come and go, clinicians will continue to have to find workarounds that benefit some and hurt others, and many people will continue to go without care.

Demanding more money for public services is, of course, a cliché. Unfortunately, it is one for a reason. As such, and in seeking to resist the discourse of inevitability that substantiates chronic underinvestment, it is one with which I am forced to conclude.

References

Abbott, A. (1988). *The system of professions: An essay on the division of expert labour*. Chicago: University of Chicago Press.

(1995). Things of boundaries. *Social Research*, *62*(4), 857–882.

Adams G., Kurtiş T., Ordóñez L. G., Molina L. E., & Oropeza I. D. (2018). Decolonizing knowledge in hegemonic psychological science. In N. Wane & K. Todd (Eds.), *Decolonial pedagogy: Examining sites of resistance, resurgence, and renewal* (pp. 35–53). Cham: Palgrave.

Adamson, C. (1997). Existential and clinical uncertainty in the medical encounter: An idiographic account of an illness trajectory defined by inflammatory bowel disease and avascular necrosis. *Sociology of Health & Illness*, *19*, 133–159.

Adetimole, F., Afuape, T., & Vara, R. (2005). The impact of racism on the experience of training on a clinical psychology course. *Clinical Psychology Forum*, *48*, 11–15.

Adshead, G. (2001). Murmurs of discontent: Treatment and treatability of personality disorder. *Advances in Psychiatric Treatment*, *7*(6), 407–415.

Allen, D. (2000). Doing occupational demarcation: The "boundary work" of nurse managers in a district general hospital. *Journal of Contemporary Ethnography*, *29*(3), 326–356.

Allen, D., Griffiths, L., & Lyne, P. (2004). Accommodating health and social care needs: Routine resource allocation in stroke rehabilitation. *Sociology of Health & Illness*, *26*(4), 411–432.

American Psychological Association. (2021). *Historical chronology: Examining psychology's contributions to the belief in racial hierarchy and perpetuation of inequality for people of color in U.S.* American Psychological Association. Retrieved 30 April 2025 from www.apa.org/about/apa/addressing-racism/historical-chronology.

Amouroux, R. (2017). Beyond indifference and aversion: The critical reception and belated acceptance of behavior therapy in France. *History of Psychology*, *20*, (3), 313–329.

Amouroux, R., Gerber, L., & Aronov, M. (2022). Putting psychotherapy in its place: The regionalization of behavior therapy in France, Switzerland, and Belgium, 1960s–1990s. *Journal of the History of the Behavioral Sciences*, *58*(1), 5–23.

Amouroux, R., Gerber, L., Jaccard, C., & Aronov, M. (2023) Historicizing "therapeutic culture": Towards a material and polycentric history of psychologization. *Journal of the History of the Behavioral Sciences*, *59*(3), 237–245.
Appelbaum, S. A. (1973). Psychological-mindedness: Word, concept and essence. *The International Journal of Psychoanalysis*, *54*(1), 35–46.
Armstrong, A. (1980). Madness and coping. *Sociology of Health & Illness*, *2*(3), 293–316.
Armstrong, D. (1983). *Political anatomy of the body: Medical knowledge in Britain in the twentieth century*. Cambridge: Cambridge University Press.
(1995). The rise of surveillance medicine. *Sociology of Health & Illness*, *17*(3), 393–404.
(2007). Professionalism, indeterminacy and the EBM project. *BioSocieties*, *2*(1), 73–84.
Armstrong, S. (2002). The emergence and implications of a mental health ethos in juvenile justice. *Sociology of Health & Illness*, *24*(5), 599–620.
Asante, M. K., & Vandi, A. S. (1981). *Contemporary Black thought: Alternative analyses in social and behavioral science*. Beverly Hills, CA: Sage Publications.
Ashmore, M., Brown, S. D., & MacMillan, K. (2005). Lost in the mall with Mesmer and Wundt: Demarcations and demonstrations in the psychologies. *Science, Technology, & Human Values*, *30*(1), 76–110.
Ashmore M., Mulkay M., & Pinch, T. (1989). *Health and efficiency: A sociology of health economics*. London: Open University Press.
Asimakopoulou, K. (2022). Beating your imposter syndrome to become a practitioner psychologist. In M. J. Forshaw (Ed.), *Health psychology in clinical practice* (pp. 75–86). London: Routledge.
Baekeland, F., & Lundwall, L. (1975). Dropping out of treatment: A critical review. *Psychological Bulletin*, *82*(5), 738–783.
Bailey, C., & Madden, A. (2017). Time reclaimed: Temporality and the experience of meaningful work. *Work, Employment and Society*, *31*(1), 3–18.
Bailey, S., Pierides, D., Brisley, A., Weisshaar, C., & Blakeman, T. (2019). Financialising acute kidney injury: From the practices of care to the numbers of improvement. *Sociology of Health & Illness*, *41*(5), 882–899.
Baird, J., Hyslop, A., Macfie, M., Stocks, R., & Van der Kleij, T. (2017). Clinical formulation: Where it came from, what it is and why it matters. *British Journal of Psychological Advances*, *23*(2), 95–103.
Balfe, M. (2016). Standardizing psycho-medical torture during the War on Terror: Why it happened, how it happened, and why it didn't work. *Social Science & Medicine*, *171*(12), 1–8.
Barnard, A. V. (2023). *Conservatorship: Inside California's system of coercion and care for mental illness*. New York: Columbia University Press.
Barr-Haim, S. (2021). *The Maternalists: Psychoanalysis, motherhood, and the British welfare state*. Philadelphia: University of Pennsylvania Press.
Bartlett, P. (2003). The test of compulsion in mental health law: Capacity, therapeutic benefit and dangerousness as possible criteria. *Medical Law Review*, *11*(3), 326–352.

Bateman, A., & Fonagy, P. (1999). Effectiveness of partial hospitalisation in the treatment of borderline personality disorder: A randomized controlled trial. *American Journal of Psychiatry, 156*(10), 1563–1569.

Bax, O. K., Chartonas, D., Parker, J., Symniakou, S., & Lee, T. (2023). Personality disorder. *British Medical Journal, 382*, e050290.

Béhague, B. P., & MacLeish, K. (2020) The global psyche: Experiments in the ethics and politics of mental life. *Medical Anthropology Quarterly, 34*(1), 5–20.

Behrouzan, O. (2016). *Prozak diaries: Psychiatry and generational memory in Iran.* Stanford, CA: Stanford University Press.

Bendelow, G. (2010). Ethical aspects of personality disorders. *Current Opinion in Psychiatry, 23*(6), 546–549.

Bennett, P. (2015). Clinical health psychology. In J. Hall, D. Pilgrim, & G. Turpin (Eds.), *Clinical psychology in Britain: Historical perspectives* (pp. 296–308). London: British Psychological Society.

Bentall, R. P. (2009). *Doctoring the mind: Why psychiatric treatments fail.* London: Allen Lane.

Beresford, P. (2005). Developing the theoretical basis for service user/survivor-led research and equal involvement in research. *Epidemiology and Psychiatric Sciences, 14*(1), 4–9.

Beresford, P., & Brosnan, L. (2021). Subjectivity, citizenship and metal health: UK service user perspectives. In G. Ikkos & N. Bouras (Eds.), *Mind, state and society: Social history of psychiatry and mental health in Britain 1960–2010* (pp. 118–127). Cambridge: Cambridge University Press.

Beresford, P., & Russo, J. (Eds.). (2022). *The Routledge international handbook of mad studies.* London: Routledge.

Berg, M. (1997). *Rationalizing medical work: Decision support techniques and medical practices.* Cambridge, MA: MIT Press.

Berrios, G. E. (1993). European view on personality disorders: A conceptual history. *Comprehensive Psychiatry, 34*(1), 14–30.

Bevan, G., & Hood, C. (2006). What's measured is what matters: Targets and gaming in the English public health care system. *Public Administration, 84*(3), 517–538.

Bezes, B., Demazière, D., Le Bianic, T., Paradeise, C., Normand, R., Benamouzig, D., Pierru, F., & Evetts, J. (2012). New public management and professionals in the public sector: What new patterns beyond opposition? *Sociologie du Travail, 54*(S1), e1–e52.

Biehl, J. (2007). Pharmaceuticalization: AIDS treatment and global health politics. *Anthropological Quarterly, 80*(4), 1083–1126.

Binnie, J. (2015). Do you want therapy with that? A critical account of working within IAPT. *Mental Health Review Journal, 20*(2), 79–83.

Binnie, J., & Boden, Z. (2016). Non-attendance at psychological therapy appointments. *Mental Health Review Journal, 21*(3), 231–248.

Biringer, E., Hartveit, M., Sundfør, B., Ruud, T., & Borg, M. (2017). Continuity of care as experienced by mental health service users: A qualitative study.

BMC Health Services Research, *17*(1), 763. https://doi.org/10.1186/s12913-017-2719-9

Blackburn, R. (1988). On moral judgements and personality disorders: The myth of psychopathic personality revisited. *British Journal of Psychiatry*, *153*(4), 505–512.

(2000). Treatment or incapacitation? Implications of research on personality disorders for the management of dangerous offenders. *Legal and Criminological Psychology*, *5*(1), 1–21.

Bonnington, O., & Rose, D. (2014). Exploring stigmatisation among people diagnosed with either bipolar disorder or borderline personality disorder: A critical realist analysis. *Social Science & Medicine*, *123*(12), 7–17.

Bossen, C., Pine, K. H., Cabitza, F., Ellingsen, G., & Piras, E. M. (2019). Data work in healthcare: An introduction. *Health Informatics Journal*, *25*(3), 465–474.

Bowden, G., Holttum, S., Shankar, R., Cooke, A., & Kinderman, P. (Eds.). (2020). *Understanding depression: Why adults experience depression and what can help*. London: British Psychological Society (Division of Clinical Psychology). https://explore.bps.org.uk/binary/bpsworks/3d108068ab3a95d4/4f408520d744b0f70ff0c444fc1d187fb467f2518e4cafab97f9bd45dd8526de/rep133_2020.pdf.

Bower, P., & Gilbody, S. (2005). Stepped care in psychological therapies: Access, effectiveness and efficiency. *British Journal of Psychiatry*, *186*(1), 11–17.

Bowl, R. (2007). The need for change in UK mental health services: South Asian service users' views. *Ethnicity & Health*, *12*(1), 1–19.

Boyle, M. (2002). *Schizophrenia: A scientific delusion? (2nd ed.)*. London: Routledge.

(2013). Letters. Distortions and maps of wonderland. *The Psychologist*, *26*, 466–467.

Boyle, M., & Johnstone, L. (2020). *A straight talking introduction to the power threat meaning framework: An alternative to psychiatric diagnosis*. Monmouth: PCCS Books.

Brenninkmeijer, J. (2010). Taking care of one's brain: How manipulating the brain changes people's selves. *History of the Human Sciences*, *23*(1), 107–126.

Brinkmann, S. (2005). Human kinds and looping effects in psychology: Foucauldian and hermeneutic perspectives. *Theory & Psychology*, *15*(6), 769–791.

(2008). Changing psychologies in the transition from industrial society to consumer society. *History of the Human Sciences*, *21*(2), 85–110.

British Psychological Society. (2006). *Understanding personality disorder: A professional practice board report*. London: The British Psychological Society.

(2011). *Response to the American Psychiatric Association: DSM-5 Development*. Retrieved 30 April 2025 from https://dxrevisionwatch.files.wordpress.com/2012/02/dsm-5-2011-bps-response.pdf

(2019). *Standards for the accreditation of doctoral programmes in clinical psychology*. London: British Psychological Society. www.bps.org.uk/sites/www

.bps.org.uk/files/Accreditation/Clinical%20Accreditation%20Handbook%202019.pdf

(2020). *Prescribing rights for psychologists*. Leicester: British Psychological Society.

(2021). *Qualification in health psychology (stage 2): Handbook for candidates (June 2020)*. Leicester: British Psychological Society.

(2022). *Qualification in counselling psychology: Handbook for candidates (post-2018)*. Leicester: British Psychological Society.

British Psychological Society Communications. (2023, 7 November). *BPS responds to the King's Speech*. Retrieved 30 April 2025 from www.bps.org.uk/news/bps-responds-kings-speech

(2024). *'The second reading of the Mental Health Bill is another positive step in the right direction,' says BPS*. Retrieved 30 April 2025 from www.bps.org.uk/news/second-reading-mental-health-bill-another-positive-step-right-direction-says-bps

British Psychological Society Division of Clinical Psychology. (2011). *Good practice guidelines on the use of psychological formulation*. Leicester: British Psychological Society.

(2013). *Classification of behaviour and experience in relation to functional psychiatric diagnoses: Time for a paradigm shift*. DCP Position Statement. Leicester: British Psychological Society.

(2017). *Understanding psychosis and schizophrenia*. Leicester: British Psychological Society.

(2019). *Working with a psychologist: Understanding formulation*. Leicester: British Psychological Society.

British Psychological Society Practice Board. (2019). *Minutes, 8th November 2019*. Retrieved 30 April 2025 from https://cms.bps.org.uk/sites/default/files/2022-07/PB%20Minutes%20-%20November%202019.pdf

(2020). *Minutes, 5th June 2020*. Retrieved 30 April 2025 from https://cms.bps.org.uk/sites/default/files/2022-07/PB%20Minutes%20-%20June%202020.pdf

(2022). *Minutes, 9th February 2022*. Retrieved 30 April 2025 from https://cms.bps.org.uk/sites/default/files/2022-09/PB%20Minutes%20-%20February%202022.pdf

British Psychological Society/Royal College of Psychiatrists. (2011). *Common mental health disorders: Identification and pathways to care, National Clinical Guideline Number 123*. Retrieved 30 April 2025 from www.nice.org.uk/guidance/cg123/evidence/full-guideline-181771741

Brodwin, P. (2013). *Everyday ethics: Voices from the front line of community psychiatry*. Berkeley: University of California Press.

Broer, T., Bal, R., & Pickersgill, M. (2017). Problematisations of complexity: On the notion and production of diverse complexities in healthcare interventions and evaluations. *Science as Culture*, *26*(2), 135–160.

Broer, T., & Chandler, A. (2020). Engaging experience: Mobilising personal encounters with mental ill-health in social science. *Social Theory & Health*, *18*(2), 103–109.

Broer, T., Pickersgill, M., & Cunningham-Burley, S. (2020). Neurobiological limits and the somatic significance of love: Care-givers' engagements with neuroscience in Scottish parenting programmes. *History of the Human Sciences, 33*(5), 85–109.

(2022). Temporal imaginaries in accounts of parenting practices: negotiations of time, advice, and expertise. *Catalyst: Feminism, Theory, Technoscience, 8*(1), 1–24.

Broom, D. H., & Woodward, R. V. (1996). Medicalisation reconsidered: Toward a collaborative approach to acre. *Sociology of Health & Illness, 18*, 357–378.

Brossard, B., & Chandler, A. (2022). Explaining mental illness: Sociological perspectives. Bristol: Bristol University Press.

Brown, J. S. L., Boardman, J., Whittinger, N., & Ashworth, M. (2010). Can a self-referral system help improve access to psychological treatments? *British Journal of General Practice, 60*(574), 363–371.

Brown, P. (2006). Risk versus need in revising the 1983 Mental Health Act: Conflicting claims, muddled policy. *Health, Risk and Society, 8*(4), 343–358.

Brownlie, J. (2004). Tasting the witches' brew: Foucault and therapeutic practices. *Sociology, 38*(3), 515–532.

Bruun, M. K. (2023). 'A factory of therapy': accountability and the monitoring of psychological therapy in IAPT. *Anthropology* & Medicine, 30(4), 313–329.

Buchanan, A., & Leese, M. (2001). Detention of people with dangerous severe personality disorders: A systematic review. *Lancet, 358*(9297), 1955–1958.

Buchanan, R. D. (2003). Legislative warriors: American psychiatrists, psychologists, and competing claims over psychotherapy in the 1950s. *Journal of the History of the Behavioral Sciences, 39*(3), 225–249.

(2010). *Playing with fire: The Controversial Career of Hans J. Eysenck*. Oxford: Oxford University Press.

Buchbinder, M. (2017). Keeping out and getting in: Reframing emergency department gatekeeping as structural competence. *Sociology of Health & Illness, 39*(7), 1166–1179.

Buetow, S. (2007). Non-attendance for health care: When rational beliefs collide. *The Sociological Review, 55*(3), 592–610.

Bull, E., Newman, K., Cassidy, T., Anderson, N., & Chater, A. (2020). Reflecting on the Stage 2 Health Psychology independent training route: a survey of trainee and graduate experiences of employability. *Health Psychology, 29*(12), 19–30.

Burns, T., & Hall, J. (2021). Critical friends: Anti-psychiatry and clinical psychology. In G. Ikkos & N. Bouras (Eds.), *Mind, state and society: Social history of psychiatry and mental health in Britain 1960-2010* (pp 191–200). Cambridge: Cambridge University Press.

Burr, J. (2002). Cultural stereotypes of women from South Asian communities: Mental health care professionals' explanations for patterns of suicide and depression. *Social Science & Medicine, 55*(5), 835–845.

Burri, R. (2008). Doing distinctions: Boundary work and symbolic capital in radiology. *Social Studies of Science, 38*(1), 35–62.

Busfield, J. (1991). Review: Governing the soul: The shaping of the private self. *Sociology of Health & Illness*, 13, 2, 276–278.

Byford, A. (2016). Trauma and pathology: Normative crises and the child population in late Tsarist Russia and the early Soviet Union, 1904-1924. *Journal for the History of Childhood and Youth*, *9*(3), 450–469.

Callon M. (1986). Some elements of a sociology of translation: Domestication of the scallops and the fisherman of St Brieuc Bay. In J. Law (Ed.), *Power, action and belief: A new sociology of knowledge?* (pp. 196–223). London: Routledge.

Calnan, M. (1984). Clinical uncertainty: Is it a problem in the doctor-patient relationship? *Sociology of Health & Illness*, *6*, 74–85.

Campbell, P. (2005). From little accords: The mental health survivor movement. In A. Bell & P. Lindley (Eds.), *Beyond the water tower: The unfinished revolution in mental health services, 1985–2005* (pp. 73–82). London: Sainsbury Centre for Mental Health.

Capella Palacios, M., & Jadhave, S. (2020). How coloniality shapes the making of Latin American psychologists: Ethnographic evidence from Ecuador. *International Review of Psychiatry*, *32*(4), 348–358.

Caplan, P. J. (1993). *The myth of women's masochism*. Toronto: University of Toronto Press.

Capshew, J. H. (1999). *Psychologists on the march: Science, practice, and professional identity in America, 1929–1969*. Cambridge: Cambridge University Press.

Care Services Improvement Partnership/National Institute for Mental Health in England. (2007). *New ways of working for everyone: A best practice implementation guide*. Retrieved 30 April 2025 from http://webarchive.nationalarchives.gov.uk/20130105064321/http://www.dh.gov.uk/prod_consum_dh/groups/dh_digitalassets/@dh/@en/documents/digitalasset/dh_079106.pdf

Carey, B. (2017, 24 July). *England's mental health experiment: No-cost talk therapy*. New York Times. Retrieved 30 April 2025 from www.nytimes.com/2017/07/24/health/england-mental-health-treatment-therapy.html

Carmichael, K., Rushworth, I., & Fisher, P. (2020). 'You're opening yourself up to new and different ideas': Clinical psychologists' understandings and experiences of using reflective practice in clinical work: an interpretative phenomenological analysis. *Reflective Practice*, *21*(4), 520–533.

Carr, S. (2007). Participation, power, conflict and change: Theorizing dynamics of service user participation in the social care system of England and Wales. *Critical Social Policy*, *27*(2), 266–276.

(2010). Seldom heard or frequently ignored? Lesbian, gay and bisexual (LGB) perspectives on mental health services. *Ethnicity and Inequalities in Health and Social Care*, *3*(3), 14–23.

Carr, S., & Spandler, H. (2019). Hidden from history? A brief modern history of the psychiatric 'treatment' of lesbian and bisexual women in England. *The Lancet Psychiatry*, *6*(4), 289–290.

Carter, S., Green, J., & Speed, E. (2018). Digital technologies and the biomedicalisation of everyday activities: The case of walking and cycling. *Sociology Compass*, *12*(4), e12572.

Cavadino, M. (1989). *Mental health law in context: Doctor's orders?* Aldershot: Dartmouth Publishing Company.

Cawthra, R., & Gibb, R. (1998). Severe personality disorder: Whose responsibility? *British Journal of Psychiatry*, *173*(1), 8–10.

Centre for Economic Performance. (2006). *The depression report: A new deal for depression and anxiety disorders*. Retrieved 30 April 2025 from http://cep.lse.ac.uk/pubs/download/special/depressionreport.pdf

Centre for Mental Health, Department of Health, Mind, NHS Confederation Mental Health Network, Rethink Mental Illness and Turning Point. (2012). *No health without mental health: Implementation framework*. Retrieved 30 April 2025 from www.gov.uk/government/uploads/system/uploads/attachment_data/file/213761/dh_124058.pdf

Chandler, A. (2016). *Self-injury, medicine and society: Authentic bodies*. Basingstoke: Palgrave Macmillan.

Chaparro, R. A., & Prado, M. A. M. (Eds.). (2022). *Latinx queer psychology: Contributions to the study of LGBTIQ+, sexual and gender diversity issues*. Cham: Springer.

Charura, D., & Lago, C. (2021). *Black identities + white therapies: Race, respect + diversity*. Monmouth: PCCS Books.

Cheshire, K., & Pilgrim, D. (2004). *A short introduction to clinical psychology*. London: Sage.

Chiesa, M., Drahorad, C., & Longo, S. (2000). Early termination of treatment in personality disorder treated in a psychotherapy hospital. *British Journal of Psychiatry*, *177*(2), 107–111.

Chiesa, M., & Fonagy, P. (2000). Cassel personality disorder study: Methodology and treatment effects. *British Journal of Psychiatry*, *176*(5), 485–491.

Chinn, D., & Abraham, E. (2016). Using 'candidacy' as a framework for understanding access to mainstream psychological treatment for people with intellectual disabilities and common mental health problems within the English Improving Access to Psychological Therapies service. *Journal of Intellectual Disability Research*, *60*(6), 571–582.

Chiswick, D. (1999). Preventive detention exhumed – and enhanced. *Psychiatric Bulletin*, *23*(12), 703–704.

(2001). Dangerous severe personality disorder: From notion to law. *Psychiatric Bulletin*, *25*(8), 282–283.

Clark, D. M. (2011). Implementing NICE guidelines for the psychological treatment of depression and anxiety disorders: The IAPT experience. *International Review of Psychiatry*, *23*(4), 318–327.

(2018). Realising the mass public benefit of evidence-based psychological therapies: The IAPT program. *Annual Review of Clinical Psychology*, *14*, 159–183.

Clark, D. M., Layard, R., & Smithies, R. (2007). *Improving access to psychological therapy: Initial evaluation of the two demonstration sites*. CEP discussion paper no. 897. Retrieved 30 April 2025 from http://cep.lse.ac.uk/pubs/download/dp0897.pdf

Clark, D. M., Layard, R., Smithies, R., Richards , D. D., Suckling, R., & Wright, B. (2009). Improving access to psychological therapy: Initial evaluation of two UK demonstration sites. *Behaviour Research and Therapy*, *47*(11), 910–920.

Clark, D. M., & Wells, A. (1995). A cognitive model of social phobia. In R. G. Heimberg, M. Liebowitz, D. Hope, & F. Scheier (Eds.), *Social phobia: Diagnosis, assessment and treatment* (pp. 69–93). New York: Guilford.

Clark, D. M., & Whittington, A. (2023). *What's in a name? NHS Talking Therapies, for anxiety and depression – the new name for IAPT services.* Blog, NHS England. Retrieved 30 April 2025 from www.england.nhs.uk/blog/whats-in-a-name-nhs-talking-therapies-for-anxiety-and-depression-the-new-name-for-iapt-services/

Clarke, A. (2020). More debate on prescribing rights. *The Psychologist*, *33*(3), 4–5.

Clarke, A. E., & Casper, M. J. (1996). From simple technology to complex arena: Classification of pap smears, 1917–90. *Medical Anthropology Quarterly*, *10*(4), 601–623.

Clarke, A. E., Mamo, L., Fosket, J. R., Fishman, J. R., & Shim, J. (2010). *Biomedicalization: Technoscience, health, and illness in the U.S.* Durham, NC: Duke University Press.

Clarke, A. E., Shim, J. K., Mamo, L., Fosket, J. R., & Fishman, J. R. (2003). Biomedicalization: Technoscientific transformations of health, illness, and U.S. biomedicine. *American Sociological Review*, *68*(2), 161–194.

Cloatre, E. (2013). *Pills for the poorest: An exploration of TRIPS and access to medication in sub-Saharan Africa.* London: Palgrave MacMillan.

Cohen-Tovée, E. (2020). DCP UK Chair's update. *Clinical Psychology Forum*, *334*(10), 5–11.

Cokley, K., & Garba, R. (2018). Speaking truth to power: How Black/African psychology changed the discipline of psychology. *Journal of Black Psychology*, *44*(8), 695–721.

Comeau-Vallée, M., & Langley, A. (2020). The interplay of inter- and intraprofessional boundary work in multidisciplinary teams. *Organization Studies*, *41*(12), 1649–1672.

Conrad, P. (2005). The shifting engines of medicalization. *Journal of Health and Social Behavior*, *46*(1), 3–14.

Constantine, M. G. (2007). Racial microaggressions against African American clients in cross-racial counseling relationships. *Journal of Counseling Psychology*, *54*(1), 1–16.

The Consultation and Advocacy Promotion Service (CAPS). (2011). *Much more than a label: A resource about personality disorder by people with lived experience.* Retrieved 30 April 2025 from http://capsadvocacy.org/wp content/uploads/2013/10/Sec-01-ÔÇô-Much-More-layout_DOWNLOAD.pdf

Cook, J. (2023). *Making a mindful nation: Mental health and governance in the twenty-first century.* Princeton, NJ: Princeton University Press.

Cooke, A., & Kinderman, P. (2018). "But what about real mental illness?" Alternatives to the disease model approach to "schizophrenia". *Journal of Humanistic Psychology*, *58*(1), 47–71.

Corrie, S., & Callahan, M. M. (2000). A review of the scientist–practitioner model: Reflections on its potential contribution to counselling psychology within the context of current health care trends. *British Journal of Medical Psychology*, *73*(3), 413–427.

Courtney-Walker, R. (2019). A role for psychologists on prescription? *The Psychologist*, *32*(3), 2.

(2020). A mixed bag of diverse views of psychologists prescribing. *The Psychologist*, *33*(2), 2–3.

Craciun, M. (2017). Time, knowledge, and power in psychotherapy: A comparison of psychodynamic and cognitive behavioral practices. *Qualitative Sociology*, *40*(2), 165–190.

(2018). Emotions and knowledge in expert work: A comparison of two psychotherapies. *American Journal of Sociology*, *123*(44), 959–1003.

Crawford, M. (2007). Can deficits in social problem-solving in people with personality disorder be reversed? *British Journal of Psychiatry*, *190*(4), 283–284.

Crellin, C. (1998). Origins and social contexts of the term 'formulation' in psychological case-reports. *Clinical Psychology Forum*, *112*, 18–28.

Crespo Suárez, J., & Machin Suárez, R. (2021). Medicalisation in public primary mental health care services in Chile. *Social Theory & Health*, *19*(3), 309–330.

Crichton-Browne, J. (1861). The history and progress of psychological medicine: An inaugural address. *Journal of Mental Science*, *7*(37), 19–31.

Cromarty, P., Drummond, A., Francis, T., Watson, J., & Battersby, M. (2016). New access for depression and anxiety: Adapting the UK Improving Access to Psychological Therapies Program across Australia. *Australasian Psychiatry*, *24*(5), 489–492.

Crosby, L., & Bonnington, O. (2020). Experiences and implications of smartphone apps for depression and anxiety. *Sociology of Health & Illness*, *42*(4), 925–942.

Dalal, F. (2019) *The cognitive behavioural tsunami: Managerialism, politics and the corruptions of science*. London: Routledge.

Danziger, K. (1990). *Constructing the subject: Historical origins of psychological research*. Cambridge: Cambridge University Press.

(1997). *Naming the mind: How psychology found its language*. London: Sage.

Davidson, S. E. (2002). Principles of managing patients with personality disorder. *Advances in Psychiatric Treatment*, *8*(1), 1–19.

Davis, A. E. (2013). 'It wasn't written for me': Law, debt, and therapeutic contracts in Greek psychiatry. *PoLAR*, *36*, 4–34.

De Boer, J., Whyte, S., Maden, T. (2008). Compulsory treatment of dangerous offenders with severe personality disorders: A comparison of the English

DSPD and Dutch TBS systems. *Journal of Forensic Psychiatry and Psychology*, *19*(2), 148–163.

Decoteau, C. L. (2013). Exclusionary inclusion and the normalization of biomedical culture. *American Journal of Cultural Sociology*, *1*(3), 403–430.

Dehue, T. (1995). *Changing the rules: Psychology in the Netherlands, 1900–1985*. Cambridge: Cambridge University Press.

Delamont, S. (1989). *Knowledgeable women: Structuralism and the reproduction of elites*. London: Routledge.

Dengrove, E., & Kutash, S. B. (1950). Why patients discontinue treatment in mental hygiene clinic. *American Journal of Psychotherapy*, *4* (3), 457–472.

Department of Health. (1999a). *National Service Framework for Mental Health*. Retrieved 30 April 2025 from www.gov.uk/government/uploads/system/uploads/attachment_data/file/198051/National_Service_Framework_for_Mental_Health.pdf

Department of Health. (1999b). *Report of the Expert Committee: Review of the Mental Health Act 1983*. London: The Stationery Office. https://webarchive.nationalarchives.gov.uk/ukgwa/20130107105354/ www.dh.gov.uk/assetRoot/04/02/12/00/04021200.pdf

(2000a). *Reforming the Mental Health Act Part I: The new legal framework*. London: The Stationery Office. www.gov.uk/government/publications/reforming-the-mental-health-act-part-i-the-new-legal-framework

(2000b). *Reforming the Mental Health Act Part II: High risk patients*. London: The Stationery Office. https://webarchive.nationalarchives.gov.uk/ukgwa/20130107105354/www.dh.gov.uk/assetRoot/04/13/42/33/04134233.pdf

(2004a). *Draft Mental Health Bill*. London: The Stationery Office. https://webarchive.nationalarchives.gov.uk/ukgwa/20130107105354/www.dh.gov.uk/prod_consum_dh/groups/dh_digitalassets/@dh/@en/documents/digitalasset/dh_4088914.pdf

(2004b). *Improving Mental Health Law: Towards a New Mental Health Act*. London: The Stationery Office. https://webarchive.nationalarchives.gov.uk/ukgwa/20130107105354/www.dh.gov.uk/assetRoot/04/08/89/18/04088918.pdf

(2006a). *Mental Health Bill 2006*. London: The Stationery Office. https://publications.parliament.uk/pa/ld200607/ldbills/001/2007001.pdf

(2006b). *The Mental Health Bill: Plans to amend the Mental Health Act 1983*. London: The Stationery Office. https://webarchive.nationalarchives.gov.uk/ukgwa/20130107105354/www.dh.gov.uk/assetRoot/04/13/42/33/04134233.pdf

(2007). *Mental health: New ways of working for everyone: Developing and sustaining a capable flexible workforce*. DH Progress Report. London: The Stationery Office.

(2011). *The IAPT data handbook. Appendices. version 2.0.1. Guidance on recording and monitoring outcomes to support local evidence-based practice*. Retrieved 30 April 2025 from http://webarchive.nationalarchives.gov.uk/

20160302154833/www.iapt.nhs.uk/silo/files/iapt-data-handbook-appendicies-v2.pdf

(2012). *IAPT three-year report: The first million patients.* Retrieved 30 April 2025 from www.mhinnovation.net/sites/default/files/content/document/Three-year-report.pdf. Accessed: 30 April 2025.

(2013). *Mental health payment by results guidance for 2013–14.* Retrieved 30 April 2025 from www.gov.uk/government/uploads/system/uploads/attachment_data/file/232162/Mental_Health_PbR_Guidance_for_2013-14.pdf

Department of Health/National Offender Management Services Offender Personality Disorder Team. (2011). Consultation on the offender personality disorder pathway implementation plan. Retrieved 30 April 2025 from http://data.parliament.uk/DepositedPapers/Files/DEP2011-0319/DEP2011-0319.pdf

Department of Health and Social Care. (2021). *Reforming the Mental Health Act: Consultation outcome.* Retrieved 30 April 2025 from www.gov.uk/government/consultations/reforming-the-mental-health-act/reforming-the-mental-health-act

(2024). *Mental Health Bill 2025: Fact sheet.* Retrieved 30 April 2025 from www.gov.uk/government/publications/mental-health-bill-2025-fact-sheet/mental-health-bill-2025-fact-sheet

Department of Health and Social Care and Ministry of Justice. (2022). *Draft Mental Health Bill, CP699.* Retrieved 30 April 2025 from https://assets.publishing.service.gov.uk/government/uploads/system/uploads/attachment_data/file/1093555/draft-mental-health-bill-web-accessible.pdf

Department of Health and Social Care and The Rt Hon Matt Hancock MP. (2021). *We must bring the Mental Health Act into the 21st Century.* Oral Statement to Parliament. Retrieved 30 April 2025 from www.gov.uk/government/speeches/we-must-bring-the-mental-health-act-into-the-21st-century

Department of Health and Social Security (DHSS). (1977). *The role of psychologists in the health service (Trethowan Report).* London: HMSO.

Derksen, M. (2000). Clinical psychology and the psychological clinic: The early years of clinical psychology at the Maudsley. *History & Philosophy of Psychology, 2*(1), 1–17.

(2001). Discipline, subjectivity and personality: An analysis of the manuals of four psychological tests. *History of the Human Sciences, 14*(1), 25–47.

Derksen, M., Vikkelsø, S., & Beaulieu, A. (2018). Social technologies: Cross-disciplinary reflections on technologies in and from the social sciences. *Theory & Psychology, 22*(2), 139–147.

De Swaan, A. (1990). *The management of normality: Critical essays in health and welfare.* London: Routledge.

De Vos, J. (2012). *Psychologisation in times of globalisation.* London: Routledge.

Dew, K., Stubbe, M., Macdonald, L., Dowell, A., & Plumridge, E. (2010). The (non) use of prioritisation protocols by surgeons. *Sociology of Health & Illness, 32*(4), 545–562.

Dingwall, R. (1977). *The social organisation of health visitor training*. London: Croom Helm.

(2016). *Essays on professions*. London: Routledge.

Dingwall, R., & Murray, T. (1983). Categorization in accident departments: 'Good' patients, 'bad' patients and 'children'. *Sociology of Health & Illness*, *5*(2), 127–148.

Dixon-Woods, M., Cavers, D., Agarwal, S., Annandale, E., Arthur, A., Harvey, J., Hsu, R., Katbamna, S., Olsen, R., Smith, L., Riley, R., & Sutton, A. J. (2006). Conducting a critical interpretive synthesis of the literature on access to healthcare by vulnerable groups. *BMC Medical Research Methodology*, *6*, 35. https://doi.org/10.1186/1471-2288-6-35

Dolan, B., & Coid, J. (1993). *Psychopathic and antisocial personality disorders: Treatment and research issues*. London: Gaskell.

Dooley, C., & Farndon, H. (2021). We've got vacancies and we're missing out on the right people. *The Psychologist*, *34*(3), 62–63.

Doward, J. (2013). *Psychiatrists under fire in mental health battle. The Guardian*. Retrieved 30 April 2025 from www.theguardian.com/society/2013/may/12/psychiatrists-under-fire-mental-health

DSPD Programme (Department of Health, Home Office, HM Prison Service). (2005). *Dangerous and severe personality disorder (DSPD) high secure services for men: Planning and delivery guide*. London: Home Office.

Duncan, W. L. (2018). *Transforming therapy: Mental health practice and cultural change in Mexico*. Nashville, TN: Vanderbilt University Press.

Dyer, C. (2024). Mental Health Bill promises more tailored and dignified treatment for people detained. *British Medical Journal*, *387*, q2463, http://dx.doi.org/10.1136/bmj.q2463

Eastman, N. (1999). Public health psychiatry of crime prevention? *British Medical Journal*, *318*(7185), 549–551.

Eastman N., & Starling, B. (2006). Mental disorder ethics: Theory and empirical investigation. *Journal of Medical Ethics*, *32*(2), 94–99.

Easton, M. (2013). *Is England a nation on antidepressants?* BBC News. Retrieved 30 April 2025 from www.bbc.co.uk/news/uk-23553897

Ecks, S. (2016). Commentary: Ethnographic critiques of global mental health. *Transcultural Psychiatry*, *53*(6), 804–808.

Edwards, C., & Imrie, R. (2008). Disability and the implications of the wellbeing agenda: Some reflections from the United Kingdom. *Journal of Social Policy*, *37*(3), 337–355.

Egbert, S., & Paul, B. (2015). Devices of lie detection as diegetic technologies in the 'War on Terror'. *Bulletin of Science, Technology & Society*, *35*(3–4), 84–92.

Ehrenberg, A. (2020). *The mechanics of passions: Brains, behaviour, and society*. Montreal: McGill-Queen's University Press.

Ellis, D., & Tucker, I. (2021). Emotion in the digital age: Technologies, data and psychosocial life. Abingdon: Routledge.

Erickson, P., Klein, J. L., Daston, L., Lemov, R., Sturm, T., & Gordin, M. D. (2013). *How reason almost lost its mind: The strange career of cold war rationality*. Chicago: University of Chicago Press.

Esteban-Guitart, M. (2014). Technologies of self/subjectivity. In T. Teo (Ed.), *Encyclopaedia of critical psychology* (pp. 1903–1933). New York: Springer.

Evans, C., Connell, J., Barkham, M., Margison, F., McGrath, G., Mellor-Clark, J., & Audin, K. (2002). Towards a standardised brief outcome measure: psychometric properties and utility of the CORE-OM. *British Journal of Psychiatry*, *180*(1), 51–90.

Evans, C., Mellor-Clark, J., Margison, F., Barkham, M., Audin, K., Connell, J., & McGrath, G. (2000). CORE: Clinical outcomes in routine evaluation. *Journal of Mental Health*, *9*(3), 247–255.

Evans, J. (2013a). *Richard Layard on happiness, CBT and Christianity*. Retrieved 30 April 2025 from https://emotionsblog.history.qmul.ac.uk/2013/04/richard-layard-on-happiness-cbt-and-christianity/

(2013b). *David Clark on improving access to psychological therapy (IAPT)*. Retrieved 30 April 2025 from www.philosophyforlife.org/blog/david-clark-on-improving-access-for-psychological-therapy-iapt?

Eyal, G. (2013). For a sociology of expertise: The social origins of the autism epidemic. *American Journal of Sociology*, *118*(4), 863–907.

Eysenck, H. (1949). Training in clinical psychology: An English point of view. *American Psychologist*, *4*(6), 173–176.

(1950). Function and training of the clinical psychologist. *Journal of Mental Science*, *96*(404), 710–725.

(1953). *Uses and abuses of psychology*. Harmondsworth: Penguin Books.

(1959). Learning theory and behavior theory. *Journal of Mental Science*, *105*(438), 61–75.

Eysenck, H., & Rachman, S. (1965). *The causes and cures of neurosis: An introduction to modern behaviour therapy based of learning theory and the principles of conditioning*. London: Routledge.

Fallon, P., Bluglass, R., Edwards, B., Daniels, G. (1999). *Report of the Committee of Inquiry into the Personality Disorder Unit, Ashworth Special Hospital, Cm. 4194-II*. London: Stationery Office.

Farmer, P., & Blackshaw, E. (2021). How the voice of people with mental health problems, families and the voluntary sector changed the landscape. In G. Ikkos & N. Bouras (Eds.), *Mind, state and society: Social history of psychiatry and mental health in Britain 1960–2010* (pp. 128–136). Cambridge: Cambridge University Press.

Fassin, D. (2012). *Humanitarian reason: A moral history of the present*. Berkeley: University of California Press.

Fassin, D., & Rechtman, R. (2009). *The empire of trauma: An inquiry into the condition of victimhood*. Princeton, NJ: Princeton University Press.

Fernando, S. (2017). *Institutional racism in psychiatry and clinical psychology: Race matters in mental health*. Cham: Springer.

Fine, M. (1985). Reflections on a feminist psychology of women: Paradoxes and prospects. *Psychology of Women Quarterly*, *9*(3), 167–183.
Fleming, I. (2012). Reflections on 25 Years working in the NHS. In E. Emerson, C. Hatton, K. Dickson, R. Gone, A. Caine, & J. Bromley (Eds.), *Clinical psychology and people with intellectual disabilities* (pp. 181–201). Chichester: John Wiley & Sons.
Fonagy, P. (2007). Personality disorder. *Journal of Mental Health*, *16*(1), 1–4.
Fonagy, P., & Clark, D. M. (2015). Update on the Improving Access to Psychological Therapies programme in England. *British Journal of Psychology Bulletin*, *39*(5), 248–251.
Forshaw, M. J. (Ed.). (2022). *Health psychology in clinical practice*. London: Routledge.
Foster, J. (2015). Engaging with the views and needs of users of psychological services. In J. Hall, D. Pilgrim, & G. Turpin (Eds.), *Clinical psychology in Britain: Historical perspectives* (pp. 20–38). London: British Psychological Society.
Foucault, M. (1988). Technologies of the self. In L. H. Martin, H. Gutman, & P. H. Hutton (Eds.), *Technologies of the self: A seminar with Michel Foucault* (pp. 16–49). Amherst: The University of Massachusetts Press.
(1989). *Foucault live: Interviews, 1966–84*. New York: Semiotext(e).
Fox, R. C. (1980). The evolution of medical uncertainty. *The Millbank Memorial Fund Quarterly*, *58*, 1–49.
Frank, A. W. (2013). From sick role to practices of health and illness. *Medical Education*, *47*, 18–25.
Frankel, S., Farrow, A., & West, R. (1989). Non-attendance or non-invitation? A case-control study of failed outpatient appointments. *British Medical Journal*, *298*(6684), 1343–1345.
Frauenfelder, C. (2006). UK mental health charities call for more talking treatments. *British Medical Journal*, *333*(7575), 936.
Frayne, D. (Ed.). (2019). *The work cure: Critical essays on work and wellness*. Monmouth: PCCS Books.
Freestone, M. (2005). Overview of an ethnographic study of the UK DSPD Pilot Units. *Therapeutic Communities*, *26*(4), 449–464.
Freidson, E. (1988). *Profession of medicine: A study of the sociology of applied knowledge*. Chicago: University of Chicago Press.
Friedli, L., & Stearn, R. (2015). Positive affect as coercive strategy: Conditionality, activation and the role of psychology in UK government workfare programmes. *Medical Humanities*, *41*(1), 40–47.
Fujimura, J. H. (1987). Constructing 'do-able' problems in cancer research: Articulating alignment. *Social Studies of Science*, *17*(2), 257–293.
Furber, G., Jones, G. M., Healey, D., & Bidargaddi, N. A. (2014). Comparison between phone-based psychotherapy with and without text messaging support in between sessions for crisis patients. *Journal of Medical Internet Research*, *16*(10), e219.
Gardner, J., Samuel, G., & Williams, C. (2015) Sociology of low expectations: Recalibration as innovation work in biomedicine. *Science, Technology, & Human Values*, *40*(6), 998–1021.

Gauthier-Mamaril, E. (2022). Reframing patient-doctor relationships: Relational autonomy and treating autonomy as a virtue. *Journal of Global Ethics, 18*(1), 32–47,

Gerrity, M. S., Earp, J. A. L., DeVellis, R. F., & Light, D. W. (1992). Uncertainty and professional work: Perceptions of physicians in clinical practice. *American Journal of Sociology, 97*, 1022–1051.

Ghosh, P. (2009). Improving access to psychological therapies for all adults. *British Journal of Psychology Bulletin, 33*(5), 186–188.

Gieryn, T. (1983). Boundary work and the demarcation of science from non-science: Strains and interests in professional ideologies of scientists. *American Sociological Review, 48*(6), 781–795.

Gilburt, H. (2015). *Mental health under pressure*. The King's Fund Briefing. Retrieved 30 April 2025 from https://web.archive.org/web/20170829011804/kingsfund.org.uk/sites/default/files/field/field_publication_file/mental-health-under-pressure-nov15_0.pdf

Glover-Thomas, N. (2006). Treating the vulnerable in England and Wales: The impact of law reform and changing policy. *International Journal of Law and Psychiatry, 29*(1), 22–35.

Goddard, J. (2024). *Mental Health Bill [HL]: HL Bill 47 of 2024–25*. Research Briefing, House of Lords Library. Retrieved 30 April 2025 from https://lordslibrary.parliament.uk/research-briefings/lln-2024-0069/

Goldie, N. (1977). The division of labour among the mental health professions: A negotiated or an imposed order? In M. Stacey, M. Reid, C. Heath, & R. Dingwall (Eds.), *Health and the division of labour* (pp. 141–161). Abingdon: Routledge.

Goodin, R. E., Rice, J. M., Parpo, A., & Eriksson, L. (Eds.). (2008) *Discretionary time: A new measure of freedom*. Cambridge: Cambridge University Press.

Goodwin, D., Pope, C., Mort, M., & Smith, A. (2005). Access, boundaries and their effects: Legitimate participation in anaesthesia. *Sociology of Health & Illness, 27*(6), 855–871.

Greene, J. A. (2011). Making medicines essential: The emergent centrality of pharmaceuticals in global health. *BioSocieties, 6*(1), 10–33.

Greener, I. (2009). Towards a history of choice in UK health policy. *Sociology of Health & Illness, 31*(3), 309–324.

Greener, J., & Moth, R. (2022). From shame to blame: Institutionalising oppression through the moralisation of mental distress in austerity England. *Social Theory & Health, 20*, 152–170.

Greer, S. L., Wilson, I., & Donnelly, P. D. (2016). The wages of continuity: Health policy under the SNP. *Scottish Affairs, 25*, 28–44.

Greer, S. L., Wilson, I., Stewart, E. A., & Connelly, P. D. (2014). 'Democratizing' public services? Representation and elections in the Scottish NHS. *Public Administration, 92*(4), 1090–1105.

Greig, D. N. (2002). *Neither bad nor mad: The competing discourses of psychiatry, law and politics*. London: Jessica Kingsley Publishers.

Grey, G. C., & Silbey, S. S. (2014). Governing inside the organisation: Interpreting regulation and compliance. *American Journal of Sociology, 120*(1), 96–145.

Grob, G. N. (2008). Mental health policy in the liberal state: The example of the United States. *International Journal of Law and Psychiatry, 31*(2), 89–100.

(2009). *Mental institutions in America.* New Brunswick, NJ: Transaction Publishers.

Grounds, A. (1987). Detention of 'psychopathic disorder' patients in special hospitals: Critical issues. *British Journal of Psychiatry, 151*(4), 474–478.

(2001). Reforming the Mental Health Act. *British Journal of Psychiatry, 179*(5), 387–389.

Grzanka, P. R., & Mann, E. S. (2014). Queer youth suicide and the psychopolitics of 'It Gets Better'. *Sexualities, 17*(4), 369–393.

Gunn, J., & Felthous, A. R. (2000). Politics and personality disorder: The demise of psychiatry? *Current Opinion in Psychiatry, 13*(6), 545–547.

Guthrie, R. V. (1976). *Even the rat was white: A historical view of psychology.* New York: Harper and Row.

Gyani, A., Shafron, R., Layard, R., & Clark, D. (2013). Enhancing recovery rates: Lessons from year one of IAPT. *Behaviour Research and Therapy, 51*(9), 597–606.

Haarmans, M., Nazroo, J., Kapadia, D., Maxwell, C., Osahan, S., Edant, J., Grant-Rowles, J., Motala, Z., & Rhodes, J. (2022). The practice of participatory action research: Complicity, power and prestige in dialogue with the 'racialised mad'. *Sociology of Health & Illness, 44*(S1), 106–123.

Hacking, I. (1995). *Rewriting the soul: Multiple personality and the sciences of memory.* Princeton, NJ: Princeton University Press.

(2002). *Historical ontology.* Cambridge, MA: Harvard University Press.

Haddock, A., Snowden, P., Dolan, M., Parker, J., & Rees, H. (2001). Managing dangerous people with severe personality disorder: A survey of forensic psychiatrists' opinions. *Psychiatric Bulletin, 25*(8), 293–296.

Hale, N. (1971). *Freud and the Americans: The beginning of psychoanalysis in the United States, 1876–1917.* Oxford: Oxford University Press.

Hall, J. (2015). Colleagues, competitors and offspring: Relationships with other professions. In: J. Hall, D. Pilgrim, & G. Turpin (Eds.), *Clinical psychology in Britain: Historical perspectives* (pp. 111–124). London: British Psychological Society.

Hall, J., & Wang, M. (2015). Professional organisation and communication. In J. Hall, D. Pilgrim, & G. Turpin (Eds.), *Clinical psychology in Britain: Historical perspectives* (pp. 65–79). London: British Psychological Society.

Hall, J., Pilgrim, D., & Turpin, G. (2015). Introduction. In J. Hall, D. Pilgrim, & G. Turpin (Eds.), *Clinical psychology in Britain: Historical perspectives* (pp. 3–19). London: British Psychological Society.

Halpin, M. (2022). Countervailing medicalization: A relational approach to the medicalization of psychosis. *SSM – Qualitative Research in Health, 2*, 100118. https://doi.org/10.1016/j.ssmqr.2022.100118

Halvorsrud, K., Nazroo, J., Otis, M., Brown Hajdukova, E., & Bhui, K. (2018). Ethnic inequalities and pathways to care in psychosis in England: A systematic review and meta-analysis. *BMC Medicine*, *16*, 223. https://doi.org/10.1186/s12916-018-1201-9

Ham, C. (2023). *The rise and decline of the NHS in England 2000-20: How political failure led to the crisis in the NHS and social care.* London: The King's Fund. www.kingsfund.org.uk/sites/default/files/2023-04/Rise_and_Decline_of_the_NHS_April_2023.pdf

Hanley, T., & Amos, I. (2017). The scientist-practitioner and the reflective-practitioner. In V. Galbraith (Ed.), *Topics in applied psychology: Counselling psychology* (pp. 167–182). London: Routledge.

Harding, S. (1986). *The science question in feminism.* Ithaca, NY: Cornell University Press.

Harper, D. (2010). Clinical psychology in context: A commentary on David Pilgrim's 'British clinical psychology and society'. *Psychology, Learning & Teaching*, *9*(2), 13–14.

Harper, D., & Cromby, J. (2022). From 'what's wrong with you?' to 'what's happened to you?': An introduction to the special issue on the Power Threat Meaning Framework. *Journal of Constructivist Psychology*, *35*(1), 1–6.

Harper, D., & Moss, D. (2003). A different kind of chemistry? Reformulating 'formulation'. *Clinical Psychology*, *25*, 6–10.

Harper, D. J. (2005). The critical professional and social policy: Navigating dilemmas in the UK Mental Health Act campaign. *International Journal of Critical Psychology*, *13*(1), 55–75.

Harper, D. J., & Townsend, S. (2021). From the margins to the NICE guidelines: British clinical psychology and the development of cognitive behaviour therapy for psychosis, 1982–2002. *History of the Human Sciences*, 35(3–4), 260–290.

Harrison, S., & Dowswell, G. (2002). Autonomy and bureaucratic accountability in primary care: What English general practitioners say. *Sociology of Health & Illness*, *24*(2), 208–226.

Harrison, S., & Ahmad, W. I. U. (2000). Medical autonomy and the UK State 1975–2025. *Sociology*, *34*(1), 129–146.

Hayes, J., McCabe, R., Ford, T., & Russell, G. (2020). Drawing a line in the sand: Affect and testimony in autism assessment teams in the UK. *Sociology of Health & Illness*, *42*, 825–843.

Hayward, R. (2014). *The transformation of the psyche in British primary care, 1880–1970.* London: Bloomsbury Academic.

Health and Care Professions Council. (2023). *The standards of proficiency for practitioner psychologists.* Retrieved 30 April 2025 from www.hcpc-uk.org/standards/standards-of-proficiency/practitioner-psychologists/

Health and Social Care Information Centre. (2016). *Prescriptions dispensed in the community: 2005-15.* Retrieved 30 April 2025 from https://files.digital.nhs.uk/publicationimport/pub20xxx/pub20664/pres-disp-com-eng-2005-15-rep.pdf

Healy, D. (2004). Shaping the intimate: Influences on the experience of everyday nerves. *Social Studies of Science, 34*(2), 219–245.

Hearnshaw, L. S. (1964). *A short history of British psychology, 1840–1940*. London: Methuen.

(1987). *The shaping of modern psychology: An historical introduction*. London: Routledge.

Hedgecoe, A. (2004). *The politics of personalised medicine: Pharmacogenetics in the clinic*. Cambridge: Cambridge University Press.

Hegarty, P. (2018). *A recent history of lesbian and gay psychology: From homophobia to LGBT*. London: Routledge.

Helén, I. (2011). Is depression a brain disorder? Neuroscience in mental health care. In M. Pickersgill & I. van Keulen (Eds.), *Sociological reflections on the neurosciences* (pp. 123–152). Bingley: Emerald.

Henriques, J., Hollway, W., Urwin, C., Venn, C., & Walkerdine, V. (1984). *Changing the subject: Psychology, social regulation and subjectivity*. London: Methuen.

Herman, E. (1995). *The romance of American psychology: Political culture in the age of experts*. Berkeley: University of California Press.

Hess, D. J. (2015). Publics as threats? Integrating science and technology studies and social movement studies. *Science as Culture, 24*(1), 69–82.

Hillman, A. (2014). 'Why must I wait?' The performance of legitimacy in a hospital emergency department. *Sociology of Health & Illness, 36*(4), 485–499.

Hilton, C. E., & Johnston, L. H. (2017). Health psychology: It's not what you do, it's the way that you do it. *Health Psychology Open*, 1–10. https://doi.org/1doo.i.101rg7/71/02.10157571/20259510727914797 1409

Hird, M. J. (2003). A typical gender identity conference? Some disturbing reports from the therapeutic front lines. *Feminism & Psychology, 13*(2), 181–199.

Hirshbein, L. D. (2009). *American melancholy: Constructions of depression in the twentieth century*. New Brunswick, NJ: Rutgers University Press.

HM Government. (2005). *Health, work and well-being: Caring for our future*. Retrieved 30 April 2025 from www.gov.uk/government/uploads/system/uploads/attachment_data/file/209570/health-and-wellbeing.pdf

HM Treasury. (2023). *Autumn Statement 2023, CP 977*. London: HM Stationary Office. Retrieved 30 April 2025 from https://assets.publishing.service.gov.uk/media/6568909c5936bb00133167cc/E02982473_Autumn_Statement_Nov_23_Accessible_Final.pdf

Hodges, I., & McManus, J. (2006). Psychology at the crossroads. *The Psychologist, 19*(1), 24–26.

Hoeyer, K., Jensen, A. M. B., & Olejaz, M. (2015). Transplantation as an abstract good: Practising deliberate ignorance in deceased organ donation in Denmark. *Sociology of Health & Illness, 37*(4), 578–593.

Hogle, L. (2019). Accounting for accountable care: Value-based population management. *Social Studies of Science, 49*(4), 556–582.

Hogue, T., Jones, L., Talkes, K., & Tennant, A. (2007). The Peaks: A clinical service for those with dangerous and severe personality disorder. *Psychology, Crime and Law, 13*(1), 57–68.

Hollin, G. (2014). Constructing a social subject: Autism and human sociality in the 1980s. *History of the Human Sciences, 27*(4), 98–115.

(2017). Autistic heterogeneity: Linking uncertainties and indeterminacies. *Science as Culture, 26*, 209–231.

Home Office and the Department of Health. (1999). *Managing dangerous people with severe personality disorder: Proposals for policy development.* London: Home Office.

Horwitz, A., & Wakefield, J. C. (2007). *The loss of sadness: How psychiatry turned normal sorrow into depressive disorder .Oxford: Oxford University Press.*

Houghton, S., Saxon, D., & Smallwood, A. (2010).Effects of opt-in letters in a National Health Service psychotherapy service. *The Psychiatrist, 34*, 507–510.

House of Commons. (1999). *Debate (15 February 1999), vol 325, col 602.* Retrieved 30 April 2025 from https://hansard.parliament.uk/Commons/1999-02-15/debates/9fdd9dfb-649e-4793-a404-c3562e59eec5/SeverePersonalityDisorders

Howells, K., Krishnan, G., & Daffern, M. (2007). Challenges in the treatment of dangerous and severe personality disorder. *Advances in Psychiatric Treatment, 13*(5), 325–332.

Howitt, D., & Owusu-Bempah, K. (1994). *The racism of psychology*. London: Harvester Wheatsheaf.

Hubbard, K. (2017). Queer signs: The women of the British projective test movement. *Journal of the History of the Behavioral Sciences, 53*(3), 265–285.

Hubbard, K. A., & Griffiths, D. A. (2019). Sexual offence, diagnosis, and activism: A British history of LGBTIQ psychology. *American Psychologist, 74*(8), 940–953.

Hughes, D., & Griffiths, L. (1997). 'Ruling in' and 'ruling out': Two approaches to the micro-rationing of health care. *Social Science & Medicine, 44*(5), 589–599.

Illouz, E. (2008). *Saving the modern soul: Therapy, emotions, and the culture of self-help*. Berkeley: University of California Press.

International Mad Studies Community. (2022). An introduction to the *International Mad Studies Journal*: A collective reflection on processes, movements, journeys, futures, and unfurlings. *International Mad Studies Journal, 1*(1), e1–e8. https://imsj.journals.publicknowledgeproject.org/index.php/imsj/article/view/5237

Jackson, S., & Rees, A. (2007). The appalling appeal of nature: The popular influence of evolutionary psychology as a problem for sociology. *Sociology, 41*(5), 917–930.

Jain, S., & Orr, D. M. R. (2016). Ethnographic perspectives on global mental health. *Transcultural Psychiatry, 53*(6), 685–695.

Jameton, A. (1984). *Nursing practice: The ethical issues*. Englewood Cliffs, NJ: Prentice-Hall.

Jimena Mantilla, M. (2023). Consciousness, healing and personal growth: How 'therapeutic mothering' impacts on raising children for Argentinean natural mothers. *Subjectivity*, *30*(1), 39–53.

Jenkins, T. M. (2020). *Doctor's orders: The making of status hierarchies in an elite profession*. New York: Columbia University Press.

Jensen, M. C. F., & Vabø, M. (2024). Making assessment protocols workable: Navigating transparency and person-centredness in Norwegian reablement. *Sociology of Health & Illness*, 46(2), 333–350.

Johannessen, L. E. F. (2017). Beyond guidelines: Discretionary practice in face-to-face triage nursing. *Sociology of Health & Illness*, *39*(7), 1180–1194.

Johnstone, L. (2016). 'I knew I was in the right place': One on one. . .with Lucy Johnstone. *The Psychologist*, *29*(9), 732.

(2017). Psychological formulation as an alternative to psychiatric diagnosis. *Journal of Humanistic Psychology*, *58*(1), 30–46.

(2021). *Users and abusers of psychiatry: A critical look at psychiatric practice* (3rd ed.). Hove: Routledge.

Johnstone, L., & Boyle, M. with Cromby, J., Dillon, J., Harper, D., Kinderman, P., Longden, E., Pilgrim, D., & Read, J. (2018). *The power threat meaning framework: Towards the identification of patterns in emotional distress, unusual experiences and troubled or troubling behaviour, as an alternative to functional psychiatric diagnosis*. Leicester: British Psychological Society.

Johnstone, L., Boyle, M., Cromby, J., Dillon, J., Harper, D., Kinderman, P., Longden, E., Pilgrim, D., & Read, J. (2019). Reflections on responses to the power threat meaning framework one year on. *Clinical Psychology Forum*, *313*(1), 47–54.

Johnstone, L., & Dallos, D. (Eds.). (2014). *Formulation in psychology and psychotherapy: Making sense of people's problems* (2nd ed.). Hove: Routledge.

Joint Committee on the Draft Mental Health Bill. (2023). *Draft Mental Health Bill 2022: Report of Session 2022-23, House of Commons/House of Lords*. Retrieved 30 April 2025 from https://committees.parliament.uk/publications/33599/documents/182904/default/

Jolley, S., Garety, P., Peters, E., Fornells-Ambrojo, M., Onwumere, J., Harris, V., Brabban, A., & Johns, L. (2015). Opportunities and challenges in Improving Access to Psychological Therapies for people with Severe Mental Illness (IAPT-SMI): Evaluating the first operational year of the South London and Maudsley (SLaM) demonstration site for psychosis. *Behaviour Research and Therapy*, *64*(1), 24–30.

Jones, E. (2004). War and practices of psychotherapy: The UK experience 1939–1960. *Medical History*, *48*(4), 493–510.

(2010). Shell shock at Maghull and the Maudsley: Models of psychological medicine in the UK. *Journal of the History of Medicine and Allied Sciences*, *65*(3), 368–395.

Jones, R., Pykett, J., & Whitehead, M. (2013). *Changing behaviours: On the rise of the psychological state*. Cheltenham: Edward Elgar.

Joyce, P. (2001). Governmentality and risk: Setting priorities in the new NHS. *Sociology of Health & Illness*, *23*(5), 594–613.

Kamens, S. R., Elkins, D. N., & Robbins, B. D. (2017). Open letter to the DSM-5. *Journal of Humanistic Psychology*, *57*(6), 675–687.

Kamp, A., Grosen, S. L., & Hansen, A. M. (2023). Tinkering with (in)visibilities: Caring for older people with surveillance technologies. *Sociology of Health & Illness*, *45*(3), 605–622.

Kellogg, K. C. (2011). *Challenging operations: Medical reform and resistance in surgery*. Chicago: Chicago University Press.

Kat, B., & Wang, M. (2021). *ACP-UK response to the British Psychological Society's Guidance 'Best Practice in Psychology Recruitment'.* Retrieved 30 April 2025 from https://acpuk.org.uk/psychology_recruitment_response/

Kelly, A. H. (2018). Ebola vaccines, evidentiary charisma and the rise of global health emergency research. *Economy & Society*, *47*(1), 135–161.

Kendell, R. E. (2002). The distinction between personality disorder and mental illness. *British Journal of Psychiatry*, *180*(2), 110–115.

Kendall, T., Pilling, S., Pettinari, C., & Whittington, C. (2004). Clinical guidelines in mental health I: The National Collaborating Centre for Mental Health. *Psychiatric Bulletin*, *28*(5), 156–159.

Kinderman, P. (2014). *A prescription for psychiatry: Why we need a whole new approach to mental health and wellbeing*. London: Palgrave Macmillan.

(2015). Imagine there's no diagnosis, it's easy if you try. *Psychopathology Review*, *2*(1), 154–161.

(2017). *The British Psychological Society and the UK Association of Clinical Psychologists.* Retrieved 30 April 2025 from http://peterkinderman.blogspot.com/2017/08/the-british-psychological-society-and.html

(2019). *A manifesto for mental health: Why we need a revolution in mental health care*. London: Palgrave.

Kinderman, P., Allsopp, K., & Cooke, A. (2017). Responses to the publication of the American Psychiatric Association's DSM-5. *Journal of Humanistic Psychology*, *57*(6), 625–649.

Kinderman, P., Read, J., Moncrieff, J., & Bentall, R. P. (2013). Drop the language of disorder. *Evidence-Based Mental Health*, *16*(1), 1–2.

King, C. (2001). Severe mental illness: Managing the boundary of a CMHT. *Journal of Mental Health*, *10*(1), 75–86.

Kirkham, P. (2017). The line between intervention and abuse': Autism and applied behaviour analysis. *History of the Human Sciences*, *30*(2), 107–126.

Kitanaka, J. (2012). *Depression in Japan: Psychiatric cures for a society in distress.* Princeton, NJ: Princeton University Press.

Kitzinger, C. (1987). *The social construction of lesbianism*. London: Sage.

(1991). Feminism, psychology and the paradox of power. *Feminism & Psychology*, *1* (1), 111–129.

Kitzinger, C., Coyle, A., Wilkinson, S., & Milton, M. (1998). Towards lesbian and gay psychology. *The Psychologist*, *11*, 529–533.

Knapstad, M., Nordgreen, T., & Smith, O. R. F. (2018). Prompt mental health care, the Norwegian version of IAPT: Clinical outcomes and predictors of change in a multicenter cohort study. *BMC Psychiatry, 18*, 260. https://doi.org/10.1186/s12888-018-1838-0

Koczanowicz, L., & Koczanowicz-Dehnel, I. (2021). Ideology and science: The story of Polish psychology in the communist period. *History of the Human Sciences, 34*(3–4), 195–217.

Kovandžić, M., Chew-Graham, C., Reeve, J., Edwards, S., Peters, S., Edge, D., Aseem, S., Gask, L., & Dowrick, C. (2011). Access to primary mental health care for hard-to-reach groups: From 'silent suffering' to 'making it work'. *Social Science & Medicine, 72*(5), 763–772.

Kroenke, K., Spitzer, R. L., & Williams, J. B. W. (2001). The PHQ-9: Validity of a brief depression severity measure. *Journal of General Internal Medicine, 16*(9), 606–613.

Kugelmass, H. (2016). 'Sorry, I'm not accepting new patients': An audit study of access to mental health care. *Journal of Health and Social Behavior, 57*, 168–183.

Kuijper, S., Felder, M., Bal, R., & Wallenburg, I. (2022). Assembling care: How nurses organise care in uncharted territory and in times of pandemic. *Sociology of Health & Illness, 44*, 1305–1323.

Kuiper, J. M. L., Borry, P., Vears, D. F., Van Esch, H., & Van Hoyweghen, I. (2023). Navigating the uncertainties of next-generation sequencing in the genetics clinic. *Sociology of Health & Illness, 45*(3), 465–484.

Kusch, M. (1999). *Psychological knowledge: A social history and philosophy*. London: Routledge.

The Labour Party. (2005). *The Labour Party manifesto 2005: Britain forward not back*. Retrieved 30 April 2025 from news.bbc.co.uk/2/shared/bsp/hi/pdfs/13_04_05_labour_manifesto.pdf

Laing, J. (2000). Rights versus risk? Reform of the Mental Health Act 1983. *Medical Law Review, 8*(2), 210–250.

Lakoff, A. (2005). *Pharmaceutical reason: Knowledge and value in global psychiatry*. Cambridge: Cambridge University Press.

Lambert, N., & Carr, S. (2018). 'Outside the original remit': Co-production in UK mental health research, lessons from the field. *International Journal of Mental Health Nursing, 27*(4), 1273–1281.

Lamont, M. (2000). *The dignity of working men: Morality and the boundaries of race, class, and immigration*. New York: Russell Sage Foundation.

Lamont, M., & Molnár, V. (2002). The study of boundaries in the social sciences. *Annual Review of Sociology, 28*, 167–195.

Lane, R. (2020). Expanding boundaries in psychiatry: Uncertainty in the context of diagnosis-seeking and negotiation. *Sociology of Health & Illness, 42*(S1), 69–83.

Latour, B. (2004). Why has critique run out of steam? From matters of fact to matters of concern. *Critical Inquiry, 30*(2), 225–248.

Latimer, J. (1997). Giving patients a future: The constituting of classes in an acute medical unit. *Sociology of Health & Illness, 19*(2), 160–185.

Lavender, A. (2002). Developing services for people with dangerous and severe personality disorders. *Criminal Behaviour and Mental Health, 12*(2 Suppl), S46–S53.

Lavender, T., & Turpin, G. (2015). The development and training of the clinical psychological workforce: From probationers to practitioner doctorates. In J. Hall, D. Pilgrim, & G. Turpin (Eds.), *Clinical psychology in Britain: Historical perspectives* (pp. 93–110). London: British Psychological Society.

Layard, R. (2005a). *Mental health: Britain's biggest social problem?* Paper presented at Strategy Unit Seminar on Mental Health, 20 January. Retrieved 30 April 2025 from http://eprints.lse.ac.uk/47428/

(2005b). *Happiness: Lessons from a new science.* London: Allen Lane.

(2006a). The case for psychological treatment centres. *British Medical Journal, 332*(7548), 1030–1032.

(2006b). *Depression, a disease that we must defeat. The Guardian.* Retrieved 30 April 2025 from www.theguardian.com/commentisfree/2006/jun/18/comment.socialcare

Layard, R., & Clark, D. (2014). *Thrive: The power of evidence-based psychological therapies.* London: Allen Lane.

Layard, R., Clark, D., Knapp, M., & Mayraz, G. (2007). Cost-benefit analysis of psychological therapy. *National Institute Economic Review, 202*(1), 90–98.

Lee, S. (1999). Diagnosis postponed: Shenjing Shuairuo and the transformation of psychiatry in post-Mao China. *Culture, Medicine and Psychiatry, 23*(3), 349–380.

LeFrançois, B. A., Reaume, G., & Menzies, R. J. (Eds.). (2013). *Mad matters: A critical introduction in Canadian mad studies.* Toronto: Canadian Scholars' Press.

Lemov, R. (2005). *World as laboratory: Experiments with mice, mazes, and men.* New York: Hill & Wang.

Leonardi, P. M. (2008). Indeterminacy and the discourse of inevitability in international technology management. *Academy of Management Review, 33*(4), 975–984.

Lester, H., Tritter, J. Q., & Sorohan, H. (2005). Patients' and health professionals' views on primary care for people with serious mental illness: Focus group study. *BMJ, 14*(330), 1122. https://doi.org/10.1136/bmj.38440.418426.8F

Lester, R. J. (2019). *Famished: Eating disorders and failed care in America.* Berkeley: University of California Press.

Lewis, G., & Appleby, L. (1988). Personality disorder: The patients psychiatrists dislike. *British Journal of Psychiatry, 153*(1), 44–49.

Lewis, L. (2009). Politics of recognition: What can a human rights perspective contribute to understanding users' experiences of involvement in mental health services? *Social Policy and Society, 8*(2), 257–274.

(2014). User involvement in mental health services: A case of power over discourse. *Sociological Research Online, 19*(1), 6. www.socresonline.org.uk/19/1/6.html

Liberati, E., Richards, N., Parker, J., Willars, J., Scott, D., Boydell, N., Pinfold, V., Martin, G., Jones, P. B., & Dixon-Woods, M. (2022). Qualitative study of candidacy and access to secondary mental health services during the

COVID-19 pandemic. *Social Science & Medicine*, 296, 114711. https://doi.org/10.1016/j.socscimed.2022.114711.

Liberati, E., Richards, N., Ratnayake, S., Gibson, J., & Martin, G. (2023). Tackling the erosion of compassion in acute mental health services. *BMJ*, *382*, e073055. https://doi.org/10.1136/bmj-2022-073055

Lindberg. K, Walter. L, & Raviola, E. (2017). Performing boundary work: The emergence of a new practice in a hybrid operating room. *Social Science & Medicine*, *182*(7), 81–88.

Linstrum, E. (2016). *Ruling minds: Psychology in the British Empire*. Cambridge, MA: Harvard University Press.

Littoz-Monnet, A. (2022). Exclusivity and circularity in the production of global governance expertise: The making of 'global mental health' knowledge. *International Political Sociology*, olab035. https://doi.org/10.1093/ips/olab035

Livesley, W. J. (2007). The relevance of an integrated approach to the treatment of personality disordered offenders. *Psychology, Crime and Law*, *13*(1), 27–46.

Lloyd, S. (2006). The clinical clash over social phobia: The Americanization of French experiences? *BioSocieties*, *1*(2), 229–249.

Lorber, J. (1975). Good patients and problem patients: Conformity and deviance in a general hospital. *Journal of Health and Social Behavior*, *16*(2), 213–225.

Loughran, T. (2016). *Shell-shock and medical culture in First World War Britain*. Cambridge: Cambridge University Press.

Lovell, A. M., Read, U. M., & Lang, C. (2019). Genealogies and anthropologies of global mental health. *Culture, Medicine, and Psychiatry*, *43*, 519–547.

Luhrmann, T. (2000). *Of two minds: The growing disorder in American psychiatry*. New York: Alfred A. Knopf.

Mackay, H., Carne, C., Beynon-Davies, P., & Tudhope, D. (2000). Reconfiguring the user: Using rapid application development. *Social Studies of Science*, *30*(5), 737–757.

MacKenzie, D. (2015, 15 April). Science and Technology Studies Stream Plenary Lecture, British Sociological Association Annual Conference, Glasgow Caledonian University.

MacKenzie, D., & Pardo-Guerra, J. P. (2014). Insurgent capitalism: Island, bricolage and the re-making of finance. *Economy and Society*, *43*(2), 153–182.

Mackenzie, M., Conway, E., Hastings, A., Munro, M., & O'Donnell, C. (2013). Is 'candidacy' a useful concept for understanding journeys through public services? A critical interpretive literature synthesis. *Social Policy & Administration*, *47*(7), 806–825.

MacLean, K. (2021). *Giving back or fighting back? A transatlantic, qualitative study exploring citizenship, social movement learning and mental health*. Unpublished PhD thesis, University of Strathclyde.

Mad Youth Organise. (2025). *The Mad Youth Manifesto*. Retrieved 30 April 2025 from https://heyzine.com/flip-book/54f71178f7.html

Maden, A. (2007). Dangerous and severe personality disorder: Antecedents and origins. *British Journal of Psychiatry, 190*(S49), s8–s11.

Madsen, O. J. (2018) *The psychologization of society: On the unfolding of the therapeutic in Norway*. London: Routledge.

Maltman, L., Stacey, J., & Hamilton, L. (2008). Peaks and troughs: An exploration of patient perspectives of dangerous and severe personality disorder assessment (Peaks Unit, Rampton Hospital). *Personality and Mental Health, 2*(1), 7–16.

Management Advisory Service. (1989). *Review of clinical psychology services*. Cheltenham: Management Advisory Services.

Manning, N. (2000). Psychiatric diagnosis under conditions of uncertainty: Personality disorder, science and professional legitimacy. *Sociology of Health & Illness, 22*(5), 621–639.

Manning N. (2002). Actor networks, policy networks, and personality disorder. *Sociology of Health & Illness, 24*(5), 644–666.

(2006). DSM-IV and dangerous and severe personality disorder: An essay. *Social Science & Medicine, 63*(7), 1960–1971.

Margison, F. R., Barkham, M., Evans, C., McGrath, G., Clark, J. M., Audin, K., & Connell, J. (2000). Measurement and psychotherapy: Evidence-based practice and practice-based evidence. *British Journal of Psychiatry, 177*(2), 123–130.

Marks, S. (2012). Cognitive behaviour therapies in Britain: The historical context and present situation. In W. Dryden (Ed.), *Cognitive behaviour therapies* (pp. 1–24). London: Sage.

(2015). Psychologists as therapists: The development of behavioural traditions in clinical psychology. In J. Hall, D. Pilgrim, & G. Turpin (Eds.), *Clinical psychology in Britain: Historical perspectives* (pp. 194–207). London: British Psychological Society.

(2017). Psychotherapy in historical perspective. *History of the Human Sciences, 30*(2), 3–16.

Martin, E. (2022). *Experiments of the mind: From the cognitive psychology lab to the world of Facebook and Twitter*. Princeton, NJ: Princeton University Press.

Martin, G. P., Currie, G., & Finn, R. (2009). Reconfiguring or reproducing intra-professional boundaries? Specialist expertise, generalist knowledge and the 'modernization' of the medical workforce. *Social Science & Medicine, 68*(7), 1191–1198.

Marzillier, J., & Hall, J. (2009). The challenge of the Layard initiative. *The Psychologist, 22*(5), 396–399.

Matza, T. (2018). Shock therapy: Psychology, precarity, and well-being in post-socialist Russia. Durham, NC: Duke University Press.

McBride, R.-S. (2017). On the advancement of therapeutic penality: Therapeutic authority, personality science and the therapeutic community. *Sociology of Health & Illness, 39*(7), 1258–1272.

McCallum, D. (2001). *Personality and dangerousness: Genealogies of antisocial personality disorder*. Cambridge: Cambridge University Press.

McClelland, L. (2013). Reformulating the impact of social inequalities: Power and social justice. In L. Johnstone & D. Dallos (Eds.), *Formulation in psychology and psychotherapy: Making sense of people's problems* (2nd ed., pp. 121–144). Hove: Routledge.

McCrone, P. (2013). IAPT is probably not cost-effective. *British Journal of Psychiatry, 202*(5), 383.

McDermott, I., Astbury, J., Jacobs, S., Willis, S., Hindi, A., Seston, E., & Schafheutle, E. (2023). To be or not to be: The identity work of pharmacists as clinicians. *Sociology of Health & Illness, 45*(3), 623–641.

McEvoy, P., & Richards, D. (2007). Gatekeeping access to community mental health teams: A qualitative study. *International Journal of Nursing Studies, 44*, 387–395.

McGivern, G., Currie, G., Ferlie, E., Fitzgerald, L., & Waring, J. (2015). Hybrid manager-professionals' identity work: The maintenance and hybridization of medical professionalism in managerial contexts. *Public Administration, 93*(2), 412–432.

McKay, R. (2016). The view from the middle: Lively relations of care, class, and medical labour in Maputo. *Critical African Studies, 8*(3), 278–290.

McWade, B. (2020). Was it autoethnography? The classificatory, confessional and mad politics of lived experience in sociological research. *Social Theory and Health, 18*(2), 123–137.

Mental Health Foundation, Mind, Rethink, Salisbury Centre, & Young Minds. (2006). *We need to talk: The case for psychological therapy on the NHS*. Retrieved 30 April 2025 from https://web.archive.org/web/20120511153304/www.centreformentalhealth.org.uk/pdfs/we_need_to_talk.pdf

Mills, C. (2014). *Decolonizing global mental health: The psychiatrization of the majority world*. London: Routledge.

Miller, P., & Rose, N. (1988). The Tavistock Programme: The government of subjectivity and social life. *Sociology, 22*(2), 171–192.

(2008). *Governing the present*. London: Polity.

Mind. (2023). *UK government shelves the Mental Health Bill*. Retrieved 30 April 2025 from www.mind.org.uk/news-campaigns/news/uk-government-shelves-the-mental-health-bill/

(2024). *The Big Mental Health Report: 2024*. Retrieved 30 April 2025 from www.mind.org.uk/media/vbbdclpi/the-big-mental-health-report-2024-mind.pdf

Mind, Mental Health Foundation, Relate, British Psychoanalytic Council, UK Council for Psychotherapy, British Association for Counselling and Psychotherapy, British Psychological Society, Young Minds, Royal College of Psychiatrists, Centre for Mental Health, St. Mungo's, Tavistock Centre for Couple Relationships, and Rething Mental Illness. (2013). *We still need to talk: A report on access to talking therapies*. Retrieved from www.mind.org.uk/media-a/4248/we-still-need-to-talk_report.pdf

Ministry of Justice. (2011). *Research Summary 4/11. The early years of the DSPD (Dangerous and Severe Personality Disorder) Programme: results of two process studies*. Retrieved 30 April 2025 from https://assets.publishing.service.gov

.uk/media/5a7cc281e5274a2f304efe51/early-years-dspd-programme-research-summary.pdf

Mitchell, A., & Selmes, T. (2007). Why don't patients attend their appointments? Maintaining engagement with psychiatric services. *Advances in Psychiatric Treatment, 13*(6), 423–434.

Mladovky, P. (2023). Mental health coverage for forced migrants: managing failure as everyday governance in the public and NGO sectors in England. *Social Science & Medicine, 319*, 115385. https://doi.org/10.1016/j.socscimed.2022.115385

Mohtashemi, R., Stevens, J., Jackson, P. G., & Weatherhead, S. (2016) Psychiatrists' understanding and use of psychological formulation: a qualitative exploration. *BJPsych Bulletin, 40*(4), 212–216.

Mol, A. (2008). *The logic of care: Health and the problem of patient choice*. London: Routledge.

Molinaro, M. L., Polzer, J., Rudman, D. L., & Savundranayagam, M. (2023) 'I can't be the nurse I want to be': Counter-stories of moral distress in nurses' narratives of pediatric oncology caregiving. *Social Science & Medicine, 320*, 115677. https://doi.org/10.1016/j.socscimed.2023.115677

Mollon, P. (2009). The NICE guidelines are misleading, unscientific, and potentially impede good psychological care and help. *Psychodynamic Practice: Individuals, Groups and Organisations, 15*(1), 9–24.

Moloney, P. (2013). *The therapy industry: The irresistible rise of the talking cure, and why it doesn't work*. London: Pluto Press.

Moncrieff, J. (2003). The politics of a new Mental Health Act. *British Journal of Psychiatry, 183*(1), 8–9.

Montgomery, C. M., Chisholm, A., Parkin, S., & Locock, L. (2020). Wild data: How front-line hospital staff make sense of patients' experiences. *Sociology of Health & Illness, 42*(6), 1424–1440.

Moran, P., Jarrett, M., Vamvakas, G., Roberts, S., Barrett, B., Campbell, C., Khondoker, M., Trebilcock, J., Weaver, T., Walker, J., Crawford, M., & Forrester, A. (2022). *National Evaluation of the Male Offender Personality Disorder Pathway Programme, Ministry of Justice Analytical Series, HM Prison and Probation Service*. Retrieved 30 April 2025 from https://assets.publishing.service.gov.uk/media/634677ee8fa8f5346f4fe9c5/national-evaluation-of-the-male-opd-pathway.pdf

Morawski, J. G. (1994). *Practicing feminisms, reconstructing psychology: Notes on a liminal science*. Ann Arbor: University of Michigan Press.

(1997a). The science behind feminist research methods. *Journal of Social Issues, 53*(4), 667–681.

(1997b). White experimenters, white blood, and other white conditions: locating the psychologist's race. In M. Fine, L. Weis, L. C. Powell, & L. M. Wong (Eds.), *Off white: Readings on power, privilege, and resistance* (pp. 215–231). New York: Routledg,.

(2015). Epistemological dizziness in the psychology laboratory: Lively subjects, anxious experimenters, and experimental relations, 1950–1970. Isis, *106*(3), 567–597.

Moreira, T. (2011). Health care rationing in an age of uncertainty: A conceptual model. *Social Science & Medicine, 72*(8), 1333–1341.

(2012). *The transformation of contemporary health care: The market, the laboratory, and the forum.* New York: Routledge.

Moreira, T., May, C., & Bond, J. (2009). Regulatory objectivity in action: Mild cognitive impairment and the collective production of uncertainty. *Social Studies of Science, 39*, 665–690.

Moth, R., Greener, J., & Stoll, T. (2015). Crisis and resistance in mental health services in England. *Critical and Radical Social Work, 3*(1), 89–102.

Moutaud, B. (2022). Cognitive optimisation and schizophrenia: Assembling heterogeneity, overcoming the precariousness of life, and challenging public health policies in psychiatry in France. *Culture, Medicine, and Psychiatry, 46*, 710–738.

Mukuria, C., Brazier, J., Barkham, M., Connell, J., Hardy, G., Hutten, R., Saxon, D., Dent-Brown, K., & Parry, G. (2013). Cost-effectiveness of an improving access to psychological therapies service. *British Journal of Psychiatry, 202*(3), 220–227.

Mulkay, M., Ashmore, M., & Pinch, T. (1987). Measuring the quality of life: A sociological invention concerning the application of economics to healthcare. *Sociology, 21*(4), 541–564.

Mullen, P. (1999). Dangerous people with severe personality disorder. *British Medical Journal, 319*(7218), 1146–1147.

Nader, L. (1972). Up the anthropologist: Perspectives gained from studying up. In D. Hymes (Ed.), *Reinventing anthropology* (pp. 284–311). New York: Pantheon Books.

Nancarrow, S. A., & Borthwick, A. M. (2005). Dynamic professional boundaries in the healthcare workforce. *Sociology of Health & Illness, 27*(7), 897–919.

National Collaborating Centre for Mental Health. (2009). *Borderline personality disorder: Treatment and management.* National Clinical Practice Guideline Number 78. London: British Psychological Society and the Royal College of Psychiatrists. www.nice.org.uk/guidance/cg78/evidence

(2024). *Ethnic inequalities in improving access to psychological therapies (IAPT).* Retrieved 30 April 2025 from https://raceequalityfoundation.org.uk/wp-content/uploads/2023/11/Ethnic-Inequalities-in-Improving-Access-to-Psychological-Therapies-IAPT.Full-report.pdf

National Institute for Clinical Excellence (NICE). (2004). Depression: Management of Depression in Primary and Secondary Care. NICE Clinical Guideline 23.

(2005). Post-Traumatic Stress Disorder: Management. NICE Clinical Guideline 26.

(2009a). Antisocial Personality Disorder: Treatment, Management and Prevention. NICE Clinical Guideline 77.

(2009b). Depression in Adults: The Treatment and Management of Depression in Adults, NICE Clinical Practice Guideline 90.

(2011). Common Mental Health Disorders: Identification and Pathways to Care. NICE Clinical Guideline 123.

(2013). Social Anxiety Disorder: Recognition, Assessment and Treatment. NICE Clinical Guideline 159.

(2022). Depression in Adults: Treatment and Management. NICE Guideline 222.

National Institute for Mental Health in England. (2003a). *Personality disorder: No longer a diagnosis of exclusion*. London: Department of Health. https://webarchive.nationalarchives.gov.uk/ukgwa/20120503145059/www.dh.gov.uk/en/Publicationsandstatistics/Publications/PublicationsPolicyAndGuidance/DH_4009546

(2003b). *Breaking the cycle of rejection: The personality disorder capabilities framework*. London: Department of Health. https://webarchive.nationalarchives.gov.uk/ukgwa/20200501103151/http://personalitydisorder.org.uk/wp-content/uploads/2015/06/personalitydisorders-capabilities-framework.pdf

(2008). *Mental health outcomes compendium*. Retrieved 30 April 2025 from http://webarchive.nationalarchives.gov.uk/20130124045059/www.dh.gov.uk/prod_consum_dh/groups/dh_digitalassets/documents/digitalasset/dh_093677.pdf

(2015). *Working with offenders with personality disorder: A practitioners guide, second edition*. Retrieved 30 April 2025 from www.england.nhs.uk/commissioning/wp-content/uploads/sites/12/2015/10/work-offndrs-persnlty-disorder-oct15.pdf

Nature. (2012). Editorial: Therapy deficit. *Nature*, *489*(7417): 473–474.

Nazroo, J. Y., Bhui, K. S., & Rhodes, J. (2020). Where next for understanding race/ethnic inequalities in severe mental illness? Structural, interpersonal and institutional racism. *Sociology of Health & Illness*, *42*(2), 262–276.

New Savoy Partnership. (2007). *The New Savoy Declaration*. Retrieved 30 April 2025 from https://web.archive.org/web/20121224051509/www.newsavoypartnership.org/docs/The_New_Savoy_Declaration.pdf

Neyland, D., & Coopmans, C. (2014). Visual accountability. *The Sociological Review*, *62*(1), 1–23.

NHS Business Services Authority. (2022). *Medicines used in mental health – England – 2015/16 to 2021/22*. Retrieved 30 April 2025 from www.nhsbsa.nhs.uk/statistical-collections/medicines-used-mental-health-england/medicines-used-mental-health-england-201516-202122

NHS Digital. (2024). *Improving access to psychological therapies (IAPT) data set*. Retrieved 30 April 2025 from https://digital.nhs.uk/data-and-information/data-collections-and-data-sets/data-sets/improving-access-to-psychological-therapies-data-set

NHS Education for Scotland. (2022). *Psychology services workforce in Scotland: Quarter ending March 2022*. Retrieved 30 April 2025 from https://turasdata.nes.nhs.scot/media/womjqn3w/2022-06-07-psychologyworkforce-report.pdf

NHS England. (2014). *NHS England using technology to beat cost of missed appointments*. NHS England News. Retrieved 30 April 2025 from www.england.nhs.uk/2014/03/missed-appts/

(2023a). *The offender personality disorder (OPD) pathway: A joint strategy for 2023 to 2028*. Retrieved 30 April 2025 from www.england.nhs.uk/long-read/the-offender-personality-disorder-pathway/

(2023b). *Reducing did not attends (DNAs) in outpatient appointments*. Retrieved 30 April 2025 from www.england.nhs.uk/long-read/reducing-did-not-attends-dnas-in-outpatient-services/

NHS Health Scotland. (2015). *Who is least likely to attend? An analysis of outpatient appointment 'Did Not Attend' (DNA) data in Scotland*. Edinburgh: NHS Health Scotland. https://web.archive.org/web/20221013065517/www.healthscotland.scot/media/1131/5317_dna-analysis_national.pdf

NHS Lothian. (2025). *Child and adolescent mental health services: Referral information*. Retrieved 10 January 2025 from https://services.nhslothian.scot/camhs/referral-information/

Nielson, J. D. J., & Nicholas, H. (2016). Counselling psychology in the United Kingdom. *Counselling Psychology Quarterly, 29* (2), 206–215.

Norman, A. H., Russell, A. J., & Merli, C. (2016). The Quality and Outcomes Framework: Body commodification in UK general practice. *Social Science & Medicine, 170*(12), 77–86.

Oakes, G. (1994). *The imaginary war: Civil defense and American Cold War culture*. New York: Oxford University Press.

O'Carroll, R. E. (2014). Health psychology interventions. *British Journal of Health Psychology, 19* (2), 235–239.

O'Donnell, A., & MacLean, K. (2019). Reclaiming agency through Oor Mad History. In L. Sapouna, H. Gijbels, & G. Sidley (Eds.), *Inside out, outside in: Transforming mental health practices* (pp. 245–260). Monmouth: PCCS Books, pp 245-260.

Odusanya, S. O. E., Winter, D., Nolte, L., & Shah, S. (2018). The experience of being a qualified female BME clinical psychologist in a National Health Service: An interpretative phenomenological and repertory grid analysis. *Journal of Constructivist Psychology, 31*(3), 273–291,

O'Loughlin, A. (2014). The offender personality disorder pathway: Expansion in the face of failure? *The Howard Journal, 53*(2), 173–192.

O'Reilly, M., Dixon-Woods, M., Angell, E., Ashcroft, R., & Bryman, A. (2009). Doing accountability: A discourse analysis of research ethics committee letters. *Sociology of Health & Illness, 31*(2), 246–261.

Orr, J. (2006). *Panic diaries: A genealogy of panic disorder*. Durham, NC: Duke University Press.

Ossa, J. C., Salas, G., & Scholten, H. (Eds.). (2021). *History of psychology in Latin America: A cultural approach*. Cham: Springer.

Oudshoorn, N., & Pinch, T. (Eds.). (2003) *How users matter: The co-construction of users and technology*. Cambridge, MA: MIT Press.

Oudshoorn, N., Rommes, E., & Stienstra, M. (2004). Configuring the user as everybody: Gender and design cultures in information and communication technologies. *Science, Technology, & Human Values*, *29*(1), 30–63.

Owen, G. (2023). What is formulation in psychiatry? *Psychological Medicine*, *53*(5), 1700–1707.

Palmer, W., Schlepper, L., Hemmings, N., & Crellin, N. (2021). *The right track: Participation and progression in psychology career paths. Commissioned and supported by the British Psychological Society*. London: Nuffield Trust.

Pandora, K. (1997). *Rebels within the ranks: Psychologists' critique of scientific authority and democratic realities in New Deal America*. Cambridge: Cambridge University Press.

Parker, I. (Ed.). (2015). *Handbook of critical psychology*. London: Routledge.

Parlee, M. B. (1979). Psychology and women. *Signs*, *5*(1), 121–133.

Parry, G. (2015). Psychologists as therapists: An overview. In J. Hall, D. Pilgrim, & G. Turpin (Eds.). *Clinical psychology in Britain: Historical perspectives* (pp. 181–193). London: British Psychological Society.

Peay, J. (2000). Reform of the Mental Health Act 1983: Squandering of an opportunity? *Journal of Mental Health Law*, *9*(1), 5–15.

(2003).*Decisions and dilemmas: Working with mental health law*. Oxford: Hart Publishing.

Pemberton, R. (2013). Letters: Distortions and maps of wonderland. *The Psychologist*, 26(7), 467.

Pennington, D., & Hodgson, J. (2012). Non-attendance and invitation methods within a CBT service. *Mental Health Review Journal*, *17*(3), 145–151.

Perkins, D., Farr, C., Romero, J., & Ebrahimjee, A. (2015). DSPD ten years on at Broadmoor. *Prison Service Journal*, *218*(1), 10–16.

Pettit, M. (2015). Subject matter: Human behavior, psychological expertise, and therapeutic lives. *Social Studies of Science*, *45*(1), 146–158.

Pettit, M., & Young, J. L. (2017). Psychology and its publics. *History of the Human Sciences*, *30*(4), 3–10.

Pfister, J., & Schnog, N. (Eds.). (1997). *Inventing the psychological: Toward a cultural history of emotional life in America*. New Haven, CT: Yale University Press.

Pfohl, S. J. (1978). *Predicting dangerousness: The social constriction of psychiatric reality*. Lexington, MA: Lexington Books.

Pickersgill, M. (2009a). Between soma and society: Neuroscience and the ontology of psychopathy. *BioSocieties*, *4*(1), 45–60.

(2009b). NICE guidelines, clinical practice and antisocial personality disorder: The ethical implications of ontological uncertainty. *Journal of Medical Ethics*, *35*(11), 668–671.

(2010). From psyche to soma? Changing accounts of antisocial personality disorders in the *American Journal of Psychiatry*. *History of Psychiatry*, *21*(3), 294–311.

(2011). Ordering disorder: Knowledge production and uncertainty in neuroscience research. *Science as Culture*, *20*, 71–87.

(2012a). Standardising antisocial personality disorder: The social shaping of a psychiatric technology. *Sociology of Health & Illness*, *24*(4), 544–559.

(2012b). The co-production of science, ethics, and emotion. *Science, Technology, & Human Values*, *37*(6), 579–603.

(2013). Sociotechnical innovation in mental health: Articulating complexity. In M. L. Flear, A. Farrell, T. K. Hervey, & T. Murphy (Eds.). *European law and new health technologies* (pp. 323–342). Oxford: Oxford University Press.

(2014). The endurance of uncertainty: Antisociality and ontological anarchy in British psychiatry, 1950–2010. *Science in Context*, *27*(1), 134–175.

(2019a). Digitising psychiatry? Sociotechnical expectations, performative nominalism and biomedicine virtue in (digital) psychiatric praxis. *Sociology of Health & Illness*, *41*(S1), 16–30.

(2019b). Access, accountability, and the proliferation of psychological therapy: On the introduction of the IAPT initiative and the transformation of mental healthcare. *Social Studies of Science*, *49*(4), 627–650.

(2020). Uncertainty work as ontological negotiation: Adjudicating access to therapy in clinical psychology. *Sociology of Health & Illness*, *42*(S1), 84–98.

(2021). Negotiating novelty: Constructing the novel within scientific accounts of epigenetics. *Sociology*, *55*(3), 600–618.

(2024). Stalling or oiling the engines of diagnosis? Shifting perspectives on the DSM and categorical diagnosis in psychiatry. *Sociology of Health & Illness*, *46*(S1), 132–151.

Pickersgill, M., Cunningham-Burley, S., & Martin, P. (2011). Constituting neurologic subjects: Neuroscience, subjectivity and the mundane significance of the brain. *Subjectivity*, *4*(3), 346–365.

Pidd, F., & Feigenbaum, J. (2007). Personality disorder: Still everybody's business? *Mental Health Review Journal*, *12*(4), 5–12.

Pilgrim, D. (1997). *Psychotherapy and society*. London: Sage.

(2007). New 'mental health' legislation for England and Wales: Some aspects of consensus and conflict. *Journal of Social Policy*, *36*(1), 79–95.

(2009). CBT in the British NHS: Vague imposition or imposition of vagueness? *European Journal of Psychotherapy and Counselling*, *11*(3), 323–339.

(2010). British clinical psychology and society. *Psychology Learning & Teaching*, *9*(2), 8–12.

(2011). The hegemony of cognitive-behaviour therapy in modern mental health care. *Health Sociology Review*, *20*(2), 120–132.

Pilgrim, D., & Carey, T. (2012). Improving access to psychological therapies: An account of recent policy aspirations in the UK and Australia. *Advances in Mental Health*, *10*, 117–126.

Pilgrim, D., & Hewitt, D. (2001). Mental Health Act reform: Emerging challenges. *The Psychologist*, *14*(10), 526–529.

Pilgrim, D., & Parry, G. (2015). Outside the behavioural tradition: Psychodynamic, humanistic, and constructivist therapies in clinical psychology. In J. Hall, D. Pilgrim, & G. Turpin (Eds.), *Clinical psychology in Britain: Historical perspectives* (pp. 208–218). London: British Psychological Society.

Pilgrim, D., & Patel, N. (2015). The emergence of clinical psychology in the British post-war context. In: In J. Hall, D. Pilgrim, & G. Turpin (Eds.), *Clinical psychology in Britain: Historical perspectives* (pp. 52–64). London: British Psychological Society.

Pilgrim, D., & Rogers, A. (2005). Psychiatrists as social engineers: A case study of an anti-stigma campaign. *Social Science & Medicine, 61*(12), 2546–2556.

Pilgrim, D., & Treacher, A. (1992). *Clinical psychology observed.* London: Routledge.

Pilling, S. (1983). The Mental Health (Amendment) Act 1982: Reform or cosmetics? *Critical Social Policy, 3*(7), 90–96.

Player, E. (2017). The offender personality disorder pathway and its implications for women prisoners in England and Wales. *Punishment & Society, 19*(5), 568–589.

Pols, J. (2003). Enforcing patient rights or improving care? The interference of two modes of doing good in mental health care. *Sociology of Health & Illness, 25*(4), 320–347.

(2006). Accounting and washing: Good care in long-term psychiatry. *Science, Technology, & Human Values, 31*(4), 409–430

Pope, C. (1991). Trouble in store: Some thoughts on the management of waiting lists. *Sociology of Health & Illness, 13*, 193–212.

Porter, T. M. (1995). *Trust in numbers: The pursuit of objectivity in science and public life*. Princeton, NJ: Princeton University Press.

Power, M. (1999). *The audit society: Rituals of verification.* Oxford: Oxford University Press.

Prime Minister's Office. (2024). *The King's Speech 2024*. Retrieved 30 April 2025 from https://assets.publishing.service.gov.uk/media/6697f5c10808eaf43b50d18e/The_King_s_Speech_2024_background_briefing_notes.pdf

Prins, H. (2007). Fifty years 'hard labour' (a personal odyssey). *Howard Journal of Criminal Justice, 46*(2), 176–193.

Prior, L. (1991). Mind, body and behaviour: Theorisations of madness and the organisation of therapy. *Sociology, 25*(3), 403–421.

Pryma, J. (2017). 'Even my sister says I'm acting like a crazy to get a check': Race, gender, and moral boundary-work in women's claims of disabling chronic pain. *Social Science & Medicine, 181*, 66–73.

Pulido-Martinez, H. C. (2010). Psychological knowledge for the governance of the South. *Critical Perspectives on International Business, 6*(2/3), 177–189.

Pyne, J. (2020). 'Building a person': Legal and clinical personhood for autistic and trans children in Ontario. *Canadian Journal of Law and Society, 35*(2), 341–365.

Quinn, F., Chater, A., & Morrison, V. (2020). An oral history of health psychology in the UK. *British Journal of Health Psychology, 25*(3), 502–518.

Raikhel, E., & Bemme, D. (2016). Postsocialism, the psy-ences and mental health. *Transcultural Psychiatry, 53*(2), 151–175.

Ratnayake, S. (2022). 'I will never love anyone like that again': Cognitive behavioural therapy and the pathologisation and medicalisation of ordinary experiences. *Medical Humanities*, 48(2), e7. https://doi.org/10.1136/medhum-2021-012210

Reed, K., Kochetkova, I., & Whitby, E. (2016). Visualising uncertainty: Examining women's views on the role of magnetic resonance imaging (MRI) in late pregnancy. *Social Science & Medicine, 164*(9), 19–26.

Reyes, H. (2008). The worst scars are in the mind: Psychological torture. *International Review of the Red Cross, 89*(897), 591–617.

Richards, G. (1996). *Putting psychology in its place: An introduction from a critical historical perspective*. London: Routledge.

(1997). *'Race', racism and psychology: Towards a reflexive history*. London: Routledge.

Richardson, A. (2015). The historical political and NHS context. In J. Hall, D. Pilgrim, & G. Turpin (Eds.), *Clinical psychology in Britain: Historical perspectives* (pp. 80–92). London: British Psychological Society.

Richert, L. (2019). *Break on through: Radical psychiatry and the American counterculture*. Cambridge, MA: MIT Press.

Rick, J., Hutten, R., Chambers, C., Connell, J., Hardy, G., & Parry, G. (2010). *Implementing IAPT: Lessons from the demonstration sites, NIHR Evaluation Report*. Retrieved 30 April 2025 from http://eprints.whiterose.ac.uk/90775/1/IAPT%20Interim%20Report.pdf

Rieff, P. (1966). *The triumph of the therapeutic: Uses of faith after Freud*. New York: Harper and Row.

Riggs, D. W., Pearce, R., Pfeffer, C. A., Hines, S., White, F., & Ruspini, E. (2019). Transnormativity in the psy disciplines: Constructing pathology in the Diagnostic and Statistical Manual of Mental Disorders and Standards of Care. *American Psychologist, 74*(8), 912–924.

Robcis, C. (2013). *The law of kinship: Anthropology, psychoanalysis, and the family in France*. Ithaca, NY: Cornell University Press.

Robotham, D., James, K., & Cyhlarova, E. (2010). Managing demand and capacity within child and adolescent mental health services: An evaluation of the choice and partnership approach. *Mental Health Review Journal, 15*(3), 22–30.

Rogers, A., May, C., & Oliver, D. (2001). Experiencing depression, experiencing the depressed: The separate worlds of patients and doctors. *Journal of Mental Health, 10*(3), 317–333.

Rogers, A., & Pilgrim, D. (1991). "Pulling down churches': accounting for the British mental health users' movement. *Sociology of Health & Illness, 13*(2), 129–148.

(2021). *A sociology of mental health and illness* (6th ed.). Basingstoke: Open University Press.

Rohde, J. (2022). Beyond torture: Knowledge and power at the nexus of social science and national security. *History of the Human Sciences, 35*(5), 7–26.

Rose, D. (2017). Service user/survivor-led research in mental health: Epistemological possibilities. *Disability and Society, 32*(6), 773–789.

Rose, N. (1985). *The psychological complex: Psychology, politics, and society in England, 1869-1939*. London: Routledge & Keegan Paul.

(1989). *Governing the soul: The shaping of the private self*. London: Routledge.

(1992). Engineering the human soul: Analyzing psychological expertise. *Science in Context, 5*(2), 351–369.

(1996). *Inventing our selves: Psychology, power, and personhood*. Cambridge: Cambridge University Press.

(1999). *Powers of freedom: Reframing political thought*. Cambridge: Cambridge University Press.

(2007). *The politics of life itself: Biomedicine, power, and subjectivity in the twenty-first century*. Princeton, NJ: Princeton University Press.

Rose, N., O'Malley, P., & Valverde, M. (2006). Governmentality. *Annual Review of Law and Social Science, 2*, 83–104.

Rosenberg, C. (2006). Contested boundaries: Psychiatry, disease, and diagnosis. *Perspectives in Biology and Medicine, 49*(3), 407–424.

Ross, E. (2017). Provisionally pregnant: Uncertainty and interpretive work in accounts of home pregnancy testing. *Health, 22*, 87–105.

Roth, A., & Fonagy, P. (1996). *What works for whom? A critical review of psychotherapy research*. New York: Guilford Press.

Roth, J. A. (1972). Some contingencies of the moral evaluation and control of clientele: The case of the hospital emergency service. *American Journal of Sociology, 77*(5), 839–855.

Royal College of Psychiatrists. (2019). *Role of the consultant psychiatrist in medical psychotherapy*, College Report CR224. Retrieved 30 April 2025 from www.rcpsych.ac.uk/docs/default-source/improving-care/better-mh-policy/college-reports/college-report-cr224.pdf?sfvrsn=b86f8bb6_4

(2020). *PS01/20: Services for people diagnosed with personality disorder*. Retrieved 30 April 2025 from www.rcpsych.ac.uk/docs/default-source/improving-care/better-mh-policy/position-statements/ps01_20.pdf?sfvrsn=85af7fbc_2

Russell, W. (1984). Letter from Westminster: Four million patients who failed to attend. *British Medical Journal, 288*(6434), 1928.

Russo, J., & Sweeney, A. (Eds.). (2016). *Searching for a rose garden: Challenging psychiatry, fostering mad studies*. Monmouth: PCCS Books.

Rutherford, A. (2018). Feminism, psychology, and the gendering of neoliberal subjectivity: From critique to disruption. *Theory & Psychology, 28*(5), 619–644.

Sadowsky, J. (2021). *The empire of depression: A new history*. London: Polity.

Sainsbury Centre for Mental Health. (2003). *The economic and social costs of mental illness, policy paper 3*. Retrieved 30 April 2025 from www.researchgate.net/publication/308378405_The_economic_and_social_costs_of_mental_illness/download

Samelson, F. (1977). World War I intelligence testing and the development of psychology. *Journal of the History of the Behavioral Sciences, 13*(3), 274–282.

Samson, C. (1995). The fracturing of medical dominance in British psychiatry? *Sociology of Health & Illness, 17*(2), 245–268.

Sanghara, H., Kravariti, E., Jakobsen, H., & Okocha, C. (2010). Using short message services in mental health services: Assessing feasibility. *Mental Health Review Journal, 15*(2), 28–33.

Sapouna, L., Gijbels, H., & Sidley, G. (Eds.). (2019). *Inside out, outside in: Transforming mental health practices*. Monmouth: PCCS Books.

Schang, L., & Morton, A. (2017). Complementary logics of target-setting: Hierarchist and experimentalist governance in the Scottish National Health Service. *Health Economics, Policy and Law, 12*(1), 21–41.

Schatzman, L., & Strauss, A. (1966). A sociology of psychiatry: A perspective and some organizing foci. *Social Problems, 14*(1), 3–16.

Scheid, T. L. (2004). *Tie a knot and hang on: Providing mental health care in a turbulent environment*. Piscataway, NJ: Transaction Publishers.

Schiebinger, L. (1993). *Nature's body: Gender in the making of modern science*. Boston: Beacon Press.

Schlett, J. (2022). When Rollo May's 'little band' of New York psychologists fought back against organized medicine's attempts to control psychotherapy. *History of Psychology, 25*(1), 3–33.

Schneider, T., Brenninkmeijer, J., & Woolgar, S. (2022). Enacting the 'consuming' brain: An ethnographic study of accountability redistributions in neuromarketing practices. *The Sociological Review, 70*(5), 1025–1043.

Schwennesen, N., & Koch, L. (2012). Representing and intervening: 'Doing' good care in first trimester prenatal knowledge production and decision-making. *Sociology of Health & Illness, 34*, 283–298.

Scott, B. (2015). On Nikolas Rose's *Governing the Soul*. *Self & Society, 44*(4), 426–430.

Scott, S. (2006). The medicalisation of shyness: From social misfit to social fitness. *Sociology of Health & Illness, 28*(2), 133–153.

Scottish Government. (2023). *NHS Scotland waiting times guidance, November 2023*. Edinburgh: The Scottish Government. Retrieved 10 January 2024 from www.gov.scot/binaries/content/documents/govscot/publications/advice-and-guidance/2023/12/nhsscotland-waiting-times-guidance-november-2023/documents/nhsscotland-waiting-times-guidance/nhsscotland-waiting-times-guidance/govscot%3Adocument/nhsscotland-waiting-times-guidance.pdf

Scull, A. (2015). Contending professions: Sciences of the brain and mind in the United States, 1950–2013. *Science in Context, 28*(1), 131–161.

(2021). UK deinstitutionalisation: Neoliberal values and mental health. In G. Ikkos & N. Bouras (Eds.), *Mind, state and society: Social history of psychiatry and mental health in Britain 1960–2010* (pp. 306–313). Cambridge: Cambridge University Press.

Secretary of State for Health. (1999). *Reform of the Mental Health Act 1983: Proposals for consultation*. London: The Stationery Office.

Seear, K. (2020). *Law, drugs and the making of addiction: Just habits*. London: Routledge.

Shah, S. A., Robertson, C., & Sheikh, A. (2024). Effects of the COVID-19 pandemic on NHS England waiting times for elective hospital care: a modelling study. *The Lancet, 403*(10423), 241–243.

Shamdasani, S. (2017). Psychotherapy in society: Historical reflections. In G. Eghigian (Ed.), *The Routledge history of madness and mental health* (pp. 363–378). London: Routledge.

Sheard, S. (2018). Space, place and (waiting) time: Reflections on health policy and politics. *Health Economics, Policy and Law, 13*(3–4), 226–250.

Shill, M. A., & Lumley, M. A. (2002). The Psychological Mindedness Scale: Factor structure, convergent validity and gender in a non-psychiatric sample. *Psychology and Psychotherapy, 75*, 131–150.

Shuster, S. M. (2019). Performing informed consent in transgender medicine. *Social Science & Medicine, 226*(4), 190–197.

Shuster, S. M., & Lubben, N. (2022). The uneven consequences of rapid organizational change: COVID-19 and healthcare workers. *Social Science & Medicine, 315*, 115512. https://doi.org/10.1016/j.socscimed.2022.115512

Silverman, C. (2012). *Understanding autism: Parents, doctors, and the history of a disorder*. Princeton, NJ: Princeton University Press.

Simpson, A. W. B. (1976). The Butler Committee's report: I. The legal aspects. *British Journal of Criminology, 16*(2), 175–177.

Smith, R. (1988). Does the history of psychology have a subject? *History of the Human Sciences, 1*(2), 147–177.

(1997). *The Norton history of the human sciences*. New York: W. W. Norton.

(2013). *Between mind and nature: A history of psychology*. London: Reaktion Books.

Snow, D. A., & Anderson, L. (1987). Identity work among the homeless: The verbal construction and avowal of personal identities. *American Journal of Sociology, 92*(6), 1336–1371.

Soffe, J., Read, J., & Frude, N. (2004). A survey of clinical psychologists' views regarding service user involvement in mental health services. *Journal of Mental Health, 13*(6), 583–592.

Soldz, S. (2011). Fighting torture and psychologist complicity. *Peace Review, 23*(1), 12–20.

Solovey, M. (2001). Project Camelot and the 1960s epistemological revolution: Rethinking the politics–patronage–social science nexus. *Social Studies of Science, 31*(2), 171–206.

South East Coast Strategic Health Authority. (2006). *The Report of the Independent Inquiry into the Care and Treatment of Michael Stone*. Commissioned by: West Kent Health Authority, Kent County Council Social Services, and Kent Probations Services. Retrieved 30 April 2025 from https://web.archive.org/web/20120915065226/www.southofengland.nhs.uk/wp-content/uploads/2012/03/Report-of-the-independent-inquiry-into-the-care-and-treatment-of-MS.pdf

Spandler, H. (2006). *Asylum to action: Paddington Day Hospital, therapeutic communities and beyond*. London: Jessica Kingsley Publishers.

Spandler, H., & Carr, S. (2020). A history of lesbian politics and the psy professions. *Feminism & Psychology*, *31*(1), 119–139.

(2022). Lesbian and bisexual women's experiences of aversion therapy in England. *History of the Human Sciences*, *35*(3–4), 218–236.

Sreeharan, V., Madden, H., Lee, J. T., Millett, C., & Majeed, A. (2013). Improving Access to Psychological Therapies and antidepressant prescribing rates in England: A longitudinal time series analysis. *British Journal of General Practice*, *63*(614), e649–e653.

Staddon, P. (Ed.). (2013). *Mental health service users in research: Critical sociological perspectives*. Bristol: Policy Press.

Stark, L. (2017). Albert Ellis, rational therapy and the media of 'modern' emotional management. *History of the Human Sciences*, *30*(4), 54–74.

(2018). Algorithmic psychometrics and the scalable subject. *Social Studies of Science*, *48*(2), 204–231.

Steel, D., & Cylus, J. (2012). United Kingdom (Scotland): Health system review. *Health Systems in Transition*, *14*, 1–150.

Stein, G. (1992). Drug treatment of the personality disorders. *British Journal of Psychiatry*, *161*(2), 167–184.

Stewart, E. (2013). A mutual NHS? The emergence of distinctive public involvement policy in a devolved Scotland. *Policy & Politics*, *41*(2), 241–258.

Stewart, J. (2015). Psychology in context: From the First World War to the National Health Service. In J. Hall, D. Pilgrim, & G. Turpin (Eds.), *Clinical psychology in Britain: Historical perspectives* (pp. 39–51). London: British Psychological Society.

Stivers, T., & McCabe, R. (2021). Duelling in the clinic: When patients and providers disagree about healthcare recommendations. *Social Science & Medicine*, *290*, 114140. https://doi.org/10.1016/j.socscimed.2021.114140

Stone, M. (1985). Shellshock and the psychologists. In W. F. Bynum, R. Porter, & M. Shepherd (Eds.), *The anatomy of madness: Essays in the history of psychiatry* (Vol. 2, pp. 242–271). London: Tavistock.

Stone, M. H. (1993). Long-term outcome in personality disorders. *British Journal of Psychiatry*, *162*(3), 299–313.

Strauss, A., Schatzman, L., Burcher, R., Ehrlich, D., Sabshin, M., Fagerhaugh, S., Suczek, B., & Wiener, C. (1985). *Social organization of medical work*. Chicago: University of Chicago Press.

Straw, J. (1999). *Severe personality disorders*. Hansard (UK Parliamentary Reports, House of Commons), 15 February, pp. 601–613.

Strawbridge, S., & Woolfe, R. (2003). Counselling psychology in context. In R. Woolfe, W. Dryden, & S. Strawbridge (Eds.), *Handbook of counselling psychology* (pp. 3–22). London: Sage.

Strong, P. (1990). Epidemic psychology: A model. *Sociology of Health & Illness*, *12*(3), 249–259.

Styhre, A. (2013). *Professionals making judgements: The professional skill of valuing and assessing*. Basingstoke: Palgrave.

Suchman, L. (2012). Configuration. In C. Lury & N. Wakeford (Eds.), *Inventive methods: The happening of the social* (pp. 48–60). London: Taylor & Francis.

Sulik, G. A. (2009). Managing biomedical uncertainty: The technoscientific illness identity. *Sociology of Health & Illness, 31*, 1059–1076.

Sulloway, F. (1992). *Freud, biologist of the mind: Beyond the psychoanalytic legend.* Cambridge, MA: Harvard University Press.

Sushovan, R., & Tyrer, P. (2001). Treatment of personality disorders. *Current Opinion in Psychiatry, 14*(6), 555–558.

Sweeney, A. (2016). Why mad studies needs survivor research and survivor research needs mad studies. *Intersectionalities, 5*(3), 36–61.

Sweeney, A., Beresford, P., Faulkner, A., Nettle, M., & Rose, D. (Eds.). (2009). *This is survivor research.* Ross-on-Wye: PCCS Books.

Syrett, K. (2003). A technocratic fix to the 'legitimacy problem'? The Blair government and health care rationing in the United Kingdom. *Journal of Health Politics, Policy and Law, 28*(4), 715–746.

Szmukler, G. (2001). A new mental health (and public protection) act. *BMJ, 322*(7277), 2–3.

Szmukler, G., & Holloway, F. (2000). Reform of the Mental Health Act: Health or safety? *British Journal of Psychiatry, 177*(3), 196–200.

Thomas, F., Hansford, L., Ford, J., Wyatt, K., McCabe, R., & Byng, R. (2019). How accessible and acceptable are current GP referral mechanisms for IAPT for low-income patients? Lay and primary care perspectives. *Journal of Mental Health, 29*(6), 706–711.

Thompson-Lastad, A., & Rubin, S. (2020). A crack in the wall: Chronic pain management in integrative group medical visits. *Social Science & Medicine, 258*, 113061. https://doi.org/10.1016/j.socscimed.2020.113061

Thomson, M. (2000). The psychological body. In R. Cooter & J. V. Pickstone (Eds.), *Medicine in the twentieth century* (pp. 291–306). Amsterdam: Harwood Academic.

(2006). *Psychological subjects: Identity, culture and health in twentieth-century Britain.* Oxford: Oxford University Press.

Timmermans, S., & Almeling, R. (2009). Objectification, standardization, and commodification in health care: A conceptual readjustment. *Social Science & Medicine, 69*(1), 21–27.

Timmermans, S., & Angell, A. (2001). Evidence-based medicine, clinical uncertainty, and learning to doctor. *Journal of Health & Social Behavior, 42*, 342–359.

Timmermans, S., & Berg, M. (1997). Standardization in action: Achieving local universality through medical protocols. *Social Studies of Science, 27*(2), 273–305.

Torre, C. (2021). Therapy in Uganda: A failed MHPSS approach in the face of structural issues. *Forced Migration Review, 66*(1), 43–45.

Trevillion, K., Stuart, R., Ocloo, J.,Broeckelmann, E., Jeffreys, S., Jeynes, T., Allen, D., Russell, J., Billings, J., Crawford, M. J., Dale, O., Haigh, R., Moran, P., McNicholas, S., Nicholls, V., Foye, U., Simpson, A., Lloyd-Evans, B., Johnson, S., & Oram, S. (2021). Service user perspectives of community mental health services for people with complex emotional needs:

A co-produced qualitative interview study. medRxiv 2021.06.24.21259476. https://doi.org/10.1101/2021.06.24.21259476

Triebwasser, J., & Siever, L. J. (2007). Psychotherapy of personality disorders. *Journal of Mental Health, 16*(1), 5–50.

Turkle, S. (1978). *Psychoanalytic politics: Freud's French revolution*. New York: Basic Books.

(1981). *Psychoanalytic politics: Freud's French revolution* (2nd ed.). Cambridge, MA: MIT Press.

Turner, J., Hayward, R., Angel, K., Fulford, B., Hall, J., Millard, C., & Thomson, M. (2015). The history of mental health services in modern England: Practitioner memories and the direction of future research. *Medical History, 59*(4), 599–624.

Tweed, A. E., & Salter, D. P. (2000). A conflict of responsibilities: A grounded theory study of clinical psychologists' experiences of client non-attendance within the British National Health Service. *British Journal of Medical Psychology, 73*(4), 465–481.

Tyrer, P. (2001). Personality disorder. *British Journal of Psychiatry, 179*(1), 81–84.

Tyrer, P., Casey, P., & Ferguson, B. (1991). Personality disorder in perspective. *British Journal of Psychiatry, 159*(4), 463–471.

Tyrer, P., Duggan, C., Cooper, C., Tyrer, H., Swinson, N., & Rutter, D. (2015). The lessons and legacy of the programme for dangerous and severe personality disorders. *Personality and Mental Health, 9*(2), 96–106.

Tyson, P. J., Jones, D., & Elcock, J. (2011). *Psychology in social context: Issues and debates*. Malden, MA: Wiley-Blackwell.

Valasek, C. J. (2022). Divided attention, divided self: Race and dual-mind theories in the history of experimental psychology. *Science, Technology, & Human Values, 47*(2), 243–265.

Vassy, C. (2001). Categorisation and micro-rationing: Access to care in a French emergency department. *Sociology of Health & Illness, 23*(5), 615–632.

Vaughan, M. (2016). Changing the subject? Psychological counseling in Eastern Africa. *Public Culture, 28*(3), 499–517.

Veblen, T. (1983 [1921]). *The engineers and the price system*. Piscataway, NJ: Transaction Publishers.

Vidal, F., & Ortga, F. (2017). *Being brains: Making the cerebral subject*. New York: Fordham University Press.

Viding, E., & Frith, U. (2013). Letters. Debate on DSM-5: A false dichotomy? *The Psychologist, 26*(6), 382.

Vorhölter, J. (2019). Struggling to be a 'happy self'? Psychotherapy and the medicalization of unhappiness in Uganda. *Current Anthropology, 60*(2), 194–223.

(2022). Family trouble: Changing (dis)orders and psychotherapeutic interventions in Uganda. *Ethos, 49*(4), 379–400.

Waidzunas, T. (2015). *The straight line: How the fringe science of ex-gay therapy reorientated sexuality*. Minneapolis: Minnesota University Press.

Wallston, K. A. (1997). A history of Division 38 (Health Psychology): Healthy, wealthy, and Weiss. In D. A. Dewsbury (Ed.), *Unification through division:*

Histories of the divisions of the American Psychological Association (Vol. 2, pp. 239–267). Washington, DC: American Psychological Association.

Wamsiedel, M. (2020). Credibility work and moral evaluation at the ED. *Social Science & Medicine, 248*, 112845. https://doi.org/10.1016/j.socscimed.2020.112845

Waring, J. (2007). Adaptive regulation or governmentality: Patient safety and the changing regulation of medicine. *Sociology of Health & Illness, 29*, 163–179.

(2014). Restratification, hybridity and professional elites: Questions of power, identity and relational contingency at the points of 'professional–organisational intersection. *Sociology Compass, 8*(6), 688–704.

Warren, F., Preedy-Fayers, K., McGauley, G., Pickering, A., Norton, K., Geddes, J. R., & Dolan, B. (2003). *Review of treatment for severe personality disorder*. London: Home Office Online Report 30/03. Retrieved 30 April 2025 from https://web.archive.org/web/20031117133448/www.homeoffice.gov.uk/rds/pdfs2/rdsolr3003.pdf

Watkins-Hayes, C. (2009). *The new welfare bureaucrats: Entanglements of race, class, and policy reform*. Chicago: University of Chicago Press.

Weinstein, D. (2013). *The pathological family: Postwar America and the rise of family therapy*. Berkeley: University of California Press.

Werlinder, H. (1978). *Psychopathy: A history of the concepts – analysis of the origin and development of a family of concepts in psychopathology*. Stockholm: Almqvist and Wiksell International.

Wessely, S. (2017). *Modernising the Mental Health Act: Increasing choice, reducing compulsion*. Final Report of the Independent Review of the Mental Health Act 1983. Retrieved 30 April 2025 from https://assets.publishing.service.gov.uk/government/uploads/system/uploads/attachment_data/file/778897/Modernising_the_Mental_Health_Act_-_increasing_choice__reducing_compulsion.pdf

Wessely, S., Lloyd-Evans, B., & Johnson, S. (2018). Reviewing the Mental Health Act: Delivering evidence-informed policy. *The Lancet Psychiatry, 6*(2), 90–91.

White, R. G., Jain, E., Orr, D. M. R., & Read, U. M. (2017). Situating global mental health: Sociocultural perspectives. In R. G. White, E. Jain, D. M. R. Orr, & U. M. Read (Eds.), *The Palgrave handbook of sociocultural perspectives on global mental health* (pp. 1–27). London: Palgrave.

White, S. M. (2002). Preventative detention must be resisted by the medical profession. *Journal of Medical Ethics, 28*(2), 95–98.

Whitehead, M., Jones, R., Lilley, R., Pykett, J., & Howell, R. (2017). *Neuroliberalism: Behavioural government in the twenty-first century*. London: Routledge.

Whittle, A., Mueller, F., Gilchrist, A., & Lenney, P. (2016). Sensemaking, sense-censoring and strategic inaction: The discursive enactment of power and politics in a multinational corporation. *Organization Studies, 37*(9), 1323–1351.

Wigg, R. S. (2009). Enhancing reflective practice among clinical psychologists and trainees. Unpublished DClinPsych thesis, University of Warwick. Retrieved 30 April 2025 from http://wrap.warwick.ac.uk/3264/

Wiseman, M. (2013). Letters: Stepping from the shadow. *The Psychologist, 26*(7), 469.

Wood, N., & Patel, N. (2017). On addressing 'Whiteness' during clinical psychology training. *South African Journal of Psychology, 47*(3), 280–291.

(2019). Editorial: Being nice is not enough. *Clinical Psychology Forum, 323*(11), 1–2.

Woolfe, R. (2012). Risorgimento: A history of counselling psychology in Britain. *Counselling Psychology Review, 27*(4), 72–78.

Woolgar, S. (1990). Configuring the user: The case of usability trials. *Sociological Review, 38*(Suppl 1), 58.

Woolgar, S., & Neyland, D. (2013). *Mundane governance: Ontology and accountability*. Oxford: Oxford University Press.

Wootton, B. (1959). *Social science and social pathology*. Woking: George Allen and Unwin.

(1980). Psychiatry, ethics and the criminal law. *British Journal of Psychiatry, 136*(6), 525–532.

Wu, H. Y.-J., & Wang, W.-J. (2016). Making and mapping psy sciences in East and Southeast Asia. *East Asian Science, Technology and Society: An International Journal, 10*(2), 109–120.

Yang, J. (2015). *Unknotting the heart: Unemployment and therapeutic governance in China*. Ithaca, NY: Cornell University Press.

Yorston, G. (1999). Aged and dangerous: Old-age forensic psychiatry. *British Journal of Psychiatry, 174*(3), 193–195.

Young, A. (1995). *The harmony of illusions: Inventing post-traumatic stress disorder*. Princeton, NJ: Princeton University Press.

Young, I., Flowers, P., & McDaid, L. (2016). Can a pill prevent HIV? Negotiating the biomedicalisation of HIV prevention. *Sociology of Health & Illness, 38*(3), 411–425.

Young, J., & Hegarty, P. (2019). Reasonable men: Sexual harassment and norms of conduct in social psychology. *Feminism & Psychology, 29*(4), 453–474.

Younis, T., & Jadhav, S. (2020). Islamophobia in the National Health Service: An ethnography of institutional racism in PREVENT's counter-radicalisation policy. *Sociology of Health & Illness, 42*(3), 610–626.

Yule, W. (2015). Clinical psychology at the Institute of Psychiatry and the Maudsley Hospital. In J. Hall, D. Pilgrim, & G. Turpin (Eds.), *Clinical psychology in Britain: Historical perspectives* (pp. 125–139). London: British Psychological Society.

Zeavin, H. (2021). *The distance cure: A history of teletherapy*. Cambridge, MA: MIT Press.

Zhang, L. (2020). *Anxious China: Inner revolution and politics of psychotherapy*. Berkeley: University of California Press.

Zigmond, A. S. (2001). Reform of the Mental Health Act 1983: The Green Paper. *Psychiatric Bulletin, 25*(4), 126–128.

Index

Printed by Integrated Books International,
United States of America